D1599313

The Mystics of
Engelthal

The Mystics of Engelthal

Writings from a Medieval Monastery

Leonard P. Hindsley

St. Martin's Press
New York

THE MYSTICS OF ENGELTHAL: WRITINGS FROM A MEDIEVAL MONASTERY
Copyright © 1998 by Leonard P. Hindsley. All rights reserved. Printed in the
United States of America. No part of this book may be used or reproduced in any
manner whatsoever without written permission except in the case of brief quotations
embodied in critical articles or reviews. For information, address
St. Martin's Press, 175 Fifth Avenue, New York, N.Y. 10010.

ISBN 0-312-16251-0

Library of Congress Cataloging-in-Publication Data

Hindsley, Leonard Patrick, 1950-
   The mystics of Engelthal : writings from a medieval monastery /
Leonard P. Hindsley.
      p. cm.
Includes bibliographical references and index.
ISBN 0-312-16251-0
1. Mysticism—Germany—Engelthal (Hersbruck)—History—Middle
Ages, 600-1500. 2. Dominican sisters—Germany—Engelthal
(Hersbruck)—Biography—History and criticism.
4. Kloster Engelthal—History. I. Kloster Engelthal. II. Title.
BV5077.G3H56 1998
248.2'2'094332—dc21   98-21081
                                                                    CIP

Design by Acme Art, Inc.
First edition: October 1998
10 9 8 7 6 5 4 3 2 1

To
Ann-Maria Contarino
John Lavallée
Alex Naglowsky
Paul Seaver, O.P.

Ist nicht das Leben kurz genug?
Sollen die sich nicht anfassen, deren Weg miteinander geht?
—Goethe

CONTENTS

PREFACE

WITH THIS BOOK I present to an English-speaking readership an introduction to the literature and spirituality of a group of remarkable women and men associated with the Dominican monastery of Engelthal near Nuremberg in the fourteenth century. I have quoted extensively from the various texts produced by the writers at Engelthal because these mystics are so little known and their writings have never been translated into English. Because the reader has had no contact with the people, events, beliefs, and mystical happenings at Engelthal, this book provides a privileged entrance into the world that the mystics of Engelthal share with us through their writings. The reader will enter into a medieval and monastic milieu in which faith is expressed in daily worship and in which the impossible becomes the expected. This world is peopled by mystics and writers—Christina Ebner, Adelheid Langmann, Gertrud of Engelthal, Friedrich Sunder, and many more. Theirs are lives expressed in words used to tell the reader about themselves, their faith, and their love for God and for one another. To them that love of God is revealed as "everlasting" and their joy in that revelation not only sustains them in trials and suffering but also leads them to write about that everlasting love so that others may come to know and experience it.

When translating texts from the Bible I have consistently used the Revised Standard Version, which I consider to be the most accurate. When making reference to Scripture quotes I use the abbreviations appropriate to the Revised Standard text—"Song of Sol.," not "Cant." For Latin quotes I use the Vulgate unless the writers used a variant version from some liturgical text. In referring to the nuns and other women mentioned in the texts, I use a modernized version of their surnames—"Christina Ebner" instead of "Christina Ebnerin," or "Adelheid Langmann" instead of "Alheid Langmannin," for example. Sometimes I refer to paragraph numbers in parenthesis marked with a star, for instance (*42). These refer to unpublished translations and I use them only by way of showing relative position in the original text when that seems important to know. In the notes when referring to the original texts I give the reference from the pertinent manuscript along with a published transcription, for example, "FS 222v; Ringler, *Viten*, 439" gives the manuscript citation for the quote as FS (Friedrich Sunder) and refers to the only extant version of the text contained in the *Codex Scotensis Vindobon-ensis*. The reference to Ringler contains the transcription of the original in a more readily available form. There are no published transcriptions of CEN, CES, or Md1, except as short excerpts in secondary literature. This will be rectified when Ursula Peters's critical edition of Christina Ebner's works is published in 1998. Another example of the method of reference would be "AL 87a; Strauch, 1:1-15." The "AL" refers basically to Manuscript B of the *Offenbarungen* of Adelheid Langmann, a transcription of which is contained in Philipp Strauch's *Die Offenbarungen der Adelheid Langmann: Klosterfrau zu Engelthal*. See the list of abbreviations on page xi.

ABBREVIATIONS USED
FOR ENGELTHAL MANUSCRIPTS

AL — Adelheid Langmann, *Die Offenbarungen,* mgq 866 (Manuscript B) in the Staatsbibliothek Preussischer Kulturbesitz in Berlin. A transcription is printed in Strauch, Philipp, *Die Offenbarungen der Adelheid Langmann, Klosterfrau zu Engelthal,* Straßburg: Karl J. Trübner, 1878.

CEN — Christina Ebner, *Die Offenbarungen,* Codex Cent. V., App 99. (Manuscript N) in the Staatsbibliothek in Nuremberg.

CES — Christina Ebner, Codex theol. et phil. 2o 282, in the Württembergische Landesbibliothek in Stuttgart, containing both the *Offenbarungen* and a copy of Md1.

ESB — *The Sister-Book of Engelthal (Engelthaler Schwesternbuch),* Codex 1338 in the Germanisches Nationalmuseum in Nuremberg. A transcription of this manuscript is printed in Schröder, Karl, *Der Nonne von Engelthal Büchlein von der Gnaden Überlast,* Tübingen: H. Laupp, 1871, 1-44.

FS — *The Gnaden-vita of Friedrich Sunder, Chaplain at Engelthal,* Codex Scotensis Vindobonensis 308 (234) in the Bibliothek des Schottenstifts, Vienna. A transcription is printed in Ringler, Siegfried, *Viten- und Offenbarungsliteratur in Frauenklöstern des Mittelalters,* München: Artemis Verlag, 1980.

Md1 — Christina Ebner, a manuscript biography in the library of the monastery of Maria Medingen, Mödingen/Dillingen.

VGE — The *Vita of Sisters Gertrud of Engelthal,* Codex Scotensis Vindobonensis 308 (234) in the Bibliothek des Schottenstifts, 227^r–229^r.

ACKNOWLEDGMENTS

I have received the help of many people, both friends and strangers, in completing this book. I wish to thank Ann-Maria Contarino for her careful reading of the manuscript and for her insightful comments and queries about the text. Thanks also to those who helped me by their service or kind hospitality during my research period in Nuremberg, especially to Frau Elisabeth Beare and her colleagues at the Stadtbibliothek, and to Hugo Stoll, Karl Kern, and the Jesuit community at the Caritas-Pirckheimer-Haus in Nuremberg, whose welcome made my research very pleasant. Also, thanks to Dr. Franz Machilek, the director of the Stadtarchiv in Bamberg, for leading me to the Library Catalogue of Engelthal that he had discovered while working in Nuremberg. I also wish to thank the Dominican community at St. Maria Rotunda for their hospitality and welcome during my period of research in Vienna.

INTRODUCTION

DOMINICAN WOMEN PLAYED A CRUCIAL ROLE in what is admittedly the greatest flowering of mysticism in the Dominican Order and perhaps in the history of Christianity. Numerous studies have appeared about the friars of this era: Meister Eckhart (ca. 1260-1328), Henry Suso (1295-1366), and John Tauler (ca. 1300-1361). Yet while their lives and writings have been an almost continual source of interest to the scholarly world, their contemporaries and friends, women such as Christina Ebner (1277-1356), Adelheid Langmann (ca. 1312-1375), and other nuns at the Dominican monastery of Engelthal have received relatively little attention since their deaths.

The monastery of Engelthal holds a key position in this spiritual movement as a vibrant center for the literary activity and spiritual teachings of the Dominican women. Founded in 1240 and suppressed by the Protestant authorities of Nuremberg in 1565, Engelthal enjoyed the high point of its spiritual life in the fourteenth century. It was a center of mystical spirituality having connections with other Dominican monasteries (St. Katharina in Nuremberg), with Cistercian monks (Kaisheim), and with the Friends of God—an extended group of spiritually serious and like-minded individuals of every social class from Agnes, queen of Hungary, to lay sisters, and of various ecclesial categories: nuns (Margaret Ebner), Dominican preachers (John Tauler), secular priests (Henry of Nördlingen), and layfolk (Rulman Merswin and his wife). To this monastery traveled people from all walks of life for spiritual guidance: Hermann Kramer, a builder from Nuremberg; Eberhard, the lord of Hohenstein; and Charles IV, emperor of the Holy Roman Empire.

The monastic life within the Dominican cloister of Engelthal nurtured the flowering of an intense mysticism in the fourteenth century that led the nuns to experience the mystical presence of God in an immediate, personal, and affective way. This flowering of mysticism inspired Dominican nuns in other monasteries, formed the character of the mystical preaching of Dominican friars, and presented to the Friends of God confirmation of the Christian ideal of holiness of life as a lived reality. The intensity and duration of mystical experiences among so many of the nuns compelled them and their chaplains to record the events in various literary modes so that others would know the wonders of God and be encouraged to live an authentically Christian life. From this treasure of texts come the autobiography of Christina Ebner called the *Revelations;* her *Sister-Book of Engelthal,* also known as *Das Büchlein von der Gnaden Überlast,* in which Christina recorded the lives and mystical experiences of the nuns who came before her at Engelthal; *The Vita of Sister Gertrud of Engelthal; Gnaden-vita of Friedrich Sunder, Chaplain of Engelthal;* the autobiographical *Revelations* of Adelheid Langmann; and a biography of Christina Ebner. The richness of texts testifies to the intensity of religious and literary life at Engelthal and to the receptivity of the nuns and those associated with them to strive for personal and powerful contact with Christ. It also shows the desire and willingness to record these experiences for the welfare and edification of others.

Nine Dominican monasteries left extant Sister-Books (*Schwesternbücher*), and one other produced an autobiography (Maria Medingen), but the writers of Engelthal produced the greatest number of extant writings and manuscripts of an autobiographical or biographical nature. Engelthal has left posterity an abundance of texts that offer the widest possible range of documents for a cultural and spiritual study of a *locus mysticus.* Collectively they provide a corporate history of the nuns, the life stories of three significant figures, and above all the personal, historical, and spiritual reflections of two women renowned in their own time: Adelheid Langmann and Christina Ebner.

These writings were recorded as documents of faith for the edification not only of the nuns and associates of Engelthal but for a wide range of other interested parties throughout the German-speaking lands. The influence of these women spread through the letters of the Friends of God and through the dissemination of manuscript copies to other monasteries of both men and women and of various spiritual traditions—Dominican, Franciscan, Cistercian, Augustinian.

Interest in these writers and their texts waned after the Protestant Reformation when the majority of the monasteries associated with the mystical movement of the fourteenth century were closed by civil authorities. Although the influential Ebner-Eschenbach family did manage to keep the memory of Christina Ebner alive by various means, most of the writers of Engelthal sank into utter obscurity, partly because of the historical circumstances and partly because many of them were women as well as mystics. In addition, their writings and the message contained in them went out of religious fashion in the controversies of the Reformation era. Only during the Catholic renewal in the baroque era was interest in the message of the Dominican mystics revived, with new histories of the suppressed monasteries and studies undertaken in an attempt to have the Church recognize these mystics as saints. Yet for the mystics of Engelthal no such efforts were made, since Nuremberg and its environs enthusiastically and fervently accepted the teachings of Martin Luther.

In the nineteenth century Germanists began to study the rediscovered texts. Their interest in the writings of Engelthal was primarily linguistic. Texts such as Adelheid Langmann's *Revelations (Offenbarungen)* as edited by Philipp Strauch in 1878 and Karl Schröder's edition of *Das Büchlein von der Gnaden Überlast* in 1871 provided Germanists with examples of ordinary written German in the later Middle Ages. In 1872, Karl Lochner produced a study with brief excerpts from Christina Ebner's *Revelations (Offenbarungen)*. In the early twentieth century writers such as Wilhelm Oehl and Margarete Weinhandl also published translations of the *Sister-Book of Engelthal (Engelthaler Schwesternbuch)*. Studies on the history of the monastery of Engelthal by Martin Grabmann, Hieronymus Wilms, and Gustav Voit appeared in the early twentieth century. More recently Siegfried Ringler and Ursula Peters have begun in-depth studies of the literature of Engelthal. Peters's critical edition of the manuscripts of Christina Ebner should appear in 1998. Susanne Bürkle's study of the literature of Engelthal should also appear in that year. Interest in the works produced by the writers of Engelthal now transcends the merely linguistic. Modern scholars study these texts as revelatory documents of the lives of women and men living in a monastic milieu during a unique era in history, enlivened and made remarkable by the prevalence of mystic fervor.

Even with these translations and studies, relatively little is known in the English-speaking world about Engelthal and its writers. Almost no other work has appeared in English on the writers of Engelthal. There have been a few studies on aspects of other fourteenth-century Dominican mystic women, such as Debra Stoudt's article on the letter exchange between Margaret Ebner and Henry of Nördlingen, and Dewey Kramer's article on the call to ministry among Dominican women at Engelthal. German scholarship on the women by Wilhelm Oehl and Margarete Weinhandl dates mainly from the first decades of the twentieth century and, while useful, is dated. More recently scholars such as Peter Dinzelbacher, Siegfried Ringler, and Margot Schmidt have turned their attention to this and related topics and have begun to publish studies on aspects of *Frauenmystik* of the fourteenth century. They agree, however, with Ringler that a study of the unique contribution of Engelthal needs to be done since Engelthal "during the first half of the fourteenth century appears as a place of intense literary activity," the fruits of which contain "teaching on the mystical life set forth in *Lives*.[1]

Ringler calls for more study on the literary works produced at Engelthal and also for critical editions of each work.[2]

This present volume builds on the works of these scholars but focuses attention on the entire corpus of literary works of Engelthal under the dual aspects of their literary integrity and their spiritual message. This book will interest scholars of women's studies since it concentrates on the lives and writings of undeservedly obscure medieval women who ably produced extraordinary accounts of their lives. Scholars interested in autobiographies will find the study interesting as a prelude to reading the actual works in Middle High German or in English translation.[3] Anyone interested in theology, spirituality, or mysticism would want to know what these female contemporaries thought and wrote about in an era of spiritual history renowned for great writings and significant teachings on mystical experiences. Social historians interested in the Middle Ages will welcome an entrée into the hidden lives of nuns in the late Middle Ages. Scholars in Dominican studies and spirituality will value the revelation of lives from that spiritual tradition lived during the apex of Dominican spiritual history.

According to the focus of my study, I have divided this work into two parts. In Part One I begin with an introductory chapter entitled "The Monastery as *Locus Mysticus*" (chapter one), that is as a center of literary and spiritual richness that became the setting for and indeed fostered the mystical life and writings. This chapter includes a study of the legal basis of the nuns' spirituality contained in the *Rule of St. Augustine* and especially in the *Constitutions for the Nuns*, promulgated by the fifth Master of the Order, Humbert of Romans, in 1259. Also important for understanding Engelthal as place is consideration of the impact of the architectural aspects of the buildings on the formation of spirituality. An appreciation of the nuns' daily activities as expressions and temporal formators of the monastic ideals helps to show the milieu in which the nuns moved. Following this, I concentrate on the literary texts, devoting one chapter to each distinct work produced at Engelthal beginning with the *Sister-Book of Engelthal* (chapter two); then *The Vita of Sister Gertrud of Engelthal* (chapter three); the *Revelations* and *Prayer* of Adelheid Langmann (chapter four); the *Revelations* and Biography of Christina Ebner (chapter five); and *The Gnaden-vita of Friedrich Sunder, Chaplain at Engelthal* (chapter six). I examine each literary document according to the manuscript tradition, sources, and spiritual teaching. Part Two begins with a study of the scriptural sources for the spirituality and shows how the nuns appropriated and used scriptural texts for spiritual and literary guidance (chapter seven). Chapter eight treats the nonscriptural, literary sources of the writings and spirituality of Engelthal. The important texts considered here are the sermons of Bernard of Clairvaux on the Song of Songs, the *St. Trutperter Song of Songs*, various versions of the *Song of the Daughter of Zion*, and *The Flowing Light of the Godhead* by Mechthild of Magdeburg. Chapter nine posits four important aspects in the definition of the spirituality of Engelthal: the importance of the Trinity; the images of Christ as Child, Lover, and Lord; the degrees and uniqueness of being chosen; and images of union and divine indwelling. I conclude with an Epilogue that shows the influence of Engelthal on other contemporary monastic communities and on the subsequent reform movements of the fifteenth century.

Since so little is known about these mystics, their writings, and their monastery, I provide here as background to the literary texts a brief overview of the history of the monastery of Engelthal from a fledgling community of beguines in Nuremberg to the closing of the Dominican monastery by the civil authorities of Nuremberg.

THE HISTORY OF THE COMMUNITY OF ENGELTHAL

With the election of Diemut of Gailenhausen as prioress some time after 9 June 1244, the history of the monastery of Engelthal as a specifically Dominican foundation began.[4] However, its history as a religious house had its beginning some years earlier when a group of beguines gathered around Adelheid Rotter in Nuremberg. Frequently such groups of beguines would progressively commit themselves to a deeper and more organized form of religious life. Many groups of beguines decided to associate themselves with the monastic orders, such as the Cistercians, but the majority chose to adopt the way of life of the Dominican Order. These women, like so many others in the thirteenth century, were greatly inspired by the new ideal of imitating Christ in poverty, for they believed that apostolic poverty freed them to serve others and to inspire others to works of charity. Adelheid Rotter had been originally in royal service and had accompanied Princess Elizabeth from Hungary to Thuringia in 1211. Somewhat later she gave up her "sinful life" and became a penitent in Nuremberg, living as a beguine. The gradual development toward the Dominican Order in Adelheid's group of followers began when they left the free imperial city of Nuremberg because Emperor Frederick II had been placed under interdict and excommunication on 11 April 1240.[5] They found protection and assistance from Ulrich II of Königstein, who permitted them to stay on his dairy farm at Engelschalksdorf near Swinach. According to the *Sister-Book* of the monastery, written by Christina Ebner still within the memory of the founding nuns, the beguines struggled for survival on the dairy farm. "There God tried them as gold is tested in fire. They had to work hard and had to cut the corn themselves and wash and bake and do all the daily chores. They did this with reverence and patience. They built a chapel in honor of St. Lawrence."[6] Despite their own hardships, these beguines also cared for the sick and the poor of the surrounding area.[7] Some time between 6 October 1241 and Easter 1243, the beguines nursed Ulrich III of Königstein, the grandson of their patron, Ulrich II. The boy had fallen from his horse near to Engelschalksdorf and had been removed nearby to the beguines for care. Eventually he died, and with his death all hope of a Königstein heir perished as well, since his father, Werntz II of Königstein, had predeceased him. Christina Ebner recorded this in the *Sister-Book*: "That made him [Ulrich II] very sad because he had no heir other than a daughter."[8] Much saddened, Ulrich II often visited the beguines and, despite the fact that he could neither read nor write, sang along with the beguines as they chanted the divine office.[9] This surprised both Ulrich and the sisters. After Easter 1243, Ulrich II of Königstein decided to bequeath his entire estate at Swinach to the beguines while granting them the revenues from the property during his lifetime. His wife Adelheid and his daughter Elizabeth agreed. The document was witnessed by Walter of Klingenburg, his son-in-law.[10] In exchange the nuns had to pray *in perpetuum* for the soul of the founder, his ancestors and descendants. The newly founded monastery would provide a suitable place of burial for family members. Ulrich also expected the nuns to accept unmarriageable daughters and to establish a working scriptorium for all manner of correspondence.[11]

That Cistercians visited the beguines with the intention of convincing them to associate themselves with their order offers evidence for the genuine feasibility of a monastic foundation at that time. The Cistercians did not succeed in convincing the beguines, however, perhaps because the inclination and religious sentiment of these women led them in the direction of the newly founded Dominican Order. From the fact that the nuns began to call their house "Engelthal" (valley of the angels) Voit asserts that they already had an inclination to become Dominicans, who often named their monasteries in a similar way (Klingenthal, Wonnenthal, Engelthal in the Black Forest, Löwenthal).[12] At any rate the association of a monastery with angels (Engelthal) must have seemed more appropriate than one with swine (Swinach). Whatever may have prompted the beguines to take this course, Bishop Frederick II of Eichstätt granted the request of Adelheid Rotter and her companions to found a monastery at Engelthal according to the *Rule of St. Augustine* and the statutes of the Sisters of San Sisto in Rome.[13] This *Rule of San Sisto* had its origins with St. Dominic himself when he used it to found the first monastery of Dominican nuns at Prouille in 1206/7 and later for the reform foundation of San Sisto. By association with the Order of Friars Preachers (Dominicans), the new nuns of Engelthal had the right of spiritual care from the preachers and initially came under the care of the Dominicans at Regensburg.[14] This was the result of a papal bull dated 4 April 1246 that redefined the relationship of nuns and friars.[15] Henceforth all monasteries of nuns would come directly under the care of the Master of the Order and the provincial of the province in which the monastery was located. The provincial was required to make an annual visitation and to assign educated preachers to care for the spiritual needs of the nuns. However, Dominican friars were neither required nor encouraged to reside at a monastery of nuns, and thus the daily spiritual ministrations had to be met by a chaplain.[16] In the inner life and administration of the monastery, the friars, chaplains, or bishop played no role. The sisters who were professed longer than twelve years had the right and obligation to elect the prioress for a set term of office. Only then did the bishop or the provincial confirm the election. A prioress had to be at least thirty years old. She chose her own subprioress and counselors.

   With the decision to become Dominican nuns and the election of Diemut of Gailenhausen, a delegation consisting of the prioress, a sister companion, and a lay brother made the arduous journey to Lyons to ask the pope to grant approval to associate the community at Engelthal with the Dominican Order. According to Christina Ebner, they found a sponsor at the papal court who helped them. "There was a brother . . . who perceived their serious intention and their holiness and made known their desires to the Pope . . . and the Pope confirmed their privileges with a letter."[17] Voit suggests this may have been Cardinal Hugo of St. Cher, who was known to have sponsored many monasteries in just such a request.[18] Whoever their advocate may have been, Innocent IV published a letter on 20 September 1248 placing the prioress and monastery "de Swina et Engeldal . . . of the Order of St. Augustine" under the care of the Master of the Order of Friars Preachers and also of the prior provincial of Germany.[19] However, unlike the friars, the nuns of the order could own property for their living and sustenance. A further papal letter was procured by the prioress, Diemut, on 10 October 1248, which not only guaranteed their properties but freed the nuns from any interference from the noble families who had supported them. No longer could these benefactors make a claim on rents and revenues from the lands they had previously donated. Of course, this set the stage for numerous disputes between the monastery and those benefactors whose daughters were admitted as nuns there. The well-intentioned directives of a distant pope often proved ineffective in protecting the rights and claims of the nuns throughout the course of the history of Engelthal, especially when the powerful Schenk family in its various branches made claims upon the revenues of the monastic holdings. These heirs of Ulrich II, the founder of Engelthal, had among their family members the local bishop, and at least seven nuns of Engelthal—Ursula Schenk of Geyern, Elsbet Schenk of Klingenburg, Anna, Elsbet, another Elsbet, and Katharina and Maria Schenk of Reicheneck, three of whom held the office of prioress a total of six times.[20] Despite the papal bull, the Schenks and other powerful families continued to exact revenues from lands donated to the monastery. The conflict with the Schenk of Reicheneck family may well be the reason for the possibility of flight from the monastery that Adelheid Langmann recorded in her autobiography. "The need was so great that the nuns were threatened that the monastery would be set afire and the animals would be taken."[21] As Adelheid reported, the prioress wished to flee. These threats against the nuns were not carried out then, however, and the nuns remained safely in their monastery. Ironically, the last of the Schenk of Reichenecks died in 1458, a nun of Engelthal.[22]

The monastery buildings date from the second half of the thirteenth century and are still visible today, having been rebuilt following a fire in the sixteenth century. They are located across from the former chapel of St. Willibald consecrated between 1057 and 1060.[23] Although the Sister-Book mentions an original chapel dedicated to St. Lawrence, the monastic church was dedicated in 1265 to St. John the Baptist. The monastery consisted of two cloisters—one connected to the chapel for the nuns and another for all the buildings needed for work and the maintenance of the complex. Around the entire monastery the nuns had a wall with three towered gates built, of which two remain. Over the years the monastery received gifts of land and dowries from the wealthy families associated with it. Recorded in the first account book of the monastery in 1312 are 175 properties in 54 locations. By 1350 the nuns had added 70 more farms and estates. By the end of the thirteenth century the monastery possessed almost the entire valley of Hammerbach.[24]

The life of each nun was inextricably united with the life of the community whose history, ethos, and ideals in turn affected the nuns individually and collectively. The families, the city of Nuremberg, and the monastery formed an extended social unit that depended upon all three parts. However, the families generally identified themselves first as citizens of the free imperial city and secondarily as devotees of Engelthal. This connection depended upon their family interest often because a daughter or a sister had become a nun. When a woman sought entrance into the religious community, her family had to provide a dowry of land with revenues that would be used for the support of the monastery. This was the expected offering from the noble families whose daughters became choir sisters. At Engelthal, entrance was restricted to daughters of the noble classes, which included not only landed nobility and gentry but also patrician families from the city and families of the imperial or royal ministerial classes. Despite the fact that the nuns had distanced themselves from their families through religious profession and enclosure, and despite the distance between the monastery and the walls of Nuremberg, familial and civil bonds remained strong; strong enough, in fact, to be at the root of the monastery's downfall.

Perhaps the high point of the political history of the monastery of Engelthal was the visit of King (later Emperor) Charles IV to Christina Ebner on 28 May 1350.[25] "On the same day the Roman King, a bishop, three dukes and many counts came and knelt down before her greatly desiring that she give them something to drink and a blessing."[26] That same year Johann II, the burgrave of Nuremberg, also came to visit Christina.[27] Likewise, Henry of Nördlingen, the spiritual father, friend, and later follower of Margaret Ebner, also visited Christina Ebner in 1351 and introduced Christina to the teachings of Suso and Tauler.[28]

In the fourteenth century Engelthal was probably the foremost center of mystical life among the nuns of Germany, if not all of Europe, and was held in high regard, as the visits of spiritual and great persons attest. More importantly, however, its reputation drew many young women to take the veil as nuns at Engelthal, and it may well be that over 100 nuns and lay sisters led the religious life within the cloistered walls of the monastery. So great was their number that it became necessary to found a daughter house. In 1269, nuns from Engelthal led by Mechthild Krumpsit, the new foundation's prioress, began a new monastery at Frauenaurach. Frauenaurach in turn prospered and founded the later famous reform monastery of St. Katharina in Nuremberg in 1295.[29] By the late Middle Ages, however, Engelthal had become simply a home for daughters of the nobility, where the rigor previously practiced and the intensity of private and public prayer ceased. The enclosure was eventually ignored. The nuns began to ride for sport, and the cloister garden was transformed into a stable for horses. Worst of all, the celebration of masses for the dead was often forgotten. Several nuns even bore children. However, in the sixteenth century nuns from St. Katharina's monastery in Nuremberg led a great Dominican reform movement and sent sisters to the monasteries of Maria Medingen in Swabia, Adelhausen near Freiburg, Töß and Ötenbach in Switzerland, Unterlinden in Colmar, Katharinenthal near Konstanz, and even its own mother house Engelthal.[30]

With this renewal of spirit the nuns of Engelthal and other monasteries strongly resisted the onslaught of the Protestant Reformation. The nuns of Engelthal and St. Katharina found themselves isolated in overwhelmingly Protestant Nuremberg, which had been the first free imperial city to accept the Reformation in 1524. From that time on the monasteries were forbidden by the city fathers to accept novices. Some nuns, such as the daughter of Veit Stoss, the famous woodcarver of Nuremberg, left the monastery willingly and married a former Dominican priest. In their isolation, the nuns of Engelthal were forced to accept a Lutheran chaplain. In 1530 there were still 24 choir sisters in the monastery. Three of these wanted to leave immediately. The others resisted the city fathers, and Christina of Königsfeld, the prioress, wanted to remain loyal to the Catholic Church. Eventually in 1565 the last prioress, Anna Tucher, and the last nun, Ursula Zeissen, had to surrender the monastery and its extensive possessions to the civil authorities.[31] Engelthal was suppressed, and with the revenues from the monastery the authorities had the means to establish an academy, later university, at Altdorf.[32] Engelthal's closing marked the end of this remarkable place of witness to the power of God's grace to transform human beings into holy beings.

After Engelthal's surrender, the monastic chapel became the Lutheran parish church of the village of Engelthal. Like many medieval German churches, it was baroquified and modified for the use of a Protestant service. The nuns' choir, for example, was replaced with a balcony. Almost the entire structure of the monastery as rebuilt from 1557 to 1563 is still extant; only one side of the main cloister is missing. The buildings are currently used as residences, garages, and storage facilities for farm equipment.

PART ONE

THE TEXTS

THE MONASTERY
AS *LOCUS MYSTICUS*

THAT SO MANY WOMEN AND MEN associated with the monastery of Engelthal report lives of Christian perfection to the level of mystical experience has to do not only with the teachings that they received and believed but also with the sort of monastic life they vowed to lead. The ideals of that life expressed in legal documents and in inspiring texts along with the lived regimen of Dominican monastic life foster an environment of intense spirituality and mystical experience. The practical basis of Engelthal mysticism is grounded in Dominican monasticism in its temporal and spatial expression—that is, in the monastery.

DOMINICAN MONASTICISM

Dominic de Guzman (ca. 1171-1221) gathered a group of women convert-ed from the Albigensian heresy into the first monastery of Dominican nuns at Prouille.[1] In 1221 he reformed various groups of nuns into a single monastery at San Sisto in Rome. The Primitive Constitutions of these nuns was edited by Dominic himself out of a desire to establish Dominican monasticism in way that would revive among the nuns the apostolic life reported in the Acts of the Apostles. The opening lines and themes of the Primitive Constitutions derived from the Rule of St. Augustine and also referred to the biblical ideal of apostolic life. "Just as from the very beginning of the early Church the multitude of believers had but one heart and one soul, and placed all that they had in common, so must you also observe the same practices and the same way of life in the house of the Lord."[2] The

Constitutions delineated the interpretation of the *vita apostolica* in some detail. With the rapid spread of new foundations of Dominican nuns throughout Europe, it became necessary to revise and adapt the Constitutions to the new state of affairs, making that document the legal and spiritual basis not of a single foundation but of the many and diverse Dominican monasteries of nuns. This task fell to the fifth successor of St. Dominic, Humbert of Romans (ca. 1200-1277).

The Constitutions of 1259

Having become Master of the Dominican Order in 1254, Humbert of Romans inherited the care and responsibility of the entire Dominican family, including all those independent monasteries of nuns that won association with the friars. In his concern for the nuns and their spiritual welfare, he promulgated the revised Constitutions for Dominican nuns in 1259. He enjoined the observance of the new Constitutions on all monasteries already following the Dominican Rule and upon all those who wished to align themselves with the Order of Friars Preachers in the future. Humbert revealed his intentions for the nuns in his letter of promulgation: "To the devoted Servants of Christ, to all the Sisters confided to the care of the Order of Preachers, Friar Humbert, unprofitable servant of the same Order, wishes you new growth in all the works of salvation."[3] His initial admonition shows a desire to set the Dominican monastic life in a teleological context in which a sister would practice the observances or "works of salvation" so that she might grow in holiness. The whole purpose of the set of laws compiled by Humbert from various usages at different Dominican monasteries formed the practical and legal basis of the spirituality of Dominican nuns. Humbert made it clear that the practical mysticism outlined here required a nun to begin to understand herself in a new relationship to Christ.

> By an admirable effect of Divine Mercy, the Son of the Eternal King has chosen the daughters of men to be His Spouses. Because He is the pattern of all Beauty, He wishes that His betrothed should be pure and beautiful, that they be holy in body and mind, that no stain appear in them. Since the same Son of God in His infinite bounty has united you indissolubly to Himself by the bonds of religious profession, you should carefully recall with what interior beauty the Spouses of the spotless Lamb should sparkle. What purity, what fragrance should cling to those who wish to enter into the house of the true Asuerus; how becoming

it is for those who wish to please such a Spouse to be adorned with
virtue and holiness.[4]

Humbert explicated his purpose in greater detail here, writing phrases that
linked the sister with Christ using bridal imagery and spousal vocabulary
and emphasized the special nature of the sister's relationship to Christ. Given
this passage, it should not be surprising to find that Adelheid Langmann and
other Dominican writers employed the same constructs to conceive of their
personal relationship to Christ in a Dominican monastic setting. Adelheid
understood herself as a chosen spouse who should become holy. She wrote
of the beauty of Christ and frequently imaged him as the Lamb. Adelheid
also emphasized the image of adornment with virtues as a metaphor for the
nun's privileged status as recipient of Christ's grace and also as an image for
her growth in perfection. Humbert reinforced the notion of the sister's
special powers stemming from this relationship by referring to King Ahasuerus. Christ has the power of a king over all who are subject to him. The
sister has the power of Queen Esther to intercede before the king on behalf
of others who need his help. Just as Esther found favor with King Ahasuerus
(Esther 5:1-8), so nuns such as Adelheid Langmann intercede before their
divine spouse for the deliverance of souls from purgatory, for the conversion
of sinners on earth and for the strengthening in holiness of the elect who
already share on earth in the joys of heaven.

Humbert emphasized the role of beauty and linked the interior beauty
of the perfect Christ with the attainment of purity and the adornment of virtues
in the nun. Union with Christ transforms the nun by Divine Mercy into a holy
woman, a spouse of Christ. The use of the word *fragrance* links the nun to the
bridal imagery of the Song of Songs (Song of Sol. 1:3, 3:6). The reference to
the beauty of the spouses of the spotless Lamb who must sparkle with virtue
associates the vocation of the nun to the Book of Revelation and prophesies
her inclusion among the elect. The vocabulary of the "marriage feast of the
Lamb" corresponds to Humbert's choice of words: "'. . . for the marriage of the
Lamb has come, and his Bride has made herself ready; it was granted her to
be clothed with fine linen. bright and pure'—for the fine linen is the righteous
deeds of the saints." (Rev. 19:6-8). He places the vocation of the nun freely
bound by profession of vows within an eschatological context.

Humbert continued with a description of the characteristics of a
spouse of Christ:

Courage! Courage! It is this that the Spouse of Christ, modest in her
speech, chaste in her affections, immaculate in her thoughts, pure in

her intentions, desiring only to please her Spouse, deserves to come to Him, and to hear the words of the divine alliances; to be admitted to the eternal nuptuals, from which the foolish virgins are excluded; and to enjoy forever the vision of Him Whom the Angels desire to contemplate ceaselessly, Whom the multitude of the elect adore and Whom every creature blesses forever and ever.[5]

Humbert's letter served as a preamble to place the more mundane and detailed rules in the Constitutions within a spiritual frame and to give the "letter of the Law" life with an eschatological goal in mind. Humbert considered the legal observance of the rules laid down in the constitutions of such vital importance for fostering personal holiness and for attaining the end of the religious life that he clearly defined association with the Order of Friars Preachers by acceptance of the new Constitutions. He believed that "uniformity observed outwardly in our manners fosters and brings to mind that unity which ought to be preserved inwardly in our hearts."[6]

Having established the theological and eschatological framework of the Constitutions in his letter, Humbert then delineated the rules by which the Dominican nun must live out her monastic profession. These rules formed the practical mysticism upon which all progress in religious life would be based. The keeping of these rules concerned all the mystic nuns of the fourteenth century. In the Sister-Books of the various monasteries, each nun was often portrayed as a heroine of observance. Christina Ebner praised Christina of Kornburg for her diligence in performing all things necessary in choir.[7] Adelheid of Ingolstadt kept the rule strictly especially with regard to silence.[8] In her *Revelations* Adelheid Langmann praised a sister Elsbet who was rewarded in heaven for going to choir regularly although she disliked doing it.[9] The nuns listened to the Constitutions each week in refectory and were constantly reminded of the connection between the observances and the call to spiritual progress. They were reminded of how a nun should live in the most minute detail. In the Constitutions Humbert set forth the authority of the prioress in her monastery and detailed every aspect of daily life paying particular attention to prayer (chapters I-III), fasting (chapters IV-VII), and silence (chapter XIII). He devoted five chapters (VIII-XII) to attire and washing, three chapters (XIV-XVI) to entrance into the monastery, six chapters (XVII-XXII) to faults and penances for them, and the remaining nine chapters (XXIII-XXXI) to offices, tasks, and buildings. The nuns adhered to the principles, practice, and spirit of the Constitutions, which enabled them to be ready for the coming of the Bridegroom.

   While the nuns of the Order of Preachers did not preach as the friars
did, both the friars and the nuns shared a common spirituality in the observances of monastic life. For the nuns in particular this way of life was very
similar to that of the Cistercians. Although mystical experiences may occur
wherever the Spirit blows, the nuns and friars of the Dominican Order in the
fourteenth century promoted mystical experience by the everyday practice of
a monastic life that was meant to bring about ever deeper conversion to Christ
and his way of life. The nun should expect to be changed and made holy by
faithfully living her monastic vocation.[10] The life of a nun at that time was
regulated with the goal of union with Christ in mind. St. Paul encouraged all
Christians to use the same kind of effort and sacrifice that an athlete uses to
gain a crown of laurel. How much more should the nun strive to "win the race"
for an imperishable crown in heaven (1 Cor. 9:24-25). The daily regimen in
a monastery was a grand training session for winning the heavenly crown.
Monastic life was both an ascetic struggle to "put on Christ" (Gal. 3:27) and
also a foretaste of the heavenly banquet.
   Dominican monasteries built both by friars and nuns were arranged
architecturally to support the goal of monastic life. The most prominent
structure of the monastic complex at Engelthal was the chapel, which occupied
fully one side of the main part of the cloister square and in height rose above
all other parts of the compound. Architecturally it symbolized the reason for
the existence of the entire structure and for the kind of life to which the nuns
dedicated themselves. The predominance of the chapel preached architecturally that the things of God were preeminently important and that all the rest
of life by comparison served to support contact with God.
   The most important part of the chapel was the choir, which at
Engelthal took up two thirds of the area of the chapel. At the center of
monastic combat with temptation and conversion to Christ was the work of
God in the choir, where the nuns gathered for the celebration of Mass and
for the canonical hours of prayer. Each day they chanted the appointed
hymns, psalms and canticles at matins, lauds, prime, terce, sext, none,
vespers, and compline. The Mass at the altar in choir or in chapel was
celebrated as the high point of the liturgical and spiritual life. Above all the
nun believed she met Christ there since he made himself present as God and
Man in the Eucharist.[11] In the choir the nuns gathered as a community to
unite themselves with the universal church, both on earth and in heaven or
purgatory to join in the praise of the Triune God. In the choir the community
heard the Word of God proclaimed and preached. There the individual nun
kept watch before the Blessed Sacrament. Alone in the choir many nuns had
mystical experiences in prayer. Adelheid Langmann mentioned the choir

numerous times and often experienced mystical ecstasy there, having to be
led away to her cell.[12] Margaret Ebner, among many others, also experienced visions while alone in choir.[13] The choir was all the more important
when one considers that the rest of the chapel was not for the use of the
nuns, but for the priests and lay people associated with the monastery. The
religious life of the nun was centered not in the chapel as such but in this
enclosed portion of the chapel cut off from the view of outsiders. The
enclosed and usually raised choir also contained articles of devotion—holy
pictures of Christ, the Virgin, the saints. Central to its architectural symbolism was the crucifix as a representation of the importance of the death of
Christ. The nuns understood the Crucifixion as the turning point in the
whole drama of salvation history, since at the moment of Christ's death he
showed the totality of his obedience to his Father's will to save the world
and the depth of his own love in offering up his life as the new sacrificial
Lamb slain for the forgiveness of sins. The physical enclosure of the nuns at
Engelthal in a cloister garden bounded by the chapel on the north, the
dormitory on the east, the refectory on the south, and the infirmary on the
west symbolized the life cut off from the outside world so that the concen-
tration of the nun's day and every detail of life might serve the goal of growth
in Christian life toward union with God. Even the work area was enclosed
in a second cloister, and the entire monastery itself was surrounded by a wall
with three gates by which contact could be made with the outside world.
Family members, workers, visitors, and dignitaries could gain access to the
monastic compound but not to the cloister itself. By rule and by practice,
the sanctity and privacy of the enclosure were carefully maintained. The
Constitutions clearly stated: "Above all else care should be taken that the
enclosure should be high and strong, so that there will be no opportunity
to pass over it either for coming in or going out of the enclosure. There is
to be but one door in the Sister's enclosure, and this door must be strong
and solidly locked with at least two or more keys. . . ."[14] The inner part of
the cloister was comprised of a garden and a walkway totally cut of from the
view of the world. The cloister walk was truly a way of the cross for the nun.
Walking around this path while meditating symbolized following the path
of life. The garden itself could symbolize the reestablishment of the Garden
of Eden, itself a symbol of the perfection of Christian life. It could also
symbolize the enclosed garden where Bride and Bridegroom meet in secret.
This garden space at the core of the monastery no doubt served as the real
basis for much of the visionary imagery employed by the nuns in their Sister-
Books and autobiographies.[15] Adelheid Langmann recorded several visions
in which a symbolic tree played a significant role.[16] She often mentioned

flowers with symbolic qualities, and the word "garden" was automatically associated with love.[17] Christ told her: "I will lead my Love into the garden of love and will show her the fruit of love and will make her a wreath of white lilies from my divine and human purity and will crown my love and set upon her head a crown of diverse fruits."[18]

The chapter room was the administration and communication center of the monastery and ranked second in importance to the chapel. The nuns met in the prayerful environment of the chapter to discuss community matters and work, to be addressed by the prioress on practical and spiritual issues, and on occasion to elect a new religious superior. The nuns also proclaimed their own faults against the rule and accepted penances to perform as a consequence. The Constitutions (chapter XXX) carefully set down the activities proper to the chapter. "Chapter will be held after Matins, or Prime, or Terce and Mass. . . . The community having entered, the reader will read the day of the moon and the Martyrology. The Hebdomadarian will then say the Pretiosa and the rest."[19] After numerous prayers, "the one who presides will say briefly whatever she thinks appropriate for the good of the house and the correction of the Sisters."[20] Then followed the proclamation of faults, penances, and prayers. The chapter room symbolized the democratic ideal of the Dominican Order whose members had always elected their superiors. This room also gave each nun the chance to remember and evaluate her own responsibility toward God and her sisters in a democratic community.

The refectory functioned not simply as a place of nourishment for the body but also for the soul. Because of this, meals were always taken in silence, accompanied by readings. The architectural arrangement of the refectory as well as the activities performed there reinforced the double nature of nourishment of body and soul. The sisters sat at table in precisely the same way that they took their places in the choir. In both rooms the sisters sat according to the order of religion, sitting side by side down both sides of the room, facing inward. The act of hearing the reading in refectory while eating reflected the hearing of the Word of God and the eating of the Eucharist during Mass in the choir. The refectory was a holy setting that, while serving to meet the bodily needs of the nun for nourishment, sought more importantly to feed the nun on the spiritual food from the readings. The Constitutions prescribed the proper ritual for meals. "After the Sisters wash their hands, she who presides rings the refectory bell, and then the Sisters will enter. After they have entered, the Versicularian says the Benedicite and the community will continue with the prayers for the blessing of the table. The servers, however, begin from the lower end and go up to the

Prioress's table."[21] In imitation of the liturgy, the meal began with the recitation of public prayers and blessings and continued with reading, during which the meal was served to each sister in her place. Physical nourishment was quite limited for the nuns, and frequently the food was of poor quality. Nuns ate meat only with special permission for reasons of health. They fasted not only according to the calendar of the church but kept the great monastic fast from the Triumph of the Cross (14 September) until Easter. The main meal was at midday while breakfast and evening collation were little more than snacks. The quality of the food as testified in the Sister-Books and autobiographies could be very poor. For spiritual nourishment the nuns listened to all manner of possible texts among which would be saints' legends such as the *Legenda aurea* by Jacobus de Voragine, the *Vitae Fratrum* by Gerard de Frachet, the *Life of St. Dominic* by Jordan of Saxony or more popularly by Theodoric of Apoldia. They might also hear readings from the *Dialogus Miraculum* by Caesarius of Heiterbach, portions of the Fathers of the Church, various books from the Bible, homilies and regularly the Rule of St. Augustine and the Constitutions of the Order.[22]

Absolute silence reigned in the dormitory where, in the first flowering of Dominican monastic life, all the sisters slept in one room. It seems that Engelthal initially followed this practice but, like most monasteries, eventually provided a cell for the individual nun, especially for the sick. The Constitutions (chapter X) clearly stated that, "No one may be allowed to have a special place to sleep in the community, unless . . . necessity should require it. In this case at least three Sisters will sleep near one another."[23] Adelheid Langmann mentioned both the dormitory and her cell. Upon arising at the call from the exetatrix, the nuns recited *The Little Office of the Blessed Virgin Mary* in the Church. This Little Office remained basically the same throughout the year and was eventually memorized by the nuns.

Dominicans considered the rule and practice of silence in the monastery as absolutely necessary to the spiritual welfare of the individual and the community as a whole. Without exterior and interior silence, no spiritual progress could be made and it should not be surprising that the Constitutions should emphasize the necessity of silence. "The Sisters will keep silence in the oratory, in the cloister, in the dormitory, and in the refectory. In all other places they may speak with special permission, when and as often as it is permitted."[24] The Constitutions also prescribed penances for those who broke the silence willfully. "If anyone deliberately breaks silence, or gives permission to speak, she will drink water during one dinner and will receive a discipline in the presence of all in Chapter. And from this there is no dispensation, except in the case of the sick who are bedridden."[25] In all other cases the Dominican Constitutions always provided for dispensation from rules and did not bind any rule under sin. That the punishment for breaking silence allowed for no dispensation emphasized the importance given to keeping silence. Dominic himself gave example of the practice of silence. The testimony of Brother William of Montferrato for the canonization process of Dominic in 1233 gave to the Order one of the key statements about the character of Dominic. "He always observed silence in the times laid down in the Order, and he avoided idle words and spoke always with God or about God."[26] Adelheid Langmann wished to keep all the observances of the Order and frequently spoke of the foolishness of idle conversation, preferring, like Dominic, to maintain silence or to pray. With every reform movement of the Dominican Order the keeping of silence played a major role for the reformers believed it to be the primary means to foster a spirit of continual prayer.

Every part of the monastic complex served the goal of spiritual perfection of the nuns. According to the Constitutions (chapter XXVIII) the "buildings of the Sisters will be humble, not remarkable for their elegance of style or superfluity." However, "great care must be taken to have them so arranged throughout so as to further religious observance as much as possible."[27] The Constitutions also provided for another type of religious observance by providing a *locatorium*. "Moreover, there should also be, in some proper place, a parlor *(locatorium)* for communicating with outsiders. Here there will be a window with iron gratings similar to that of the larger grille placed in the church."[28] At this window Adelheid Langmann counseled Marquard Tockler and Eberhard Schutz of Hohenstein.

THE MONASTIC HORARIUM

Even as the monastic buildings had to be arranged to foster religious observance, so too the horarium functioned to sanctify every moment of the day in a balanced rhythm of community prayer, private prayer, and *lectio divina*, labor, eating, and sleeping. Of greatest importance for the monastic revival of the *vita apostolica* was the solemn chanting of the psalms, an activity that had always characterized Christian monastic life. The psalm verse, "Seven times a day I praise thee for thy righteous ordinances" (Ps. 119:165) gave scriptural foundation to the daily sequence of liturgical ceremonies. As mentioned by Adelheid Langmann, the nuns gathered in choir for the offices of matins, prime, terce, sext, none, vespers, and compline. The Constitutions devoted an entire chapter to the office of the Church (chapter I). "The Sisters assist all together at Matins and at all the canonical hours, unless some are dispensed for a reasonable cause. All the canonical hours must be recited in the church, distinctly and without precipitation, so that the Sisters will not lose devotion and that other duties may not be impeded."[29]

These hours, observed seasonally according to the rising and the setting of the sun, formed the framework of the nun's day around which all other activities took place. Of these activities the most important was the celebration of Mass, usually after prime. Also the nun devoted time to private prayer in the choir and to *lectio divina* or the prayerful memorization of Scripture and liturgical texts. Each sister had work duties in the monastery so that the affairs of the community would run smoothly. Matins interrupted the time for sleep in the middle of the night, and many considered this interruption to be the most severe penance among Dominican observances.

Just as the day was divided by the canonical hours of prayer, so the year progressed according to liturgical seasons and feast days. In the autobiographies and biographies of the fourteenth century, this annual cycle of feasts and fasts gave a definite liturgical rhythm to life. The Advent season brought special grace to Margaret Ebner. Good Friday was the climax of the Lenten fast and the Passion cycle. Adelheid Langmann and Christina Ebner frequently made references to feast days and ecclesiastical seasons. The nun always lived in anticipation of the coming feast, especially Christmas and Easter.

MONASTIC PRACTICES

Dominicans professed obedience as the primary vow, poverty and chastity being understood as part of obedience. According to the Dominican profession formula the nun promised only obedience.

> I, _____, make profession and promise obedience to God, to the Blessed Mary, and to the Blessed Dominic, and to you, _____, Prioress, in the place of _____, Master of the Order of Friars Preachers, according to the rule of Blessed Augustine and the Constitutions of the Sisters whose care is committed to the Order of Preachers that I will be obedient to you and to my other Prioresses until death.[30]

Obedience had preeminence because it more perfectly imitated Christ himself who, by dying on the cross, offered total conformity of his will to that of the Father by "obediently accepting even death—death on a cross" (Phil. 2:8). The consent of his will and the shedding of his blood constituted the sacrifice by which Christ saved the world. By comparison, poverty and chastity seemed less important for the imitation of Christ. However, poverty as a guiding ideal of Dominic and the Order helped to separate the nun from the things and people of the world and from attachment to them. Adelheid Langmann and the people whom she advised constantly needed to choose between God's will and the world. Poverty then served as an aid in achieving the necessary detachment from the world in order to cling to the things of God. Chastity functioned as an eschatological symbol of the nun's attachment to God and to the things of God, and it showed a preference for the things of heaven over earthly things.

Although a library catalogue exists for the monastery of Engelthal, no list of readings for refectory survives.[31] However, sample lists do exist from Engelthal's daughter house, St. Katharina in Nuremberg. Since close ties existed between the two houses, the list of readings at St. Katharina offers a glimpse into what may have been done at almost any Dominican monastery.[32] This list can only hint at what may have been read at Engelthal since it was drawn up for another monastery for the years 1429 to 1431. The recommendations for reading were carefully worked out using numerous books from the extensive library at St. Katharina's. In general, for a particular feast day the appointed epistle and gospel would be read along with a sermon on the day and perhaps a devotional work appropriate to the theme. For example, on Pentecost Sunday at the first meal, the epistle "In those days . . ." was read followed by the *Veni Creator;* then the Gospel of the day, followed by a reading from the Book of Prophets, "There is a question. . . ." Then came a reading taken from the Song of Solomon, "Rise up rushing wind . . ." and a reading beginning with *Spiritus sanctus hodie* followed by sermons by John Tauler: *Qui spiritans puer iste erit, Emitte spiritum tuum, Qui spiritu Dei;* and finally a reading from the Acts of the Apostles, presumably the text reporting the Pentecost event.[33]

The plan for readings covered the entire liturgical year and included readings from all the Gospels plus the Gospel of Nicodemus, the Acts of the Apostles, Paul's First Letter to the Corinthians, the Song of Solomon, unspecified prophetic books, and the Apocalypse; liturgical texts such as the *Exultet;* sermons by John Tauler, St. Gregory, St. Thomas; and other sorts of texts: the Rule of St. Augustine, the *Constitutions of the Sisters,* and devotional works such as "On the Name of Jesus" and a life of St. Dominic. These readings were taken from manuscripts at hand in the monastery library. It should also be noted that the texts chosen were not only in Latin. Frequently the Gospel, Epistle, homily, or tract was in German, making it more likely that the hearers would learn from the readings. Although Adelheid

Langmann made no reference to reading, *lectio divina,* or study in her *Revelations,* her use of Scripture quotes and allusions as well as the numerous resonances of the sermons of Bernard of Clairvaux, the writings of Mechthild of Magdeburg, *The Song of the Daughter of Zion,* and other religious works make it clear that she learned much from these influential texts and made use of them in her life and literary work. Also of particular note with regard to the education of Adelheid Langmann is the fact that excerpts from the Song of Solomon occurred more frequently in the cycle of refectory readings than other texts. In all likelihood this was also the practice at Engelthal and may account for Adelheid's numerous references to the biblical text.

Dominican monastic life as regulated by the Rule of St. Augustine and especially by the *Constitutions of the Sisters* formed the practical mysticism of nuns such as Adelheid Langmann, which in turn was the basis for the ecstatic mysticism described in her *Revelations.* These texts and the spirit of religious fervor of the age established an ideal of mystical life unparalleled in the history of Christianity.

MYSTICAL LIFE AS IDEAL

The religious fervor of the fourteenth century produced a culture and an atmosphere in which mystical life of an ecstatic sort became idealized. Martin Grabmann described the mystics of that time in a favorable light. "These were the mystics . . . who yearned for knowledge of God and the love of God and who strove by leading a life of virtues to be as united with God as was possible on earth. They set down their religious inner life in compelling writings."[34] Above all, this ideal of ecstatic mystical life occurred among Dominican nuns along the Rhine and the Danube and in Franconia, especially at the monasteries of Töß and Ötenbach in Switzerland, Katharinenthal near Konstanz, Unterlinden in Colmar, Adelhausen near Freiburg in Breisgau, Maria Medingen in Swabia, and Engelthal near Nuremberg. In fact, almost all written evidence of *Frauenmystik* derive from the Dominican Order.[35] In all of these Dominican monasteries of nuns, strict discipline of life was the ideal in order to foster spiritual growth even to a mystical level, but also to ground mystical experience in the liturgical routine of the daily round of prayers and praise offered by the whole community.

Hieronymus Wilms posited several reasons why such a unique flowering of mysticism should occur in the German-speaking lands in the fourteenth century and why Dominican men and women should play such a major role. He believed that the age fostered a turning away from earthly cares to heavenly matters since that entire period of church history was so tragic because the popes ruled from Avignon and were under the influence of the French kings. The conflict between emperor and pope and especially the interdict imposed upon the lands subject to Louis the Bavarian, with the subsequent imperial reaction supported by the theories of Franciscan Spirituals, tested the loyalties of every Christian and brought many faithful people into confusion or indifference. Natural causes also contributed to the malaise of the times—famine, earthquakes, floods, strange diseases, comets and prophecies about them, and the Black Death.[36] While all these reasons have sociopolitical importance, they really do not fully explain the incredible spiritual movement of that time. In fact, most of the reports about mystical life and experiences of Dominican nuns were written prior to the Black Death. The plague actually did more to destroy the fabric of religious life in the monasteries and consequently helped to diminish or even to destroy the monastic culture that fostered mysticism. The reasons for this flowering of German mysticism had more to do with the preaching of Dominicans and the educational level of the nuns than with sociopolitical influences. Scholars differ as to the reasons why mystical life developed so powerfully in Dominican cloisters. Some ascribed this development to the influence of Meister Eckhart, Henry Suso, and Mechthild of Magdeburg, while others attributed it to the practical mysticism of the nuns expressed in their use of the Divine Office, *The Little Office of the Blessed Virgin Mary*, the reading of the Church Fathers, *The Song of the Daughter of Zion*, the practice of *lectio divina*, and contact with the friars.[37] I assume that all of these factors contributed to setting the stage for a flowering of mystical life, but they do not explain why mystical life flourished in Dominican monasteries of the fourteenth century. The nuns and friars of the time would more than likely have ascribed the entire mystical movement to God's providence. They viewed themselves as recipients of his special graces and as his special friends chosen by God to enjoy intimacy with the divinity. This belief arose from the mutual influence of the friars and the nuns and had much to do with the advancement of learning.

Many of the nuns in these monasteries enjoyed a high level of education and could read Latin.[38] Also, they possessed and studied copies of theological works such as the *Summa Theologicæ* by St. Thomas Aquinas and *The Flowing Light of the Godhead* by Mechthild of Magdeburg, among others. Henry of Nördlingen, the translator of Mechthild's work, sent copies to Margaret Ebner at Maria Medingen and possibly to Christina Ebner at Engelthal.[39] Christina mentioned *The Flowing Light of the Godhead* twice in her *Revelations*. In the summer of 1346, she related that God spoke to her: "My eternal Love, I have sent you the book that is called an outflowing light of the Godhead before your death so that you will become even bolder."[40] During Easter week in 1348, she related the following words from God: "I have sent you that book so that your spiritual joy and hope be the more increased. And I meant the book that is called an outflowing light of the Godhead."[41] Other scholars have also suggested that Adelheid Langmann was influenced by this work. Wilhelm Preger stated that the book was sent to Engelthal in 1345 and that certain details such as Adelheid's singular desire for God described in contrast to the inadequacy of consolation from heaven, earth, and angels and the insistent request that God come to console her without any intermediaries suggest Mechthild's influence.[42] Also Siegfried Ringler noted his belief that certain portions of the *Revelations* of Adelheid Langmann were written under the influence of Mechthild of Magdeburg.[43]

That the Dominican nuns who took part in this flowering of mysticism were educated in spiritual matters is certain. Sufficient evidence has been given to note some of the texts they possessed and used in their own writings. In her *Revelations*, Adelheid Langmann showed knowledge especially of the Song of Solomon, the Gospel of John, the Gospel of Luke, the Gospel of Matthew, and the Book of Revelation. Evidently she also knew St. Bernard's *Sermons on the Song of Songs* since she employed allusions to and direct quotes from them in her autobiography.

The level of education of the Dominican nuns also had to do with the influence of the Dominican friars. The *cura monialium* was given only to highly educated and gifted Dominican priests. "The best of the Dominican preachers . . . found in the monasteries of Dominican nuns a grateful audience for their religious zeal."[44] These preachers, among whom were John Tauler and Henry Suso, spoke of the love of God in less speculative terms, appealing to the emotions and affections of the audience. They were also aware, especially because of the training given Dominican preachers and the advice from Humbert of Romans, that they should direct their preaching and formulate its content and expression according to the abilities and spiritual maturity of the audience.[45] Hence a sermon delivered to the general public in the city square on a Sunday afternoon differed greatly from what might be preached to a community of nuns. Even with the nuns, the emphasis would be on a practical mysticism that should be experienced by the hearer. There was nothing academic about the mysticism preached. The message was not meant to be discussed and politely critiqued over a glass of Rhine wine; it was meant to be applied directly to the conditions of the life of the sisters. Because of the level of education and religious observance of the nuns, the preacher's words, like the seed in the parable of the sower, found fertile ground in the minds and hearts of the Dominican nuns. The preaching of the friars centered on several indispensable themes that then fashioned and supported the ideal life of a Dominican nun. She was to renounce all earthly things, to renounce the false Self completely, to pick up her cross in imitation of Christ and to proceed along the "narrow way" by growing in the practice of virtues, ultimately in order to be graced with the mystical experience of seeing God "face to face."[46] Even in this life moments of union could occur during which all cares, worries and self-consciousness would disappear. The human spirit, in rapture ("out of itself"), sees God and forgets self. This rapture, which Paul and Moses experienced, represents the highest happiness in this life. For this the mystic longed—the experience of God in knowledge and love.[47] Like the athlete who sacrificed all to gain merely a wreath of laurels, the mystic sacrificed all earthly things to gain all heavenly things.

THE INFLUENCE OF
THE FRIARS: ECKHART, TAULER, AND SUSO

The nuns received guidance in their mystical awareness from the friars who preached to them, the most famous of whom were Meister Eckhart, John Tauler, and Henry Suso. Of these three Meister Eckhart had the least direct influence on the nuns. According to Otto Langer, Eckhart's teachings diverged significantly from the teachings gleaned from the various Sister-Books in four significant areas. (1) The religious conversion (*ker*) of the nun signified a new beginning or new existence for her. In the Sister-Books this change is an interior act symbolized by the flight from the world and the entrance into a monastery. For Eckhart, however, "the real new beginning of life consists not in a flight into the monastery, but rather in the breaking of self-will."[48] The nun's problem was not with the world but with herself. While Adelheid Langmann did write extensively about her entrance into the monastery, she never portrayed it as a flight from the world. In fact, she resisted Christ's will for her to enter Engelthal and could be induced to take the veil only because of revelations received by herself and by a friend. The entire pattern of her spiritual growth approximated more closely Otto Langer's description of Meister Eckhart's teachings. Adelheid clearly struggled with her self-will, and even though desirous of conforming her will to Christ's, she continually grappled with this problem. Even though Adelheid prayed to conform her will to Christ's, she could not do it. After a series of revelations in which Christ asked her to choose between going to heaven or remaining on earth, she finally responded, "I want whatever you want."[49] This was the right answer at last, and Christ immediately delivered his lengthiest response thus far and rewarded Adelheid with association with his mother, saints, and angels, since she had finally conformed her will to his. Likewise Margarete Weinhandl emphasized the importance of conformity of will for the nuns as demonstrated in the Sister-Books.[50]

(2) The ascetic practices or penitential observances (uebunge) as presented in the Sister-Books showed a tendency to destroy the body, the greater extent of which would lead to greater happiness. Eckhart distinguished the external work of penance from the intention. Love, rather than severe penance, is the measure of perfection. "The real penitential work is the destruction of the (false) Self, the only good is a good will."[51] While she practiced the normal penances prescribed by the Constitutions of the Sisters and also practiced severe penance in the form of the discipline, Adelheid Langmann clearly did such things precisely as a "discipline" to destroy her false self, and her motive was always love for Christ. Through her revelations she learned to connect suffering and love as the perfect imitation of Christ who suffered and died on the cross out of a motive of love. Christ taught her, "Gladly bear suffering for my sake. See what I have suffered for you."[52] In another revelation the virgin Caritas taught her of Christ's love. "Love compelled him to give himself into the hands of his enemies and let himself be martyred in such anguish and need that no one can ponder it."[53] She went on to explain every moment of the passion as done out of love. "When he died out of love, his side was pierced and water and blood flowed from it. This he gives as a gift to all those who love him."[54]

(3) Using a term from von Balthasar, Langer claimed that Eckhart would prefer an "Entphantasierung des Glaubens" or "a faith stripped of images" as opposed, apparently, to the visions and private revelations granted to the nuns. Adelheid Langmann reported almost innumerable visions and revelations throughout the text in dialogue form. For her the imaginative power of fantasy supported what was even more important to Eckhart's mysticism—a union of God and soul at the level of being. Adelheid imaged this union primarily in the heart. On her heart Christ wrote his name, never to be erased.[55] Mary placed her child in Adelheid's heart. "Our Lady placed herself in front of the sister and it seemed to this sister that her own heart opened up and Our Lady took her little Child and placed him in her heart. Then her heart closed up again and Our Lady made the sign of the cross over her heart saying, 'You will remain in this heart forever.'"[56] Further, Adelheid prayed to Christ, "Dearly beloved Lord, for the sake of the love that you showed me yesterday, let me

see you," to which Christ responded simply, "Look into your own heart."[57] These non-bridal images reinforce the idea that Adelheid and Christ are united at the very core of her being, a much more Eckhartian approach than evidence gleaned from the monastery Sister-Books would allow.

(4) Langer's fourth differentiation between the mystical teachings in the Sister-Books and those of Meister Eckhart had to do with the role of ecstasy. Ecstasy played no role in Eckhart's mysticism. The human person should live as a "Son of God" according to his human nature, which has attained an inestimable dignity by the incarnation of God.[58] If Langer was correct in his description of Eckhart's teaching, clearly Adelheid Langmann's ecstatic mysticism has no connection with those teachings. Her ecstasies were clearly important as symbols of spiritual progress and imaged her relationship to Christ as that of bride and bridegroom, lover and beloved.

John Tauler, a disciple of Meister Eckhart, had a more personal and lasting impact on the Dominican nuns. He exercised his ministry of the care of souls in his native Strasbourg and had frequent contact with the seven monasteries of Dominican nuns in the city, and he exerted a wide influence on monasteries elsewhere and on the Friends of God. His only extant letter was written to Margaret Ebner, a nun and mystic at Maria Medingen in Swabia.[59] Christina Ebner, a nun of Engelthal, spoke of Tauler's "fiery tongue that kindled the entire world."[60] Of the three great German mystics, "Tauler is the one who has exercised the greatest influence on the German-speaking countries as well as on the rest of Europe."[61] A Carthusian, Laurentius Surius, translated Tauler's works into Latin in 1548. In his dedicatory preface he wrote of Tauler:

> Tauler's attraction lies in the fact that he (who certainly had reached the heights of Christian perfection) never tires to encourage all, as strongly as possible, in the love of God and neighbor; that he exhorts them to eradicate vice, to be attentive to their innermost ground, to strive for virtue and to deny their self-will and inordinate desires; that he invites them to imitate Christ by taking up His Cross and following Him humbly but faithfully in spite of many obstacles and mortifications; until finally the soul becomes so united to Him as to be one spirit with Him, in a most wondrous way. All this is nothing else but loving God with heart and soul and mind, with all one's strength, and one's neighbor as oneself.[62]

This approach obviously differs greatly from Eckhart's more cerebral *Entphantisiering des Glaubens*, for it stressed the path of identification with the passion of Christ, of union with Christ's perfect humanity so that the believer may come to know Christ in his divinity. Tauler directed his Sermon 59, "*Ego si exaltatus fuero*" for the feast of the Triumph of the Holy Cross (14 September) to an audience of cloistered religious women, presumably at one of the monasteries in Strasbourg. He preached to the nuns about bearing the Cross within themselves in imitation of Jesus:

> We meet people who indeed carry the Cross outwardly, performing good and pious exercises and having taken upon themselves the burden of monastic life. They do a lot of chanting and reading, they take their place in choir and in the refectory, but they do our Lord a minor service because they are only externally involved. Do you suppose that God has created you like so many songbirds? You were to be his beloved brides and spouses.[63]

Tauler led up to a lesson on the interiorization of the monastic observances. It was not enough to take up the Cross externally by entering the monastery or by chanting psalms; the Cross should also be taken up internally. He admonished the nuns to "accept this cross from God and bear it in the depth of your heart."[64] He set forth his argument using images, examples, and quotes from Scripture and the Fathers and Doctors of the Church. He showed concern that the sisters learn the ways of the mystical life correctly in order to persevere in the true practice of monastic observances that would lead to an interior change in the individual nun, helping her to live more closely united to Christ.

While Tauler preached extensively about Christian life and mysticism to the nuns, Henry Suso apparently lived more in keeping with those teachings and seems to have identified with the nuns in ways not expressed by Eckhart or Tauler. In style and content, Suso's writings were closer to the kind of literature produced by the nuns when writing biographies or autobiographies. His biography was written by a nun of the monastery of Töss, Elsbeth Stagel, and, like the autobiographies of Margaret Ebner, Adelheid Langmann, and Christina Ebner, offers a more complete account of the life than those offered of the nuns in the Sister- Books of the monasteries. His 100 meditations and petitions resemble the prayers of Margaret Ebner and Adelheid Langmann, although thematically he concentrated solely on the passion of Christ rather than on events from the course of Christ's entire life as preferred by the nuns.[65] Events from Suso's life matched similar mystical experiences of Adelheid Langmann. He underwent a spiritual espousal with Eternal Wisdom (chapter three) whereas Adelheid was espoused to Christ her beloved.[66] Suso branded the name of Jesus on his heart (chapter four) whereas Christ wrote his name on Adelheid's heart.[67] Suso's use of images and choice of vocabulary resonated with those used by the nuns. Quotes from Suso's *The Soul's Love-Book* might just as easily have been written by a nun.

> Open my heart for the sake of your precious blood, so that I may behold you, King of kings and Lord of lords, with the eyes of faith. Place all my understanding and wisdom in your wounds, so that henceforth I may draw closer to your death and cut myself off from all earthly things until at last it will be no longer I that live, but you who live in me and by me. Thus, bound with the cords of love, I will remain ever fixed in you.[68]

All three of these preachers, as representative of many others, ministered to the needs of Dominican nuns by preaching and teaching. Each left a legacy of benefit for his sisters: Eckhart's example and inspiration to Tauler and Suso, Tauler's preaching and instruction on religious life, Suso's experiential compatibility with the sensibilities of the nuns. Each helped to bring to life and to direct a monastic culture that supported a flourishing of mysticism in a positive way. The reason for this extraordinary flowering in the fourteenth century has more to do with faith than with sociopolitical circumstances. The preachers and the nuns believed that nothing was impossible with God.

MYSTICAL PHENOMENA

Among numerous possible mystical phenomena Margarete Weinhandl ascertained eleven mystical motifs common among Dominican nuns of the fourteenth century: (1) the appearance of God and the saints at the deathbed; (2) the gift of tears; (3) Mary's mantle of protection; (4) the ability to perceive the spiritual state of others; (5) the comparison of the Order with a garden; (6) the promise to appear after death; (7) the appearance of a dead sister and her relation of her state after death; (8) the certitude of eternal life promised by God or revealed through a saint; (9) all kinds of miracles associated with the host or with receiving communion; (10) the illumination or transfiguration of the face or body; and (11) the yearning for particular graces.[69] Adelheid Langmann experienced or yearned for many of these phenomena herself: God the Father assured her, "Be at peace. I will free you from the prison of your body and take you up into my divine grace and will lead you into the kingdom that I prepared for you from the beginning of the world"(motif one).[70] Adelheid often shed "sweet" tears and prayed for this gift, "I remind you (Christ) that you cried and ask you to give me sweet tears of love for all my sins"(motif two).[71] Kunigunde, Adelheid's nanny, related mystical events from Adelheid's childhood. "Then the most beautiful lady . . . came and she was wearing a blue mantle. This mantle was so wide that if it had ever been unfolded it would have covered the whole world"(motif three).[72] Adelheid frequently perceived the spiritual state of others despite a lack of cooperation on the part of her advisees. When Marquard Tockler refused to reveal his problem, Adelheid stated simply, "You are sorely tempted. I know for certain you want to kill yourself"(motif four).[73] Garden imagery occurred frequently throughout the work (motif five). Adelheid referred to fruits and various flowers by name and wrote of the garden of love, but she did not apply this imagery directly to the monastery. Adelheid never promised to appear after her death, but another sister, Elsbet, did appear to her after she had died to reveal, "God is so merciful and did such good for me at my end that if I had known this, I would never have had such great anxiety about my death" (motif six and seven).[74] Adelheid received certitude of eternal life directly from God the Father. "I will . . . lead you into the kingdom that I prepared for you from the beginning of the world" (motif eight).[75] Adelheid also reported various miracles with regard to the host; Christ succeeded in convincing her to enter the monastery because she could not swallow the host until she promised to become a nun. Also, while a priest was celebrating Mass, the Christ Child appeared and changed into the host (motif nine).[76]

Adelheid had a variety of mystical experiences such as mystical marriage, transport into purgatory and heaven, the writing of the name of Jesus on her heart, mystical lactation, visions, locutions, and holy fragrances. She spoke with God the Father, the Son and the Holy Spirit, the Virgin Mary, St. John the Beloved, St. Peter, and other saints. She visited or was visited by deceased members of her family and other souls. She fell into ecstasy and had to be led away to her cell. She lay like a corpse overwhelmed with revelations. Above all she heard innumerable times the salutation of love from Christ, "My Beloved!"

Such mystical experiences were considered to be the natural outcome of a nun's spiritual development if she were faithful to the Dominican way of life and allowed herself to be formed in prayer and ascetical practices. That the nun would progress in holiness, symbolized by mystical experiences was expected. Margarete Weinhandl agreed with Engelbert Krebs concerning the kind of life the nuns led and quoted him: ". . . a nun who entered the monastery in its first flowering took on a life full of exalted spiritual activity. If she was fervent, she filled her mind and her feelings with heavenly things taken daily from the Holy Scripture, the Fathers, poets, teachers, from the particularly poetic Dominican liturgy and from the innumerable legends of the saints and stories of the history of the Order. . . ."[77] The nuns of Engelthal and their chaplains and friends clearly lived in such a manner.

IDEALS REMEMBERED AND TAUGHT: THE *SISTER-BOOK*

In caritate perpetua dilexi te:
ideo attraxi te miserans.

—Jer. 31:3b Vulgata

AMONG THE NINE EXTANT SISTER-BOOKS (*Schwesternbücher*) written by Dominican nuns in the fourteenth century, the *Sister-Book of Engelthal* enjoys a unique place, since the community at Engelthal produced so many original literary works of a biographical or autobiographical nature in addition to it. Like many of the other examples of this genre, the *Sister-Book of Engelthal* was written in the vernacular by one of the nuns. The author produced a document that both recalled the original ideals of the founding community of beguines and perpetuated those ideals by including life sketches of many nuns, whose lives embodied a certain ideal of religious life and whose stories taught how to live by virtues important to the monastic ideals of the nuns.

THE MANUSCRIPTS

The *Sister-Book of Engelthal* exists in two manuscripts, one in the Germanisches Nationalmuseum in Nuremberg (N) and the second as part of the *Codex Scotensis Vindobonensis* housed in the Schottenstift in Vienna (W).[1] Manuscript N belonged to the Monastery of Engelthal and is the oldest extant copy of any Dominican *Sister-Book*.[2] The scribe, Hans Probst, included Manuscript W in his *Sammelcodex*, which also contains the *Sister-Book of Kirchberg* and that of an unknown monastery in Swabia, as well as other texts written at Engelthal, such as the *Gnaden-vita of Friedrich Sunder, Chaplain of Engelthal,* the *Vita of Sister Gertud of Engelthal,* and the shortest version of Adelheid Langmann's *Revelations.* This codex also contains numerous devotional and theological works important for anyone interested in mystical teachings. Among these texts are excerpts from Gertrude of Helfta's *Ein botte der göttlichen miltikeit,* or other works such as *Das Wirken Gottes, des Engels und des Teufels in der Seele des Menschen,* and *Vier Stufen des mystischen Aufstiegs.*[3] This manuscript can be dated precisely from the text to the year 1451, and an epilogue written by Anna Jäck dates to the year 1457. The manuscript belonged to the monastery of Inzigkofen.[4] That monastery, originally for Poor Clares, became a foundation for Augustinian canonesses in 1394 and can be counted as one of the most influential sites for mystical writings in the fifteenth century.[5] The large number of works by authors from Engelthal included in this manuscript attests to the close connection between the two monasteries of nuns and to the importance of the writings from Engelthal.

THE AUTHOR OF
THE *SISTER-BOOK OF ENGELTHAL*

The author of the text does not identify herself. However, it is certain from external and internal evidence that Christina Ebner authored the *Sister-Book of Engelthal.* Previously scholars were in doubt about her authorship, but now the evidence points to her and to no one else as the author. A postscript, written some time after the completion of the Nuremberg manuscript, identifies the author as Christina Ebner: "Kristein Ebner made a little book about the divine graces granted by our Lord to the sisters of her monastery . . ."[6] Internal evidence also shows the author to have been a nun. The author emphatically states that she is going to write this book in the first line of the text. "I begin to write a little book . . ."[7] Like so many medieval authors who pronounce their lack of learning and ability to write, Christina claims that she does not have the ability to write a book about the history of her monastery; however, she dares to undertake the task because she is writing under obedience and is compelled by that vow to do it. "Now I wanted to write something about the overburden of grace. Yet I have regrettably little understanding and do not know how to write. Only because of obedience have I been compelled to do these things."[8] Throughout the text she interjects information about herself and her role as speaking for the entire community. In the first two paragraphs Christina Ebner, using the first person singular, mentions her intention for writing the "little book" and also her inability to write it. She writes the text and no other. Later, after writing of the donation of two altars in the chapel by their chaplain, Ulschalk of Vilseck, she writes that she will inform the reader about how the third altar was erected in the chapel, "How the third altar came about, I will make known to you soon."[9] She has done the requisite research and has obtained her information from various and reliable sources.

Christina also refers to herself as part of the community, and as writer of the *Sister-Book*, she speaks for the sisters collectively: "One came here to us, who was called Reichhild of Gemmersheim, with her husband, who became a lay brother."[10] Likewise she writes collectively in speaking of their chaplain: "A Preacher was named Friar Conrad of Eichstätt and he was the guardian of our monastery for a long time . . ."[11]

THE TEXT AS CHRONICLE

Frequently the Sister-Books have been called "chronicles," a name that implies a chronological ordering of events written over a certain period of time. However, the entries recorded in the Engelthal text are not arranged chronologically. Difficulty arises in attributing specific dates and even years to the lives and events recorded in the *Sister-Book*. Analysis of the text shows that it divides naturally into two sections: the foundation story of the community and the biographical sketches of specific nuns, lay brothers, and priests. Necessarily, the texts of the two overlap, for the same people may be treated in both sections. Adelheid Rotter, the founding beguine, naturally appears in the historical section of the early days of the community, but she is also the focus of a brief sketch about her spiritual life, independent of the biographical and historical information already included in the first part.

Specific dates needed for the argument that the biographical sketches are arranged in chronological order cannot be accurately determined from documentary evidence. For many of the nuns, such as Liugart of Berg, Alheit of Roet, Reichhilt of Gemmersheim, and others, no dates whatsoever exist. For other nuns, dates gleaned from documents exist but offer little help to support a chronology based upon their date of birth, date of entry into the community, or their date of death. For example, the entry for Adelheid of Ingolstadt, who can be dated to before 1269, follows the entry for Rihza of Ellenbach, who died after 1323. Since no chronology as the structural foundation of the book can be determined, one might consider the text as "history."

THE TEXT AS HISTORY

No documentary evidence supports the thesis that the *Sister-Book of Engelthal* was written primarily as a history although it does include historical data. If it was intended to be a history, then it would be a very poor one since historical inaccuracies abound. According to the text, the first prioress traveled to the pope in Rome to obtain permission for the community of nuns at Engelthal to be incorporated into the Dominican Order.[12] The pope, however, was in Lyons from where the papal bull for the foundation of the monastery was issued on 10 October 1248, by Pope Innocent IV. Also, if the text was intended to be a history, it is quite incomplete. An analysis of the incomplete list of nuns compiled by Gustav Voit shows that there may very well have been more than fifty nuns whose biographical sketches could have been included in the *Sister-Book* but were not. Since these nuns are not included in a "history" or in a "chronicle" of Engelthal, then the structural principle of the text must lie elsewhere.

STRUCTURAL PRINCIPLE
OF THE TEXT: THE MESSAGE

The guiding structural principle of the text is neither chronology nor history. While both of these may be included and used at times in the text, the real guiding principle can be determined by the explanation of the author herself:

> I now begin to write a dear little book about the beginnings of the monastery at Engelthal and about the many graces God showed to the nuns there from its very beginning and ever since; and also about the great number of the virtues He pours out which can come as little to an end as the ocean's overflowing power.[13]

What Christina Ebner announces as the purpose of the book is the praise of God's grace for pouring out virtues. The guiding principle of the text is an account of God's grace in bringing about the foundation of a new community and monastery. It also reports the overflowing of God's grace to individual sisters and the virtues that they thereby receive. The first part of the text is not actually a history of the foundation of the monastery; it is rather a history of God's providence and action in the world to bring about a new monastery. The second part contains biographical sketches precisely as related to God's grace given to each sister, which then brings forth different virtues and mystical experiences as received by each unique sister and mystic. The text can most profitably be read as a document of faith, for matters of historicity, chronology, and completeness of the text, while important, remain merely incidental to the purpose of the *Sister-Book*.

THE FOUNDING OF THE
COMMUNITY AND THE DOMINICAN MONASTERY

Providential circumstances led to the foundation of the community and to its later incorporation into the Dominican Order. The *Sister-Book* invites the reader to become aware of the action of God's grace as the providential force that established the community, formed it into a religious house, and invited its individual members into an immediate experience of the divine. In so doing, the text performs a didactic function both by retelling and interpreting the foundation story and the life sketches of sisters who had gone before. The text is meant to inspire contemporary nuns with a clear indication of how God has related to the community in the past along with the reassuring hope that he will continue to do so in their own lives.

Christina Ebner accomplishes her theological end by showing the community of her sisters within the context of God's providence to call individuals and the community to conversion. She places this dynamic within the concept of divine mystery: "No one has achieved great holiness by her own piety, rather he [God] has brought them along by his own free will. He is powerful in doing good for his friends because he knows all things. For that reason he does good to one and not to another. Our human senses cannot grasp that without falling into error.[14] Christina clearly asserts God's initiative and guidance in the spiritual life and in the call to holiness. She likewise asserts his freedom in giving his gifts and in choosing his friends, a freedom which to human senses may seem unfair, especially to those who do not receive his gifts. However, Christina's story is precisely about those who have been favored by divine grace and the effect that grace, once received, can have on others. She carefully constructs her foundation story to illustrate God's providence and its effects on those with whom the nuns of Engelthal come in contact.

Christina Ebner introduces Adelheid Rotter as the first example of conversion. According to Christina's account, this Adelheid served as a musician to the child Princess Elizabeth of Hungary (b. 1207–d. 1231), during which time she used her playing ability, not primarily to entertain but to soothe the child when she cried. She also accompanied the princess

to her betrothal and marriage to Louis IV of Hesse and Thuringia (b.1200–
d.1227).[15] Afterward Adelheid no longer wished to continue in her musical
profession, but preferred to "give her life over to the loving God."[16] Christina
relates that Adelheid was considered to be a great sinner because of her
profession. The image of a *trobaritz* could well have been very negative
because of the content of the songs that formed the repertoire of a roving
minstrel. Knowing that Adelheid had played at a court, people might
automatically assume that she had sung such songs of courtly love, illicit
affairs, or secret love trysts as part of her duty to entertain. Christina explains
that Adelheid "was known far and wide for her sinful profession."[17] Whether
her profession actually was sinful to Adelheid or only thought to have been
sinful by others, the change from being a musician to a lover of God
represents a personal conversion experience for Adelheid and should be
understood in that way. No matter to what level of sinfulness her profession
had brought her, she had now chosen a different course dictated by love for
God. Having taken up residence in the city of Nuremberg, Adelheid
possessed a reputation for goodness that was all the more remarkable. She
soon became the leader or teacher (*magistra*) of a collection of women who
formed a community of beguines about her, since they did not have the
means to establish a monastery.[18] These women had been prompted to
change their lives and to seek a teacher by listening to preaching. The
preacher had spoken about the great reward that the Lord would give to
those who sought purity and lived by voluntary poverty.[19] Significantly,
Christina links this desire for purity and poverty with the actions of early
Christians as reported in the Acts of the Apostles (2:44-45; 4:34-35, 37) by
showing the beguines as freely seeking a *magistra* to whom they will be
obedient so that they may progress in the spiritual life, and by the willing
offering of all they possess, which they place at the feet of Adelheid.[20] This
impulse to imitate the lives of the apostles predisposes the beguines of
Nuremberg to associate themselves with the mendicant orders, especially
with the Dominicans who understood the foundation of the new Order of
Preachers precisely as a return to the *vita apostolica*, especially with regard to
the importance of poverty. Christina's association of the actions of the
beguines with those of the early Christians likewise implies the position of
Adelheid as apostolic teacher, one who knows Christ from experience and
who can impart knowledge about him and his teachings and further inspire
her followers to dedicate themselves completely to the spiritual life. Just as
the apostles had known Christ and gave witness to his resurrection, so
Adelheid by her conversion witnesses her own intimacy with Christ and
gives witness to her "resurrection to new life" in him. Her preaching becomes

powerful and persuasive because she has accepted and lived the call to holiness. Adelheid's conversion becomes a cause for the conversion of others, just as the apostles' living witness and preaching had drawn the crowds to believe in Christ. The same providential dynamic continues to work in the church in all ages, in the thirteenth as well as in the first century.

The association of Adelheid and her beguines with the apostolic community in Jerusalem continues with the opening of the next paragraph, which announces the beginning of "our community."[21] Adelheid is a mother to her community and "cares for them as if they were all her children."[22] Like the church at Jerusalem, the beguines prosper in holiness to such an extent that "everyone who saw their life were made better by it."[23] Adelheid's providential conversion bore fruit in the example of her sisters to such a degree that lords of the land come to receive the blessing of the beguines, pilgrims begin to stop at Engelthal before they set out on their journey, and pious women take instruction from them as to how to confess their sins properly.[24] The reputation of the beguines draws other women to them, and the kinds of activities that the beguines undertake link them closely with the activities of the apostles: they bless those who seek a blessing, they send forth others to spread the good news, and they instruct those who wish to make progress in Christian life. Perhaps because of these implicit associations with the activities of the apostles, Christina Ebner carefully and cautiously notes that the beguines were in the territory of the pastor of St. Lawrence, one of the two medieval parishes of Nuremberg, and "were obedient to him as their true pastor."[25] It may just as likely be that he knew of their activities and approved of them and could act as their protector if they were ever challenged or criticized.

Following the apostolic community as a model, the beguines begin to organize themselves in a more structured way. Christina writes of the beguines, somewhat anachronistically, that they elect a "subprioress," an office title used by Dominican nuns. They also begin activities that associate them with the life of the apostolic community. They share common meals and listen to edifying readings. As their leader, Adelheid sits at the head of the table, her position signifying her authority in a monastic context. They also pray the office in common, and after compline they go to their *meisterin* and ask what they should do the next day.[26] All these activities link them with the apostolic community that prayed together, took meals in common, and accepted the authority of the apostles. These activities also show a progression of the community in its eventual assimilation into a monastic way of life that intentionally seeks to imitate the *vita apostolica*. The return of the beguine community to the ideals of the apostolic church bears fruit by powerful signs. When listening to the readings in German, many in the community fell down, senseless as if dead, for, as Christina explains, "they were truly dead in God."[27] Christina further relates that this "grace of rapture" also affected them while working, praying, or listening to the word of God. She also carefully notes that this happened to all the sisters except one.[28] The beginnings of mystical experiences result from their fidelity to apostolic life.

The fame of the beguines spreads. They receive gifts from Queen Kunigunde of Bohemia (d. 1248) and also begin to attract the help of men who wished to associate themselves as members of the community.[29] A Brother Hermann serves the needs of the community. Ulschalk of Vilseck, a wealthy priest known as a public sinner (his daughter later became a nun of Engelthal), undergoes a conversion experience because of the beguines and becomes their chaplain and benefactor.[30] Conrad of Lauffenholz, a Teutonic knight, leaves his order desiring to lead a more contemplative life and associates himself with the community. Other men aid the fledgling community. Ulrich of Königstein is considered by the nuns to be the founder of the monastery, for he welcomed them and gave them shelter when they fled the interdicted city of Nuremberg. Braun of Himmelsdorf, a nobleman who experienced a powerful encounter with Christ, vows to give all he has to support the new community.[31] In a few paragraphs Christina makes the reader aware of the wide-ranging influence of the community of women headed by Adelheid. Their fame spreads from the local area to foreign lands (Bohemia). They influence a queen (Kunigunde), lords of the area, pilgrims, pious women, powerful noblemen (Ulrich and Braun), members of orders (Conrad of Lauffenholz and Conrad of Eichstätt), simple brothers (Hermann and Conrad), and a sinful priest (Ulschalk). Like the church in Jerusalem, the community of beguines and later Dominican nuns sends its message throughout the world to both genders, to all levels of medieval society, and even to foreign lands.

The community's progress continues in a providential vein. By having to leave the free imperial city of Nuremberg because of the interdict against the emperor, the sisters begin the process of association with the Dominican Order. They are tested by God in this period of confusion, having to struggle for survival by performing the most menial tasks, which would later be assigned to lay sisters. Their temporary stay under the hospitality of Ulrich of Königstein becomes permanent after the death of his only male heir, whom the beguines had nursed following his accident. Ulrich had become so taken with the community that he determined to make it possible for them to stay permanently on his lands, which he would donate to them. He is likewise credited for the choice of the name of the monastery—Engelthal (valley of the angels) instead of the place-name Swinach (place of the pigs). He earns credit also as the one who rebuffs the invitation of seven Cistercian or Franciscan "abbots" to the beguines to join their order.[32]

The community's transformation into Dominican is further indicated by the activities of the beguines. They are learning to chant Mass and the offices.[33] The activity of chanting associates them with the singing of angels, indicates the perfection of human beings, and shows love for Christ. In a passage that some believe should belong to the biographical sketches of the individual nuns, Christina clearly shows the direction in which the community progressed. The section on the first chantress of the community, Hailrat, functions more as a statement of the ideals of the fledgling community than as a life sketch:

> It was in Advent when they sang according to the Rule for the first time. Their first chantress was called Hailrat. She was incredibly beautiful and sang well above the norm and learned well and loved our Lord very much. She showed this in all her work and life. Then when it was the fourth Sunday in Advent they sang matins and when they came to the fifth response *Virgo Israel* and the versicle *In caritate perpetua* she sang in German and so superhumanly beautifully that one thought she sang with the voice of an angel. The verse means, "I have loved you with an everlasting love and therefore I have drawn you with my mercy." Our Lord spoke this verse to the human race through the mouth of the prophet. And the whole community lost its senses in profound prayer and they fell down and lay there as if dead until they all came to themselves again. They sang matins with profound reverence until the end.[34]

This verbal icon functions as a revelation of the community to itself. They live in an ecclesial and liturgical time frame. Their primary function as nuns will be the praise of God through their liturgical singing according to their Rule. Each nun will be called to imitate Hailrat to the best of her ability—to sing God's praise and to be thus transformed into the beauty of human perfection. Because of their love for the Lord, the nuns associate themselves with the chosen, the virgins of Israel, who have been called into intimacy with Christ by his mercy in making them virgin monastics according to a new Rule that places them in the tradition of the *vita apostolica*. The message of the community is to believe what Christ has spoken and to make known his promises and love to the world. They will also experience Christ's overwhelming presence to them in spiritual ecstasy.

This prophetic vision encapsulated in this visual icon comes to fulfillment in the next paragraph: "At that time it happened that the Preachers of Regensburg were wandering in the region. The ladies made known that they wished to come under their obedience.[35] Immediately Adelheid Rotter steps aside. The community begins to function as a Dominican foundation by electing its first prioress, Diemut of Geilenhausen, who then obtains approbation from the pope for the incorporation of the new monastery of Engelthal into the Order of Preachers. Pope Innocent IV proclaims the bull of confirmation on 10 October 1248. More significantly, Christina concludes her account of the foundation of the monastery with the opinion of the masters of the Dominican order who were sitting in chapter: "We should take some soil from this place to other monasteries because of the great holiness that we have found here."[36] The masters and authorities of the learned Order of Preachers consider the new monastery of Engelthal to be "holy ground" and a place whose influence will benefit both monastics and others.

THE BIOGRAPHICAL SKETCHES

In the first part of the *Sister-Book of Engelthal*, Christina Ebner mentions only four sisters by name—Adelheid, the founding beguine; Alheit of Trochau, whose biographical sketch is the lengthiest of the 48 women and men recorded in the *Sister-Book*; Diemut of Gailenhausen, the first Dominican prioress of the monastery of Engelthal; and Hailrat, the first chantress. Christina does not give a list of the original beguines who gathered around Adelheid Rotter, nor does she list the first nuns of the monastery. In the first part of the *Sister-Book*, the main character is God, who providentially brings about a community. The second part of the *Sister-Book* concentrates on what God does with individual sisters, chaplains, and brothers after the establishment of the monastery. Christina makes no attempt here to report the lives of every sister in the community. An analysis of the list of nuns at Engelthal gleaned from documentary evidence provided by Gustav Voit suggests that there may have been as many as sixty nuns whose biographical sketches could have been included in the *Sister-Book*. Among these are nuns mentioned in other works produced at Engelthal such as the *Revelations* of Adelheid Langmann or the autobiography or biography of Christina Ebner herself—Kunigunde of Forchheim, Williwirch, Gertrud Türriegel, Elsbet, Agnes and Maria of Breitenstein, Christina of Kornburg. The order of the individual sketches cannot be determined as being chronological by birth, death, or order of religion. Is there an order to the arrangement of the sketches?

Christina did not order the biographical sketches by length of entry. The lengthiest, that of Alheit of Trochau, contains nineteen paragraphs (*33-51). The entry for Diemut Ebner extends for thirteen paragraphs (*101-113), and that for Anna Vorchtel for eleven (*114-124). The entries for four of the nuns—Elisa (*131-136), Irmelin of Roet (*23-27), Mechtild Krumpsit (*58-62), and Hedwig of Regensburg (*68-72)—include five or six paragraphs. Christina of Kornburg (*94-97) and the chaplain Herr Friedrich (*137-140) both have four paragraphs devoted to their stories. Nine biographical sketches of nuns are three paragraphs each, six cover two paragraphs, and the remaining 23 sketches of nuns and brothers contain but one paragraph each. I believe the lengthier sketches derive from previous, independent, written sources, since several of these sketches are longer than the singular work on Gertrud of Engelthal. Christina Ebner gleaned her material from the earlier written accounts as well as from the verbal tradition passed on by the nuns. Independent written accounts of the lengthier sketches are no longer extant; however, the length and the completeness of each sketch show the document to have had a previous and independent existence. They are fuller in detail and develop the character of the nuns. When these sketches are contrasted with the shorter sketches, this becomes clear. The entry for Elsbeth of Klingenburg is typical for the sketches of one paragraph length:

> There was a sister named Elsbeth of Klingenburg who was the grand-daughter of the founder. She prayed diligently and especially liked to pray the psalter often. About eighteen weeks before her death she contracted a serious illness. Then Brother Conrad of Füssen, a Dominican, told her that she should give over her will to the will of God. Then she said, "Before ever I would set myself against God's will, I would rather suffer pain up to Judgment Day." Then when it came time for her to die, a trustworthy nun saw that St. John came to her. And another sister saw in spirit that he came with the twelve apostles and read the Gospel *In principio* and said, "I deliver a message to you from our Lord Jesus Christ. He has promised you certainty of eternal life." Then seven sisters heard the most sweetest string music playing in the clouds that came over her and then she died. [37]

In all biographical sketches the name of the sister or brother is given, here noting the family name. Christina identifies her as coming from a noble family, indeed as being the granddaughter of the founder of the monastery, Ulrich of Königstein, whose daughter Elisabeth had married Walter of

Klingenburg. The nun's name, station in life, family background, relation to the founder, and her status in the monastery are made known. She is a choir sister and not a lay sister. Entries for lay sisters clearly indicate their status. Then Christina includes some detail about Elsbeth's spiritual life. She, being literate, reads the psalter frequently, presumably outside the prescribed times for canonical offices. Elsbeth has immersed herself in the songs of Israel, in the inspired texts that formed the primary element of every monastic's praise of God. She has appropriated the public prayer of the community and the Church as her own prayer used for praise and meditation. In so doing, Elsbeth becomes an example of love for the psalms and of the personal appropriation of their message in her life. For Elsbeth they do not remain simply the prescribed songs of praise used in the official ceremonies of the monastery; they become her own prayer and form her own spirituality. Thus Elsbeth becomes an example of the interiorization of the message of the psalms. This Christina makes clear by reporting the conversation with the renowned preacher Conrad of Füssen, who advises Elsbeth to unite her will with that of God in view of her possible death. That Elsbeth needs no such advice or encouragement is clear. Emphatically she asserts that she would rather suffer pain until the Day of Judgment rather than set herself against the will of God. An important lesson contained in the psalms has been thoroughly learned, so that in the face of death, Elsbeth confidently entrusts her will to God. Her reading of and meditation on the psalms have prepared her for her most important profession of faith in God.

This entry, like most of the entries, portrays the subject precisely at the most important moment of choice—close to her death. How Elsbeth faces her own death comes directly from how she lived her life. She becomes a lesson in living the monastic life as it should be lived so that the monastic may face death with the assurance of eternal life. The witness borne by a "trustworthy sister" and by seven other sisters lends credence to Elsbeth's experience. For the faithful such visions typically form a part of the deathbed scene. Significantly here, Elsbeth is visited by St. John, presumably the Evangelist, who reads the prologue to his Gospel account as a consolation for the dying nun. Its message assures her of the divine plan of mercy to save. This scriptural passage functions as a preamble to the personal message that Elsbeth has yet to receive. The nun hears the plan of salvation, the loving purposes of God. "But to all who received him, who believed in his name, he gave power to become children of God (John 1:12)."[38] Elsbeth hears her personal prophecy in the context of this Gospel passage by John. Likewise from John comes the message from Christ, the savior, who assures her of eternal life. The symbolism of the string-playing links Elsbeth to the playing of David, who accompanied himself in singing the psalms. This portrayal appears frequently in deathbed scenes in monastic literature.[39] Elsbeth had loved the psalms, and now King David plays them at her death. This is heavenly music and is described as the "most sweetest" music to indicate that connection. It is music beyond what human talent could produce, and its meaning fortifies the promise of eternal life given to Elsbeth. The symbolism of the cloud coming over her at death recalls the theophany, the presence of God in the cloud, while the use of the phrase "coming over" suggests the coming of the Holy Spirit. The psalms and heavenly bliss are signified by the lovely string music. The presence of the Trinity through the promise of Christ, the theophany, and the Spirit indicates Elsbeth's union with God in heavenly glory.

Such an entry is typical of the brief biographical sketches in the *Sister-Book*. In each, the sister (or brother) is identified by name, position in the world and in the monastery, and by personal spiritual characteristic. The subject is faced with impending death, and her or his behavior at that moment teaches a lesson in how to live and how to die. The supernatural events that typically attend the death promise the reward of a good life.

Another brief example fortifies this analysis:

> A lay sister named Hosanna came to us in her old age and was a very good person. When she was dying she related that she had heard the angels singing and this was beyond all human senses. She said our Lord and our Lady were also with her and had assured her of eternal life. St. Martin had come to her in the vesture of a bishop and had given her the Body of our Lord. Then she died a holy end.[40]

Even in this brief account, the same elements as in the somewhat longer sketch of Elsbeth of Klingenburg are present. Hosanna, like many women, entered the monastery at an older age. Often women became nuns after having been widowed and having raised their family. These nuns became lay sisters rather than choir sisters. The lay sister performed all manner of manual labor for the maintenance of the monastery and for the orderly functioning of the community. Widows frequently had not benefited from the opportunity to become literate as was automatically the case with young girls who entered a monastery. Being illiterate, these older women could not function as choir sisters since they could not read the psalms and other required texts. Nonetheless, as in the case of Hosanna, lay sisters were considered holy women and their lives were included by Christina to show that even the illiterate latecomer could become holy. Hosanna, like Elsbeth, shows her mettle in the face of death. Supernatural events attend her death and signify her entrance into heaven. She hears the singing of angels (*engel*), something frequently mentioned by nuns but even more so by the nuns of Engelthal. She is assured of salvation by the Lord himself and by the Virgin. St. Martin, perhaps one of her favorite saints, attired as a bishop, "admits" her to the communion of saints and gives her holy communion—union with Christ. Thus fortified, she dies.

Hosanna's death becomes a lesson for lay sisters and for all nuns. As a widow she is most probably not a virgin and yet she can be saved despite her "sin." As a lay sister, she offers hope for salvation to other lay sisters who were not "real" nuns (choir sisters). To choir sisters her death may teach humility and bring joy to all the members of the community.

THE *VITA OF*
SISTER GERTRUD OF ENGELTHAL

Ave Maria! Gratia plena. Dominus tecum.
benedicta tu in mulieribus,
et benedictus fructus ventris tui.

THE SINGLE KNOWN EXTANT COPY OF THIS *VITA* exists in the same manuscript as the account of Friedrich Sunder's life—in the *Codex Scotensis Vindobonensis.* The text contains only five pages, 227r-229r, and the authors assure the reader that what they have written amounts to merely one-thousandth of what Gertrud had told them of her life.[1] The copy contained in the manuscript in Vienna and written by one Hans Probst certainly reproduces only the opening paragraphs of the original.

THE AUTHORS

The authors of the *Vita* identify themselves as "Cunrat Fridrich" and "bruder Heinrich," both of whom were chaplains to the nuns at Engelthal.[2] Difficulties arise in identifying these two men since the list of chaplains at Engelthal as formulated from documents in Nuremberg contains several possibilities.[3] Documentary evidence shows one Heinrich of Ekewint, a Dominican as vicar in 1323, five years prior to Gertrud's death.[4] The title "brother" given to Heinrich in the *Vita* distinguishes him as a Dominican in contrast with Cunrat, who would then be a secular priest. A Konrad appears in documents dated 14 February 1336.[5] In 1351, a Konrad designated as the "young chaplain" appears, which may indicate that the "older Konrad"

still served as a chaplain.[6] Although both Cunrat and Heinrich collaborate
and share the information they received from Gertrud herself, Cunrat does
the actual writing as the use of the first person singular pronoun indicates:
"Now I shall begin to write of this sister's life."[7] Both men hear her confession
over a period of years and have the opportunity to hear many details about
her life and her relationship to God and to the Virgin Mary. It is upon this
long association with Sister Gertrud that their authority as authors rests.

SISTER GERTRUD OF ENGELTHAL

The subject of the *Vita* may have been a woman from the village of Engelthal
itself. In the *Sister-Book of Engelthal* each nun bears either a surname of a
patrician or noble family of Nuremberg, that is, Pfinzing, Ebner, Langmann,
Schenk, or a designation from place of origin, that is, von Happurg, von
Hersbruck. These nuns, known by place of origin, do not necessarily come
from noble families and may even have been peasant women. Oddly, the
list of nuns and sisters in the documentary evidence gathered by Gustav Voit
contains no reference to Gertrud of Engelthal. Her contemporary, a
Gertraud von Stein, lived beyond the date of death for Gertrud of Engelthal.[8] A Gertrud Türriegel died soon after 1350.[9] This omission simply means
that Voit found no reference to her in the various documents relating to the
accounts and records of the monastery, such as its legal transactions and
deed records. Nor does Voit list a sister Erlint mentioned in the *Revelations*
of Adelheid Langmann. Evidently the documentary evidence is incomplete.
    The author of the *Gnaden-vita of Friedrich Sunder* also mentions Sister
Gertrud of Engelthal in several paragraphs. The author skillfully offers
information and characterization of Gertrud before ever revealing her name,
as if to imitate the process whereby Friedrich Sunder had come to know her.
Friedrich had come to the monastery as chaplain at the age of thirty and
remained there for forty years. The author reports, "he found a sister in a
nearby village who had received many wonders and graces from God."[10]
Among these wonders and graces are visions of the Christ child in Friedrich's
hands at the elevation of the host and her ability to speak with Christ, his
mother, and the saints. The author reports that "much is written about her
in another little book."[11] The author carefully shows the development of the
relationship of Friedrich and Gertud over a period of years: "Then this priest
obtained great grace and love for her and she for him in God. And she
confessed to him, received Our Lord from him. God shared the same graces
he gave to her with him, and he often wondered about this."[12] Their mutual

relationship in God progresses over time through difficulties and blessings. Gertrud wonders what kind of loyalty he has toward her and questions him about his seeming lack of loyalty to her—an issue that undoubtedly arose from past experience. Friedrich professes his loyalty to her, promising, "Every good thing I receive or ever will receive from God, I will give to you before God and I do not want anything except what is given to me by God."[13] Gertrud rejoiced that God had given her such a friend and promised to be loyal to Friedrich as long as she lived. She explained that her loyalty was not only to his soul but to his body, for she would be willing to offer up any part of her body to save any part of his. At that time an angel was standing before them in the church at Entenberg. This angel took them before God and they confirmed their loyalty to each other. The author concludes this passage with the words, "And the priest increased more and more in grace."[14] This entire passage symbolizes a marriage ceremony. Friedrich and Gertrud pledge loyalty to each other until death while standing in a church before a representative from God who then mystically presents this avowal of loyalty before God. Clearly Gertrud gives not only the consent of her will as necessary for this "sacrament of marriage" but also symbolically offers her body as a "consummation" of the marriage bond. The sacramental character of this new relationship also echoes the ultimate sacrifice as taught by Christ: "Greater love has no man than this, that a man lay down his life for his friends" (John 15:13). The author emphasizes the intensity of the relationship between Friedrich and Gertrud by portraying it as a marriage in the church of Entenberg in which they vow their mutual loyalty unto death, celebrate their union in a church, and ask God to witness their love. God's approval and "blessing" of the relationship is indicated by the ever-increasing growth in grace on the part of Friedrich.

Following this ceremony, the author reports a vision given to Gertrud that fortifies and testifies to the efficacy of the relationship. The vision of a holy virgin speaks to Gertrud and asks why Gertrud honors so many virgins, but not the speaker. Gertrud protests that she does not know who the speaker is. The personage in the vision reveals herself as Caritas. This same virgin appears to Gertrud later, when Gertrud is convinced that someone wishes to murder Friedrich. Caritas instructs her to recite five prayers over three days for each of the five sayings of Christ: "Recite a *Pater noster* and an *Ave Maria* for the words of our Lord to Peter: 'You should not forgive seven times but seventy times seven times so that our Lord will forgive the priest his sins and will protect him in body and soul.'"[15] This prayer was for Friedrich's protection from physical and eternal spiritual death. It also taught the need to forgive the would-be murderer. The basis of this teaching is the

Bible (Matt. 18:22): "I do not say to you seven times, but seventy times seven." The teaching of Caritas continues: "For the second recite the words with which our Lord asked his Father to deliver him from his passion so that he will deliver the priest from his suffering."[16] This instruction refers to the incident recorded in Luke 22:42: "Father, if thou art willing, remove this cup from me; nevertheless not my will, but thine, be done." Here the power of Christ's words reaches out to protect Friedrich, even though at their original utterance they do not bring about the end of Christ's passion. "To the third recite the words with which our Lord commended his mother to St. John so that the priest may be commended to our Lord St. John."[17] Here Caritas refers to the words of Christ: "Then he said to the disciple, 'Behold, your mother!' And from that hour the disciple took her to his own home" (John 19:27). Mary is given as protectress over Friedrich, and St. John will also protect him. "The fourth to the words with which our Lord prayed to the Father for those who crucified him to forgive them so that he will also forgive the priest all his sins."[18] Caritas refers to Christ's words; "And Jesus said, 'Father, forgive them; for they know not what they do'" (Luke 23:34). Finally, Caritas asks Gertrud to recite the prayers to the fifth saying of Christ: "Father, into thy hands I commit my spirit!" (Luke 23:46). In each case, Caritas (Love) instructs Gertrud in how to pray in order to protect Friedrich from murder. "Love" spurs Gertrud on to action made efficacious by the connection with Christ under every circumstance. Motivated by love, Gertrud meditates upon the words of Christ under the most dire circumstances for Christ and now for Friedrich. This connects the "passion" of Friedrich (and by extension also of Gertrud) with the passion of Christ, and instructs Gertrud what attitude to take in prayer. Caritas (Love) counsels 1) forgiveness of others; 2) trust in God's will; 3) reliance on others; 4) recognition of the ignorance of others; 5) surrender to God.

The author reveals that Gertrud makes all this known to Friedrich with the result that he wishes to honor this saint Caritas, unknown to him. In turn, Friedrich experiences a vision of Caritas in which he learns that he should also honor two other little known virgins—Spes and Fides. They speak of these saints as real people reporting details of the martyrdom of Spes and indicating their feast days: Caritas's feast is the day before Crispin and Crispianus (25 October); Fides's feast is on the third day after the Nativity of Mary (Sept. 11) and Spes's day is the same as All Souls (2 November). However, the conclusion of the vision makes clear what is of greater importance: "And I tell you whoever praises and honors the three virgins takes on the virtues of their names: Love, Faith and Hope."[19] Despite the fact that these saints were treated as real people, their symbolic names convey the important fact about each that is to be imitated by Friedrich. The love of Gertrud, calls forth his faith (loyalty) and offers hope, in this instance, that his life will be spared.

THE STRUCTURE OF THE TEXT

The *Vita* as it exists begins with a preamble probably composed by the scribe Hans Probst since it indicates that only a brief account of Gertrud's life will be given.[20] Then follows what may have been the introductory paragraph of the original, since it indicates the purpose for writing the life of Gertrud, identifies the authors and their relationship to her, and indicates the source of Gertrud's mysticism. In the subsequent paragraphs the authors tell of events surrounding her mother's pregnancy, Gertrud's birth, how she was nourished, the appearance of the Virgin Mary, and the appearance of an angel when Gertrud was six years old. The text ends abruptly with a formulaic statement asking the reader to recite an *Ave Maria* for the scribe, Hans Probst of Biberach.[21]

THE TEXT

The authors begin the *Vita* with a statement of their purpose in recording the life of the nun. "The wonders of God and the grace that he does and works with good people is good to know so that God will be honored and praised for it and people will be made better by it."[22] They repeat the reasons for making known Gertrud's life, so important do they believe the message to be. Speaking directly of her life they report, "She did this in part to praise God and [in part] for the salvation of our souls so that we would be made better from it. . . ."[23] Praising God for his gracious actions in her life so that she might be encouraged and made better in living out Christian life is the motive for Gertrud's revelation to Cunrat and Heinrich. They have received revelations about God's power and improvement in their own lives and wish to show the same to a wide readership so that they too will share in being made better by knowing what God has done for Gertrud. The document is both revelatory of truth and hortatory for faith. At the conclusion of the authors' introduction, they characterize Gertrud in a way that will help the reader understand the precise nature and importance of her relationship with God: "And also frequently our Lord came over her, came so that she would tell us many things."[24] The vocabulary used here allows for diverse but complementary interpretations of the text. Given the importance of the role of the Virgin Mary in the following pages, it seems reasonable to believe that the authors consciously strive to identify Gertrud with Mary at the Annunciation: "And the angel said to her, 'The Holy Spirit will come upon you, and the power of the Most High will overshadow you . . ."(Luke 1:35). Gertrud will give birth to Christ spiritually in her soul even as Mary gave birth physically to Christ in her womb. Mary brought Christ, "the Word of God," into the world for the salvation of all. Gertrud, by giving birth to the Savior in her soul, becomes a prophet of the marvels of God's grace and an "angel" or messenger of God's saving actions in her life so that people will believe in God's power and be improved in their lives. The authors identify Gertrud with Mary and with Christ. Just as Gertrud was God-bearer, so may every Christian become the bearer of Christ. And being God-bearer compels Gertrud to proclaim the good news that God acts powerfully in the here and now with the inference that this is possible for any Christian. One should conclude from this that God's power as reported in the Scriptures continues to act in the world.

The report of Gertrud's life begins with an account of her mother's dream while carrying Gertrud in the her womb. As is common, the symbolism contained in the dream and the explanation given for it predict the characteristics and mission of the child to be born. Gertrud's mother dreams that a shining star came down from heaven onto her head. The star portends the birth of a famous personage, as had the star of Bethlehem (Matt. 2:9-10). In the dream the mother understands the star to mean that the baby will become a light in Christendom.[25] The star symbolism also associates Gertrud with Christ, who is "Light of the world," and thus adds another symbolic association to her identification with Christ. The dream also continues the association with the Virgin Mary since she appears in the dream riding on a sled and promises that she will care for the child.[26] The mother awakes in a panic and, as the authors report, neither of the parents understands the meaning of the dream until both recognize the graces given to Gertrud as she grows up.[27]

The events of Gertrud's birth add to the understanding of the special nature of the child. Her mother had already given birth to eight sons in great pain. With the birth of her daughter she suffers so little pain that she does not even realize she is pregnant, thinking she has some illness in her advanced age. The lack of pain in giving birth goes contrary to the biblical punishment that women will bring forth children in pain (Gen. 3:16). In the Middle Ages many scholars believed that the Virgin Mary had given birth to Christ without any pain.[28] This grace has to do with Mary's special status as being born without original sin by virtue of the fact that she was destined to bear the Incarnate God. Gertrud's mother, in having relatively little pain, shares incompletely in the privilege of Mary by virtue of her giving birth to a child whose destiny associates her mystically with Christ himself. After the birth of the child, the authors describe her as "good" and use family stories as proof of her goodness. For example, as a baby she never woke her mother during the night with crying. As soon as her mother placed her in the crib, she became quiet and remained still.[29]

Cunrat continues with further evidence of Gertrud's special status, which symbolically prophesies her mystical life. The authors announce that, "Our Lord God began early on to share his grace with the child."[30] This grace has to do with the fact that the child frequently refrains from sucking milk from her mother's breast for as many as three days. Yet during this time, both day and night she moves her lips as if sucking nourishment. For this her mother sometimes slaps her as punishment. However, even though she lacks normal nourishment, she continues to look healthy and to act normally. Nonetheless, throughout her life Gertrud makes these movements with her lips and God reveals to her that by this means he has always fed her with his divine sweetness.[31] This movement of her lips as if she were sucking nourishment functions as a special means by which Christ feeds her with his grace. That Gertrud "sucks" this grace links her experience to that of other mystics such as Margaret Ebner and Christina Ebner, each of whom graphically describe the Christ Child as sucking from her breast or the nun as sucking from the breast of Christ.[32] Sometimes mystics describe this image in terms of St. John at the Last Supper, who leans against Christ and "sucks wisdom" from his breast, a wisdom that enables him to write of the fullness of Christ's identity in intimate terms in the Gospel according to John and in the Book of Revelation.

Continuing the theme of linking Gertrud and the Virgin Mary, the authors include a vision of Mary to Gertrud as a young child. In this vision Mary instructs the child how to pray in a very specific way. Having been assured that she can recite the Hail Mary, the Virgin directs Gertrud to recite an *Ave Maria* while making the sign of the cross over both eyes, her left and right ears, her mouth, and her heart. This symbolic action "signs" Gertrud with the cross of Christ as a protection against evil and as a blessing for good. Her senses of sight, hearing, and taste are blessed in imitation of the baptismal ritual, but here she is baptized into a mystical life. Her heart, the seat of the emotional life and the seat of love, is secured in purity and her

mouth is dedicated to praise and proclamation. The Virgin further directs
the child to recite another prayer after each *Ave Maria*. "Praised be to you,
tender, worthy and most highly to be praised queen, our Lady!"[33] The Virgin
promises Gertrud that each day when she recites this prayer, she will have
no problems with her eyes or ears. The Virgin teaches Gertrud that each
part of the prayer has a special significance:

> When you say "Praised be to you" you are praising me with the angel
> who was sent down from heaven and brought me God's greeting. When
> you say "tender" you are praising me with the Holy Spirit who began
> his tender work with me. When you say "worthy" you are praising me
> with my beloved Son, for whom I was worthy above all women. When
> you say "most highly to be praised" you are praising me with the
> heavenly Father who praised me above all the saints in heaven. When
> you say "queen, our Lady" you are praising me with all the saints whose
> queen I am.[34]

This explanation of the prayer expands on the text of the Hail Mary and
refers primarily to the Annunciation. Faithfully, Gertrud recites this prayer
every day until she dies.[35] The vision, its prayer, and instruction connect
Gertrud with Mary and with the incarnation. The Word of God (Christ)
took on flesh in order to save. The word of God through her prayer connects
Gertrud with the saved: with Mary, the angel Gabriel, the Holy Spirit, God
the Father, and with all the holy ones. Through recitation of the prayer and
by her fidelity, Gertrud associates herself with the elect.

The second vision Cunrat records concerns the apparition of an angel.
This vision also includes a prayer and an instruction: "And whenever you
recite that, our Lady will look down upon you."[36] The prayer consists of four
inexpertly rhymed couplets and is addressed to Mary. This prayer, too,
expands on the Hail Mary, offering greetings to Mary, proclaiming that she
is full of grace and stating that she is above all women. The second half, in
imitation of the Hail Mary, includes an intercessory petition asking for
Mary's help so that "we" may see Jesus. Mary should also pray to her dear
child for all sinners.[37] The concluding note states that Gertrud recites this
prayer more than once a day up to her death.

One can only speculate as to the contents of the rest of the missing
Vita. However, if the text remains true to the opening paragraphs, the
structure of the text would likely follow the same pattern used in the first
seven sections. The theology would likely build on the identification of

Gertrud with Christ and with his mother, who first believed. Because of her special calling, Gertrud shares intimacy with Christ and continues his mission of spreading the Good News. This reading, however, remains purely speculative unless an alternative complete manuscript is found.

THE *REVELATIONS* AND *PRAYER* OF ADELHEID LANGMANN

Favus distillans labia tua, sponsa;
mel et lac sub lingua tua;
et odor vestimentorum tuorum sicut odor thuris.
Cant. 4:11

WITH THE DEATH OF ADELHEID LANGMANN on 22 November 1375, the intense mystical life fostered at the monastery of Engelthal virtually came to an end. The life of Adelheid Langmann, as gleaned from her *Revelations* and from external sources, presents a picture of a particularly pious girl from the patrician burgher class of the powerful imperial city of Nuremberg. Her family members sometimes held office among the city councilors. Although not as prominent as the Ebner family, to whom they were likely related by marriage, nonetheless they held noble status in the city and are memorialized in a stained-glass window in their parish church, St. Sebaldus. Despite the opposition of family and friends, Adelheid chose to accept a monastic vocation with the Dominican nuns of Engelthal. Eventually she flourished under the cloistral regimen. There she received an education from the nuns, after which she had a sufficient knowledge of Latin and could read and write in her native tongue. Her learning, acquired through study and the normal readings in the cloister as well as from preaching and letter exchanges with spiritual friends, shows knowledge of biblical texts, especially the Song of Solomon, the Book of Revelation, and the letters of St. Paul. Adelheid made use of translations and commentaries such as the *St. Trutperter Song of Songs* and the *Sermons on the Song of Songs* by St. Bernard of Clairvaux. In addition, Mechthild of Magdeburg's *The Flowing Light of the Godhead,* among other mystical texts, certainly exerted an influence on Adelheid's thought.

The major source of information with regard to the inner life, thought and mystical experiences of Adelheid Langmann is her autobiography, called the *Revelations.* From this and from external sources it is known that Adelheid was born into a patrician family of Nuremberg around the year 1312. The Berlin manuscript of the *Revelations* does not give the exact date of birth, but it does record that she had been born in Nuremberg. As a young girl she already showed a pious nature as this description demonstrates. "Whatever seemed proper and pleasing in spiritual and divine matters this child performed and she appeared happy to all without being boisterous."[1] Further evidence of her piety and of her particular receptivity to the Word of God augments this description. "Whenever she went with her mother to hear the preaching she listened well and locked the message in the interior of her heart. Then when she came home and was alone she pondered the words of the sermon and especially liked to meditate upon the martyrdom of Our Lord according to her understanding. The people who were with the child and took care of her soon noticed this. They often said to her mother, 'The child certainly belongs in a monastery.'"[2] This suggestion did not coincide with her parents' wishes. At the age of thirteen she was engaged to a young man named Gottfried Teufel, who, as she herself reported, soon died. After a struggle with her own unwillingness to accept a monastic calling, and with the disapproval of her family, she eventually entered the monastery of Engelthal sometime between 1327 and 1330. Adelheid became a nun only after she had accepted the call according to Christ's will conveyed to her in visions and by confirmation from other spiritual people.

In the *Revelations,* Adelheid records the events of her life from 1330 to 1344, recalls memories from her childhood, and reports revelations received about herself, her sisters, her friends, the souls in purgatory, the saints in heaven, and the state of Christianity. Among the more important events of her life the following should be mentioned here. On the night before her profession of vows, Adelheid experienced diabolic temptations meant to prevent her from becoming a nun.[3] She fainted and was tended by angels. On All Saints Day, Adelheid descended into purgatory and learned that many people—including her mother, whom everyone thought had already attained heavenly bliss—were still awaiting deliverance from purgatory although they no longer suffered in any way except for the lack of the vision of God.[4] She prayed for a perfect coincidence of her will with that of Christ. She enjoyed an ever progressive intimacy with her Beloved—Jesus Christ as noted by various incidents such as the inscription of Christ's name upon her heart and her name upon his.[5] Ultimately she was taken to the heights of mystical union with Christ when he came to her marriage bed and captivated her with his beauty.[6]

In addition to Adelheid's autobiography, much information about her life and her monastery exists in public documents such as deeds, the records of the city of Nuremberg, and the account books of the monastery. These supporting documents add practical information, knowledge of which is assumed in the *Revelations*. They also provide background material that clarifies the social status of her family and reveals the rich tapestry of connections woven by the monastic community and the families of the nuns who lived out their lives according to the spirituality of Engelthal.

According to the research of Gustav Voit, documentary evidence dated 8 August 1327 reported that Adelheid was the widow of Gottfried Teufel and that she had received an estate at Happurg from her mother, Mechthild, a citizen of Nuremberg and the widow of Otto Langmann. On 20 June 1339, she purchased an estate at Traunfeld from Henry II Steinlinger from Lauterhofen.[7] In 1350 Adelheid received revenues from a house in Offenhausen, from estates at Ittelshofen, Schmiede, Traunfeld, Happurg, Speikern, and a share in the revenues from another estate in Traunfeld.[8] After Adelheid's death, revenues from Offenhausen were to be donated to the monastery to observe the anniversary of the death of Sr. Kunigunde of Forcheim. Also after her death the rents from Happurg and Speikern would fall to her nieces, Gerhaus and Margarete Sachsen, both nuns of Engelthal.

She probably began to write her *Revelations* in 1330 at the request of an unnamed but prominent Dominican lector and was probably still writing in 1350.[9] She lived uninterruptedly within the monastic enclosure until she died on 22 November 1375.

In her *Revelations*, Adelheid mentions having relatives in the monastery and states that her aunt had received an office in the monastery.[10] Her sister Sophia lived as a nun at Engelthal as did the two nieces previously mentioned. She may also have been related to Elsbet Mayer (her goddaughter) and to Gerhaus Mayer, with whom she shared revenues from an estate in Traunfeld.[11] Kunigunde of Forchheim may also have been related as well as Elisabeth of Eyb, since both nuns and their families were commemorated by the monastery at the same time. There also exists a possible relationship with Christina Ebner, since Friedrich Ebner's daughter Agnes married Hermann Langmann on 14 June 1344. The second wife of a Hermann Ebner, who died in 1403, was Kunigunde Langmann.[12] The Berlin manuscript makes the claim that the Ebners and the Langmanns were related. Also it seems evident that the church of St. Sebaldus in Nuremberg was the parish church of both families. Their coats of arms are placed side by side in one of the stained-glass windows at the east end of the church.

Chronicles from the city of Nuremberg also record a coat of arms for the family that matches those displayed in St. Sebaldus.[13] The Lang-manns seem never to have been numerous yet they held positions of responsibility in the city.[14] A Hans Langmann became a city councilor in 1349 and died in 1371. One Otto Langmann also served as a city councilor until 1370 and then hanged himself in his bedroom on 31 August 1375.[15] This Otto and Hans may have been Adelheid's brothers. From external sources it is known that Adelheid's brothers were named Hans and Otto and her sister Jutta (Geut) married Henry of Sachsen.[16] In Martini's *Historisch-geographische Beschreibung des ehemaligen berühmten Frauenklosters Engeltal* (1798), he referred to "herr Conrad Langmann (1318) and to "Mechthild Langmann from Nuremberg, nun at Engelthal (1338).[17] He also noted that a vigil and Mass were recited during the week following the feast of St. Michael (29 September) for Sister Adelheid Langmann and her family, for Sister Elisabeth of Eyb and her family, for Geut Sachsin, and for Kunigunde of Forcheim.[18] Also a vigil and Mass were recited for Adelheid Langmann and her family during Holy Week.[19]

Her mystical experiences and powerful intercessions became widely known, as evidenced by the visits of many people known or totally unknown to her asking for her advice and prayerful intercession. Three individuals in particular come to her for advice. Marquard Tockler asked Adelheid's advice with regard to his vocation. She advised him to enter the order of St. Augustine. One year after he had become an Augustinian, he returned to visit Adelheid. From their previous conversation she knew that he was sorely tempted by a very disturbing sin. Now she learned from him that he still suffered from it and now even stronger. "Immediately Our Lord revealed to her his grace and mercy in that she recognized all his suffering and said, 'Woe to you, poor man, do you want to let your body and soul be overcome by the devil? You are sorely tempted. I know for certain that you want to kill yourself.'"[20] She taught him a prayer she had learned: "With suffering I am surrounded, a cross in me is founded, in my suffering need. From this free me Lord Jesus Christ by your bitter death."[21] Thereafter the temptation left him and he became a master of theology in Paris. In 1336, a knight named Eberhard Schutz of Hohenstein sought her counsel. This lengthy episode shows Adelheid overcoming her conflict with her desire for a solitary contemplative life and the spiritual needs of someone who had been directed by a hermit to seek her out. At his third attempt to speak with Adelheid, the prioress and the sisters prevailed upon her to talk with him. After she had learned that he knew nothing about the canonical hours of prayer, scarcely recited one Our Father a day, never fasted, and now at the age of forty had never yet received Holy Communion, she gave him this counsel:

> Then she said, "You should guard your eyes against all unnecessary sights and whatever you see that is contrary to God, you should always turn to the good in your heart. You should guard yourself against all unnecessary and loose words. Whenever you hear such speech you should never say a word, but if you can not avoid it and have to speak, then you should at all times speak so that such evil talk will diminish and not be spread about. And you should guard yourself against going to any unnecessary place. Wherever you know people who are living contrary to God you should never go there, but if you must go guard yourself against sin and carry our Lord Jesus Christ in your heart and trust completely in him to turn you away from your sins and help you to become a good man."[22]

Adelheid perceived clearly what problems this man had to face and what temptations he would encounter. Her advice is sound, practical, unambiguous, and forthright. He continues to speak with her on other occasions, when she teaches him how to pray for his now deceased wife and advises him to take Our Lady as his bride, by which she encourages him to become a monk. This he misunderstands completely and seeks a young bride. In a revelation, Christ reveals to her, "I will give you the knight of Hohenstein, Eberhard, so that he will be converted from all his sins. You should tell him to go to the monastery of Kaisheim and become a monk. I will confirm the marriage of my mother with him. No other will do for him. You should tell him that when he comes again."[23] After she tells him that he is to become a monk, he grows sad and sullen, asking her to pray for him to accept this. While praying for him she receives another revelation. "With this man I will let you know how much I really love you."[24] The next day Eberhart relates to Adelheid his astounding conversion experience"

> "When I left you yesterday I was so depressed that I had to lie down immediately, but I remained awake and could not fall asleep. As I lay there I heard such a rumbling noise as when a bad storm approaches in summer. I jumped up and thought, Our Lady will certainly come to comfort me. Then I saw a blue fog that enshrouded me and filled my room. Then a ray shot down from heaven into the crown of my head and

struck deeply into my heart and was so hot and fiery from divine love that I thought I was burning alive and threw off the blanket. When the ray came into my heart it spread out into all my limbs. When I perceived the heat in all my limbs I began to laugh and to cry so that all the servants who lay near me in the room got up and asked what was wrong with me. I could say nothing to them. The laughing and crying grew ever louder so that everyone spending the night in the guest house got out of bed. All of them watched with me through the night. I forgot all worldly things completely and never can I return to the world. From that moment on I wanted nothing more than to become a monk. Beg the Lord for the monks of Kaisheim to accept me."[25]

After reporting his spiritual progress and the many graces he receives over time, Adelheid summarizes the change. "Our Beloved Lord Jesus Christ showed his love to him and did wonders with him. For that may he be praised forever! The honor is his, he gives it to whomever he wills."[26] In these encounters Adelheid shows herself to be a wise counselor, but not everyone responds so well to her wisdom. Adelheid's widowed aunt refuses to accept her advice to enter the monastery, takes another husband instead and soon suffers the predicted consequences: illness and death.

It was not only the status of the Langmann family as leaders of a free imperial city but also their attachment to the parish church that made a lifelong impression on Adelheid. The parish church of St. Sebaldus influenced and helped to form Adelheid's religious world view. From her own account she claimed to have paid careful attention to the sermons. Such a precocious child would not have failed to notice the artistic decoration of the church meant to preach the Gospel to the illiterate. When one considers the subsequent spiritual concerns of Adelheid, it is not surprising to find them displayed in the stone carvings around the exterior of the church. To enter the church one had to pass by a scene of angels rescuing souls from purgatory. This image, along with the Judgment scene above the entrance, could well have impressed the religious imagination of the child at an early age. It would not be surprising then to know that she entered the monastery of the angels (Engelthal) rather than the Dominican monastery of St. Katharina founded in 1295 and located within the city walls of Nuremberg. At Engelthal she devoted herself especially to the task of praying for the release of souls from purgatory. Adelheid also wrote about the events of the Last Day. The Trinity is prominently displayed in the carvings around the church. Adelheid's spirituality is emphatically Trinitarian rather than Christocentric, normal for her contemporaries. The image of the Virgin spreading her mantle of protection over the people also appears both in the stone carvings and in the imagery in the *Revelations*.

Adelheid is predisposed to enter the monastery of Engelthal by her family connections and by her imaginative religious world view leading her to identify with the angels, who worship before the Triune God, do his will, and intercede for others before his throne, and to associate herself with the Order of Preachers, for she loved to hear the preaching. Her entrance into the Dominican monastery also places her under the spiritual influence of its unique history. One of the chief influences of the Dominicans is to train her to write, therefore making it possible to record her special revelations and experiences with Christ.

THE MANUSCRIPTS

Although the text of Adelheid Langmann's *Revelations* has been evaluated by Wilhelm Oehl as one of the weakest of its kind in redaction, nonetheless it fills an important part in the construction of a distinctive mystical spirituality at Engelthal.[27] As the autobiography of an ecstatic mystic, it takes a major place among the documents produced at Engelthal because it reports the personal experiences and theological vision of one individual even if the various manuscripts suffer from redaction.

Manuscript M (Munich) is kept at the Staatsbibliothek in Munich (Cgm. 99). The text appears on pages 36-173, having been bound at a later date with works by Jan van Ruysbroec. Adelheid's text follows its own pagination in Roman numerals. This manuscript bears no title and remains unfinished since the red capital letters that indicate new paragraphs as they appear in this translation have not yet been filled in from page 165v to the end. At the beginning of the manuscript the scribe carefully plotted the lines so that they would be even and straight, with 15 lines to the page. Later there is no evidence of such care and the number of lines per page varies between 14 and 19 lines. After page 118 the scribe seems to exhibit new care in copying the text but soon relaxes, making unwanted marks on the page. However, numerous marginal notes indicate an effort at completing scribal omissions to correct the text after different sections had been completed. Manuscript M appears to be a copy of an earlier version.

Manuscript B (Berlin), originally belonging to the monastery of St. Katharina in Nuremberg, is now in the possession of the Staatsbibliothek Preussischer Kulturbesitz in Berlin (mgq. 866). The text was written in two hands (1. 86v-88; 105-215; and 2. 89-215) and was bound together with other texts copied in a hand from the fourteenth and fifteenth centuries and was completed according to a note on page 310, "completus est liber iste XXI junio 1404" ("this book was completed 21 June 1404"). A third hand on 86v. made the following notation: "Anno Domini MCCC or more according to the count in the city of Nuremberg there was an honorable family named Langmann that was related to the Ebners. From them was born a child who was called Adelheid. What wonders God did for her from her childhood and the Holy Spirit accomplished through her, you will presently hear. Whatever was seemly and right, spiritual or divine, the child had and was indeed happy among people without being fresh."[28]

Both manuscripts are written in Bavarian with a strong admixture of a Middle German dialect.[29] However, the two texts have considerable differences in content, chronology, and length. Strauch based his critical edition published in 1878 on M and B, preferring the Berlin manuscript but always noting the differences and distinctive features of the Munich manuscript.

The Berlin manuscript is longer than M. It contains a lengthy prayer attributed to Adelheid Langmann and the letter exchange with Ulrich of the Monastery of Kaisheim interwoven into the text and the episode in the school.[30] However, M also has texts not found in B: Eberhart of Hohenstein's first communion, the death of Elsbeth.[31] Also various episodes appear in different places in the sequence of events, that is, the temptation by devils on the night before profession of her vows appears in M immediately before the account of the day of profession, whereas in B it is reported much later in the sequence of the text.[32]

A later edition of the autobiography of Adelheid Langmann, unknown to Strauch when he prepared his critical edition, is contained in *Codex Scotensis Vindobonensis* 308 (234) at the Bibliothek des Schottenstifts in Vienna. In his detailed analysis of the manuscripts, Ringler designates this edited text as W (Wien) and asserts that this version differs to a greater degree from M and B than they do from each other. However with regard to texts deleted or added to B, W agrees with M. Manuscript W is a paper manuscript completed in 1451 with an epilogue appended in 1457.[33] The manuscript consists of 238 pages written by a single hand in a clear Bastarda from the fifteenth century. On page 229r, the scribe identifies himself as Hans Probst. The descriptive epilogue telling how the manuscript found its way to the monastery of St. Katharina was written by Anna Jäck. The number of lines per page varies between 25 and 34, and rubrics were used throughout to indicate Latin quotations, names and underlines. Originally the manuscript belonged to the Franciscan monastery of Inzigkoven. Aside from the works having to do with Engelthal, this manuscript contains numerous other spiritual texts by Gertrude the Great of Helfta, Marquard of Lindau, Gregory the Great, and Henry of Louvain. It also includes the *Sister-Book of Kirchberg* and that of another monastery in the vicinity of Ulm, and numerous other devotional texts. This version of Adelheid's work is the shortest of the three, omitting single words, abbreviating, reformulating sentence structure, and using passages in an entirely different way. The scribe intentionally abbreviated the text in order to tighten the reports by eliminating repetitions and facts known in general.[34] Manuscript W generally omits names, titles, descriptive details, and epithets such as "holy" and "divine." This tendency to abbreviate can be demonstrated especially in references to Christ and the Virgin Mary. Manuscript M typically refers to Christ as "unser lieber herre"; whereas Manuscript B has "unser herre" and Manuscript W often replaces that with "er." The same pattern occurs with references to Mary: M "unser liebe fraue," B "unser fraue," M usually agrees with B. Altogether W abbreviates passages in fifty instances. The scribe also shortens the formulaic *Gnadenfrucht Topos*, which recounts the number of individuals saved from purgatory, the number of sinners converted, and the number of believers strengthened in faith through the intercessory prayers of Adelheid or as a gift from Christ. This *topos* occurs 15 times.

More importantly, Ringler theorizes that the editor abbreviated many passages because of objectionable content. Among these are statements about Adelheid's lack of faith and her sucking from the wounds of Christ.[35] All of these passages are omitted or abbreviated because they throw doubt on the faith of Adelheid or contain erotic language or images.[36] However, the major difference of this version, according to Ringler, is the addition of an introductory paragraph and a brief conclusion. The introductory paragraph in W agrees in content with the marginal note contained in M. The content of the conclusion of M is the same as that of W. I agree with Ringler that these additions to the text show a strong tendency to historicize the text and to direct it and make it amenable to an audience. However, such a tendency, as interesting and as well-intentioned as it may be, removes the text from the autobiographical and places another level of interpretation between the author and any audience. Such an interpretation as exhibited in W while seeking to enlighten or explain the text directed to a new audience may just as easily obscure or falsify the text. In addition, it is my belief that the "naughty bits" or embarrassing passages intentionally eliminated in W because they do not conform to some preconceived notion of what religious life should be must be included precisely because they throw the reader back into the realm of wonder or mystery and thereby emphasize the reality that God works in mysterious ways and that he deals with human beings according to the fullness of human nature. The relationship between God and any mystic is a private affair. The course of events, the attitudes, the graces, and the interpretation by the individual mystic demonstrate the way that God related to one individual. To read such an autobiography offers entry into a privileged experience of a relationship; it does not necessarily teach a lesson applicable to the reader or invite the reader to imitate the same experiences. I agree with Ringler's thesis that the progression of manuscripts culminating in W shows a *Legendarisierungsprozeß*, a progressive process of formulating a legend in the sense of an edifying work for the benefit of the reader. However, because of this *Legendarisierungsprozeß* and the abbreviation and rearrangement of portions of the text, I believe the best source to be Manuscript B. Although, as Ringler noted, it was hastily written, it contains Adelheid's prayer and the letters from the prior of Kaisheim and prefers first-person narrative. Aside from that, it belonged to the monastery of St. Katharina. These facts indicate a more authentic text. Manuscript M rearranges large episodes, has numerous variations, seeks a unified style of reporting, and prefers a third person narrative. Manuscript W imposes a chronological framework with introduction and epilogue similar to those in the Munich manuscript and abbreviates the text extensively, especially because of content. In preparing his critical edition of 1878, Philipp Strauch rightly favored the Berlin manuscript.

THE AUTHOR/ADELHEID LANGMANN

No certain reference to Adelheid (or Alheid) Langmann exists in the writings of the other authors of Engelthal. There are passages about several sisters named Alheid who bear no surname in the *Sister-Book of Engelthal*, but since the biographical sketches of that text seem to cover the lives of selected individuals who died sometime around 1340-1343, it is unlikely that these Alheids refer to Adelheid Langmann. Although Adelheid Langmann mentions Christina Ebner in her *Revelations* and the two mystics mention some of the same nuns and individuals in their works, Christina never mentions Adelheid. The Library of Catalogue of Engelthal written in the fifteenth century lists Adelheid Langmann's biography simply as "a little book by Langmann."[37] This reference along with the exact knowledge of events from her life recorded in the text make it clear that Adelheid is the source for this autobiographical information and that it accurately records her experiences and thought. No other document exists in which anyone other than Adelheid assumes the authorship of the *Revelations*.

THE TEXTS

Although Manuscript B includes all three works, the *Revelations,* the *Prayer,* and the *Letters* as one document, here I shall discuss each as an independent unit. Manuscript M and W do not contain the letters and Adelheid's prayer, either by omission or by their addition to B. In the Berlin manuscript as in this translation, the *Prayer* begins after the main body of the text and serves as a mystical climax of the autobiography.[38] There was no attempt to integrate the *Prayer* into the text of the *Revelations* since the *Prayer* does form an independent unit. However, at the conclusion of the *Prayer,* the autobiographical narrative of the manuscript commences again without any title to mark the beginning of a new section.[39] The three letters were then clumsily tacked on to the main narrative. While care was taken to preserve these vestiges of Adelheid's correspondence, it would have been better to title this part of the manuscript and to separate it clearly from the autobiography.

The Revelations (AL, 87a-191a; Strauch, 1-80)

The text begins with the sign of the cross in Latin as an invocation of the Trinity. That Adelheid chooses to begin her autobiography in this way indicates three interpretive possibilities: *Revelations* as public document, prayer, or sermon.

Many public documents began by invoking the Trinity. Since Adelheid composes her *Revelations* only under obedience, this *incipit* may indicate her awareness that these events of her private relationships with heavenly and earthly personages will be made a matter of public knowledge. This "official" beginning implies that her private experiences are worthy of being recorded and revealed for the edification of others.

The *incipit* may also indicate the prayerful content of the documents. This is the autobiography of a nun whose concerns were primarily spiritual in kind. She records the events of her relationship to God and its impact on her life. Very little detail concerns secular or family matters. Adelheid seeks to show her life as a document of grace under the Trinity. Her life story functions as a prayer, for in it she records the remarkable events of temptation and grace that lead her to rise to her special status as beloved of God. She hears the Gospel preached and loves it, and indeed everyone (except her family) thinks she should become a nun.[40] Despite the family's efforts at matchmaking, Christ powerfully arranges that she should be his for he has chosen her for himself.[41] Because of advice from spiritual friends and these revelations from Christ, Adelheid overcomes her real reluctance to enter a monastery and her fear of the harshness of the monastic regimen.[42] She reports diabolic temptations and divine revelations.[43]

The *Revelations* may also be interpreted as having the qualities of a sermon, for these would typically begin by invoking the Trinity and, like a prayer, could well end with an "Amen." The structure of the text reflects a Taulerian sermon structure.[44] The opening formula may function as the *thema*. It begins in Latin, and the entire graced life of Adelheid could be interpreted as being under the care of the Triune God. The *prothema*, which amplifies the quote, would then be the initial portrayal of Adelheid, and the *introductio* would occur in the first paragraph of the *Revelations*, which contains the themes that will be developed throughout the book which will be the "account of the life of a cloistered nun showing how God displayed wonders to her from the days of her childhood and how the Holy Spirit dwelt within her."[45] The following description shows Adelheid as happy and spiritual-minded, intent on hearing the preaching and meditating, particularly on the passion of Christ. The rest of the text *(clausio)* could be interpreted as being nothing more than an expansion of the theme using numerous reports from life, experiences at prayer, visions, auditions, temptations, dialogues, and mystical phenomena to build on the theme. The *Revelations*, like innumerable sermons of the period, closes with a prayer.

Less speculative than that is the analysis of Ursula Peters, who divides the *Revelations* into an introduction (Strauch, 1:1- 3), Adelheid's background (Strauch, 1:4-4,26), followed by many reports of graced moments, dialogues meant to teach, reports from other sources, reports about various people, contemporary events such as the interdict, and the problems the nuns had with local nobles. The culmination of Adelheid's spiritual progress is the *unio mystica* event (Strauch, 51:12-66:7) followed by a prayer, accounts of visions of the Christ Child, and by various reports about her holiness up to the beginning of the prayer (Strauch, 80:20).

The Prayer *(AL 191b-209a; Strauch, 80:20-92:25)*

Adelheid's *Prayer* consists of 61 petitions addressed to the Trinity. It serves as a *summa* in brief of her personal theological vision expressed through the prayer concerns of each petition and through the progression of petitions as a whole. Each petition has a twofold structure beginning with the proclamation or rehearsal ("I remind you . . .") of some event in the course of salvation history and then concludes with the request that either some attribute stemming from that event be given to Adelheid (or to those for whom she intercedes) or some personal benefit may come through the power of that salvific event and by association with or imitation of the event. Each petition makes Adelheid present to the personage or moment invoked. She addresses individually in turn the Trinity, the Godhead, the Father, and Christ as she rehearses significant moments in history touched by divine intervention. She calls to mind events before time began as well as the episodes of the private and public life of Jesus up to the institution of the Eucharist at the Last Supper. The *Prayer* as extant may very well be incomplete. There seems to be no definitive end to the prayer, and the expectation that Adelheid should continue in the same manner by including the events of the passion, death, and resurrection of Christ and perhaps even the postresurrection events such as Pentecost and Ascension is strong. Perhaps the rest of the prayer has been lost. It may also be that Adelheid composed a separate and perhaps somewhat different prayer designed for meditation on the passion events. That would not be unusual given the predilection of fourteenth-century mystics to contemplate the saving sufferings of Christ in minute detail. Given Adelheid's theological perspective, I doubt that such a prayer exists, but if it did it would undoubtedly resemble her vision in which she asserts that love was the motive for all of Christ's sufferings and repeats the love motive in response to every action of Christ's public ministry and to every act of suffering Christ endured.[46] However, I argue that the *Prayer*, as contained in Manuscript B and in this translation, has an integrity of its own in that it expresses Adelheid's theological vision and can be interpreted as a single and complete unit.

If the *Prayer* can be understood as a summary of Adelheid's theology, the opening paragraph functions as a synopsis of the *Prayer*. Not surprisingly, Adelheid addresses the prayer to the Holy Trinity. Unlike her contemporary Dominican mystics, whose spiritual focus was directed toward Christ and particularly toward him crucified, Adelheid's spirituality is Trinitarian. In her *Prayer*, the passion of Christ in the events of Good Friday disappear from consideration. She thinks of Christ in a much broader context beginning with his presence in the Eternal Trinity and ending with his coming in glory at the end of time to judge the living and the dead. Adelheid's theological vision coextends with eternity. In this largest of contexts, everything and everyone has its place and its meaning and contributes to the progression of salvation history under God's providence.

Importantly, in her *Prayer* Adelheid interprets her own place within the scope of providential history. She prays to become the mouthpiece through which all the cries and yearnings of every human being before her time would be channeled. Their prayers for love and mercy would be collected in her and uttered through her own mouth before the Triune God. In the same breath she prays that her intercessory power extend to every human being from her own day to the end of the world and that the concerns of all people be channeled through her. "They must all come forth from my mouth . . ."[47] Adelheid assumes the Christological function of priestly intercession to herself. As intercessor she stands in a long line of powerful figures who intercede on behalf of others. Abraham wagered for the just men of Sodom (Gen. 18:22-33); Moses lifted up his hands in prayer for victory while Joshua and the Israelites waged battle with Amalek (Exod. 17:8-13); and Queen Esther pleaded the cause of the endangered Israelites before King Ahasuerus (Est. 5). All of these righteous individuals made intercession on behalf of a distinct group of people under particular circumstances during a specific period of time. Adelheid's intercession far exceeds that of these biblical personages; in fact, her intercessory prayer resembles that of Christ himself. Just as Jesus died for all for the forgiveness of sins, so Adelheid pleads for all to receive mercy and love. As his motive for dying was love for all, so now Adelheid prays that his mercy and love be extended to everyone who has ever called out for it. She calls forth the motive and the historical action of the Crucifixion into the personal and real lives of all people. What the Trinity intended (salvation for all) and Christ accomplished by his obedience and crucifixion (the possibility of and invitation to salvation), Adelheid prays to happen in reality, not simply in theology. She prays for others and she also prays for herself what she would wish for others: that God come into her heart and fill her with love and grace, remove her sins, and make it possible for her to live a holy and perfect life so that she be found perfect on the last day.[48] With this first petition, she prays for the actualization of salvation within her. Her concept of salvation cannot be minimalized, for she conceives of salvation for her and for the whole world as the union of God and herself in her heart, the effect of which is to be a total transformation of herself. She is to be set apart as holy and therefore godlike, and further she is to become completely divinized in "perfection." Such a process completes the saving work of Christ in Adelheid and therefore makes his sacrifice fruitful.

Repeatedly Adelheid prays for this to be accomplished in her search for "perfection."[49] She asks for a "holy and perfect life."[50] She needs divine grace "so that nothing will be lacking" in her.[51] She wishes to become "holy in real truth."[52] She also desires to be "found perfect" at her death.[53] Adelheid conceives of this progress toward human perfection as a gift of God's grace that gradually and continually provides her with the virtues necessary to lead a life transformed by the divine presence. To foster this process she prays for "perfect humility" and "all virtues" so she is able to benefit from God's free gift.[54] With regard to faith she also asks to "know the truth" and even to have hidden mysteries revealed to her just as had happened with the Virgin Mary. Most importantly she asks for mercy and love suspecting that Christ operates for individuals as he did for the world when he offered up his life on the Cross. Emphatically, Adelheid prays twice to receive such love from God that her "heart must burst more from love than from the pain of death."[55] She associates Christ with herself in two ways: as her Beloved or Bridegroom and as her "child" who will be "born spiritually within" her.[56] The first image links her with bridal mysticism *(Brautmystik)* and the second alludes to essence mysticism *(Wesenmystik)*, thus linking in a single prayer two contrasting symbol systems, both of which seek to describe the indescribable immediate union of God and the soul.

The reception of holy Communion functions as the prime image of the reception and conception of Christ within Adelheid. The indwelling of the divine, now motivated no longer by love for the world but by love for Adelheid individually, brings the benefits of the salvific acts of Christ in his life and on the hill of Calvary to Adelheid herself. The indwelling of Christ, like the reception of the Eucharist, brings forgiveness of sins, illumination to truth, and spiritual growth fostered by love. With such an understanding, it is not surprising that Adelheid concludes her *Prayer* with the institution of the Eucharist on Holy Thursday and its application to her and effect on her. "I ask you to give me true, perfect love to receive your Holy Body so that I may conceive you spiritually even as your mother conceived you bodily. . . ."[57]

The Letters *(AL 207b-216b; Strauch, 91-96)*

After the *Prayer* and following a break in the text of Manuscript B, the *Revelations* continues with the addition of possibly six letters worked into a redactional narrative. It was done in a clumsy way and would have been greatly improved by inserting the complete text of each of the letters, which would have clearly indicated each letter in its integrity. However, as the letters appear in the text, it is difficult to interpret them and impossible to date them or to determine whether the text contains three or more letters from Ulrich of Kaisheim to Adelheid. Wilhelm Oehl included and designated the texts as Letters 1-3 but did not include the rest of the text, which could contain excerpts from as many as three different letters.[58]

In comparison with Ulrich's five extant letters to Margaret Ebner, the letters to Adelheid seem more spiritual. Perhaps if the extant text included the greeting to each letter, the letters to Adelheid would more closely match the style of the letters to Margaret. In writing to Margaret, Ulrich passes on greetings and news in response to Margaret's inquiries but never discusses any spiritual topic. In fact he refrains from doing so, writing that he will discuss some matter known only to Margaret when he comes to visit her at Maria Medingen.[59] Kaisheim was much closer to Maria Medingen than it was to Engelthal, making it easier for Ulrich and Margaret to speak of important topics in person, while Adelheid would have had to rely on letters to communicate matters that she might have preferred to discuss in private. Thus the tone and subject matter would necessarily differ in a letter to Adelheid, since that letter had to serve as the only contact between Ulrich and Adelheid.

The letter fragments do reveal the spiritual closeness of Adelheid and Ulrich. Their relationship seems to have been one of mutual confidence and trust. Each depends upon the other for intercessory prayer and prophetic revelations. Both exhibit bridal mystic tendencies and emphasize the importance of the Holy Trinity in the spiritual life. They unite bridal mysticism and Trinitarian spirituality in the indwelling in the heart, and therefore neither would ever be separated from God or from each other. Ulrich writes of Christ being "drunk" with love for Adelheid and emphasizes her role as intercessor for all because she is able to obtain anything she wishes from her bridegroom.[60] In addition to the bridal imagery, Ulrich also writes of the birth of the Christ Child in the soul, a very popular idea among the Rhineland mystics.[61] In response to his letter, Adelheid, using first person, records that she does not understand that very well.[62] A revelation to her clarifies the result of the birth of Christ in the soul—Adelheid would receive power to convert sinners to goodness, the task for which Christ took on flesh, preached, and died. In the final revelation, Christ proclaimed ". . . no one can do anything more dear to me than to pray for sinners."[63] To be united with Christ and to accomplish the same conversion of sinners was Adelheid's task.

THE *REVELATIONS* AND *BIOGRAPHY* OF CHRISTINA EBNER

Audi, filia et vide! Inclina aurem tuam;
et obliviscere populum tuum,
et domum patris tui.
Psalm 44:11 (Vulgata)

CHRISTINA EBNER'S FAME CONTINUED after the dissolution of the monastery of Engelthal in 1596 principally because of the influence of her family, which later became ennobled with the surname von Ebner-Eschenbach. Her Protestant family erected a monument to the Catholic nun (and to themselves) in which Christina, attired in the Dominican habit, kneels before the Virgin Mary, who has the Christ Child seated upon her lap. Christina holds a book, perhaps a copy of her *Revelations*. Beneath this scene the unknown artist portrayed various Ebner men in chronological order along with their coats of arms, identifying each by text and heraldic symbol. This epitaph exists today above the interior south portal of the St. Sebaldus Church in Nuremberg. It stands as a witness to the perduring renown of Christina despite the Protestant Reformation and despite the devaluation and dissolution of her way of life. Her fame rests upon her reputation as a holy woman, documentary evidence of which is preserved in two texts— her autobiographical *Revelations* and her hagiographical biography. History also remembers her as the author of the *Sister-Book of Engelthal*. The distinction between the autobiography by and the biography about Christina Ebner is very important since one gives the reader a glimpse into the life of Christina that is undoubtedly close to the source, while the other paints a verbal picture of Christina precisely in the stance of a saint.

MANUSCRIPTS

Several manuscripts of the *Revelations* exist. The Nuremberg manuscript (CEN), dating from the second half of the fourteenth century, belonged to the Ebner family and now rests in the Staatsbibliothek in Nuremberg (cod. Cent. V., App 99). A copy of this manuscript (E1) made before 1721 exists in the Ebnersche Bibliothek in Eschenbach (cod. 89), as well as a further copy of CEN (cod 90 = E2) possibly from the fourteenth or the fifteenth century. Codex 91 (E3) from the eighteenth century is a copy of E2. A *Sammelhandschrift* containing both a copy of the Nuremberg manuscript (CES) and a copy of the hagiographical biography (Md 1) is housed in the Landesbibliothek in Stuttgart.

Manuscript Cent. V. App. 99 in the Stadtbibliothek at Nuremberg contains 163 pages and dates from the second half of the fourteenth century. Pages are numbered with Roman numerals recto and verso. The text is divided into paragraphs set off in red. Red ink is also used for capital letters, underlines, punctuation, and slashes, which may indicate pauses for public reading. Each page contains approximately nineteen lines of text. Further, there are marginal notes in a later hand of the early fifteenth century and others from the sixteenth or seventeenth century. The manuscript is bound in leather with the cover displaying the Ebner coat of arms. On the inside cover, written in a hand of the fourteenth century, it states: "This shall always belong to the oldest Ebner so that it will always remain in our family."[1] Under that, in another hand of the sixteenth century is written: "The Life of St. Christina Ebner."[2] Beneath that is written also in a hand of the sixteenth century: "This belongs to Tobias Ebner."[3]

Manuscript 282 (CES) in the Würtembergische Landesbibliothek is a *Sammelhandschrift* from the eighteenth century.[4] However, it contains material from the fourteenth century, copied rather faithfully. It collects various writings from diverse sources having to do with Christina Ebner and her family.

The manuscript begins with an illustration portraying the Virgin and Child before whom kneels the Dominican nun, Christina Ebner. This picture closely resembles the epitaph erected in St. Sebaldus Church in Nuremberg. It bears the inscription, "Blessed Christina Ebner was born as one counts after the birth of Christ one-thousand-two-hundred-seventy-seven years and was seventy-nine years old and died after the birth of Christ one-thousand-three-hundred-fifty-six years on St. John's Day after Christmas. She lived a holy life in the monastery of Engelthal where she lies buried. Pray to God and to the Mother of Mercy for your family and for all believing souls. Amen." On the next page is displayed a colored illustration of a Dominican nun kneeling in prayer with rays shining forth from around her head signifying her sanctity. Both pictures also show the Ebner heraldic shield. Pages 11-28 contain biographical and bibliographical notes about the Ebner family and other nuns at Engelthal such as Adelheid Langmann, who may have been a relative. These notes are in a hand from the eighteenth century. After this follows a copy of Manuscript CEN beginning with the notes concerning Christina's birth added before the text itself begins. The copy of CEN is faithful, and the scribe attempted to retain the antique script of the original. After this lengthy document follows a page marking the beginning of the next part of the manuscript. This states unambiguously: "This book belongs to the monastery of Maria Medingen of the Order of Preachers. This book tells about Christina Ebner who was at the monastery of Engelthal of the Order of Preachers."[5] This portion of the manscrtipt contains a copy of the text housed at Maria Medingen (Md1). The manuscript concludes with an account of her death: "She died blessedly on St. John's Day after Christmas and God gave her what he had promised—what no eye has seen nor ear heard, nor ever has come into the heart of humans what God has prepared for those who love him. To the same reward may God help us by his mercy. Amen."[6]

The archives of the monastery of Maria Medingen in Mödingen/Dillingen contain a bound manuscript (Md1) of the hagiographical biography written before 1400.[7] This copies some earlier manuscript prepared to collate all the extant written materials, eyewitness accounts, and remembrances from life about a prospective saint—Christina Ebner. The Dominicans of Maria Medingen received a copy of this life because it was also a Dominican monastery with a famous mystic—Margaret Ebner. The longstanding but falsely presumed family ties of the two mystics may also have played a role in the importance of the manuscript for the nuns of Maria Medingen, who were likewise intent upon celebrating their own Ebner. This presumed relationship, which has been disproven by J. Traber, perdured through the centuries.[8] A biographer of Margaret Ebner, Sebastian Schlettstetter, perpetuated the myth in his "Description of her Life" written in 1662.[9] The myth was promoted artistically when the monastery of Maria Medigen was totally rebuilt and baroquified in 1717. The coat of arms that decorated Margaret Ebner's burial chapel were not those of her own family, but of the Ebners of Nuremberg. This manuscript (Md1) is small in size but thick, containing 373 pages numbered later on each side—746 pages. It is bound in red leather and was produced in the fifteenth century. It contains just one work—The Life of Christina Ebner.

AUTHORSHIP

The source and author of the *Revelations* is Christina Ebner herself. The manuscript (CEN) begins *in mediae res* with the report of an ecstatic vision that took place on Easter in 1344. No background information about her birth, childhood, or entry into the monastery forms any part of this account, as it was not important in the light of the content. Immediately Christina draws the reader into the ecstatic vision of her journey to Jerusalem to the house in which the Last Supper had taken place. This text exists wholly on a spiritual plane and conveys an immediacy of experience and knowledge that could have come only from Christina herself. There is no trace of any reportage distancing the subject and the author from the event. Both Christina and the reader have immediate access to the event, Christina through experience and the reader through the account of the mystical experience unencumbered by commentary or interpretation. Later in the text, many parts of the revelations and dialogues will be explained or interpreted, sometimes by Christ, sometimes by Christina or perhaps even by a later redactor, but knowledge of these events and the content of the many revelations granted to her must come from Christina herself. Undeniably the source of the vast majority of information on these mystical events and revelatory dialogues, Christina never claims to be the author. Neither is the text attributed to her authorship in the manuscript. However, nowhere is the authorship attributed to anyone else. In the absence of other evidence, the immediacy of experience and knowledge of the content point to only one person as the author—Christina Ebner. The account of her birth and death do not form part of the original manuscript. They are simply notes added later to the inside and back covers. In addition this manuscript reports events in Christina's life only during the years from 1344 to 1352. While not always consistent and organized, there is a certain chronology overall. Some episodes may have been included from memory of past events, while others seem to be recorded closer in time to the event. By and large, however, a chronology is discernible.

The author of the *Biography* (CES, Md1) is unknown. While the source for much of the material in the Medingen and Stuttgart manuscripts must have been Christina Ebner, she could not have been the author. Integral to the text are reports about her birth, her childhood and life before entering the monastery, as well as an account of her holy death. These manuscripts begin with events prior to her birth, contain an account of her miraculous birth, and report Christina's childhood devotions and penances. After her entry into the Dominican monastery, the chronology of events breaks down completely. Ursula Peters calls this a *Mischtext*, for it contains reports in both first and third person, accounts from other sources, and the editorial commentary of a redactor during the life of Christina Ebner. It also contains fragments of letters, accounts of visions, prayers, songs, and meditations.[10] Peters believes that an anonymous brother authored the account of Christina Ebner's life. In fact he is mentioned in the text as a "brother who first wrote these things."[11] He diligently seeks out information from and about Christina. He exacts a more detailed account of a vision of the Holy Spirit than Christina had related to him earlier.[12] The brother speaks with her mother about the details of the unusual birth of her daughter.[13] He wishes to have a more precise account of Christina's childhood from Christina herself.[14] Christina looks upon him as a gift from God to help her write down her experiences.[15] To accomplish his task, he visits her sickbed and writes down her experiences.[16] This brother inquires further about the "loving discourse" of her divine partner.[17] He also serves as Christina's confessor.[18] Finally he records this: "She wants to be certain about all these things that God has accomplished with her and which I have written."[19] Both Christina and the scribe want to be sure that everything has been recorded accurately. Peters argues convincingly that the cooperation of Christina and her confessor produced the text of this manuscript.[20] She is the authoritative source, he the faithful recorder. In fulfilling this God-given task, he also helps Christina to remember and seeks to organize the diverse materials that he collects from his various other sources. It is evident that Christina depends upon him. After a particular mystical experience she says, "Lord, let me go and tell him."[21] She wishes to do this presumably because she does not want to forget the experience and wants it to be carefully recorded. Further evidence of her dependence upon this brother follows soon after. "And she often did this: she prayed to God that he let her go to him when she was overflowing in grace to the glory of God, so that these great things would not be lost, but rather be revealed to the glory of God."[22]

Peters concludes that the identity of this important confessor and scribe remains unknown.[23] She entertains the likelihood that Conrad of Füssen may have been the scribe, for he was certainly the confessor for the monastery and had encouraged Christina to record the wonders that she was experiencing.[24] This occurred in 1317 when Christina was forty years old. Conrad remained at his post as confessor of Engelthal for seven years until 1324, when he was transferred to Freiburg. The section of the manuscript (Md1) in which Conrad plays a role ends on page 27 with Christina's letter to him.[25] After that, Conrad is absent and could not have helped in the actual writing of the text. The scribe continues his activity into

Christina's old age.[26] While Conrad of Füssen could be credited with the initiative to write the book, he did not actually write it himself. Another likely candidate for the role of co-author would be Friedrich Sunder, the chaplain of Engelthal mentioned numerous times in the various texts associated with the monastery. His influence on the nuns as priest and confessor was enormous and greatly appreciated by them. However, he died in 1328 and could therefore not have been the scribe of Christina's manuscript. Another likely candidate was Henry of Nördlingen, whom Christina frequently mentions at the conclusion of both the Nuremberg and the Medingen/Stuttgart texts. He was in contact with Christina by letter as early as 1338, but he did not visit Engelthal until after the death of Margeret Ebner of Maria Medingen on 20 June 1351.[27] Christina had already been writing for many years prior to that date.

The identity of this influential scribe cannot be definitively determined. There were other chaplains at Engelthal in the fourteenth century who were also engaged in writing. Two of them, Cunrat Fridrich and Heinrich, authored the life of Sister Gertrud of Engelthal. Gustav Voit has constructed an incomplete list of the chaplains of Engelthal and its filial churches. Evidence from the text suggests that the scribe must have been a chaplain to the nuns and must have resided in the monastery complex; otherwise Christina would not have had ready access to him for purposes of advice and the quick recording of her experiences. This detail would probably eliminate those chaplains assigned to filial churches at a distance from the monastery, unless they were so close that the chaplain could reside in the chaplains' quarters at Engelthal. Even so Christina would not have ready access to someone whose duties kept him in another location each day. Using documentary evidence, Gustav Voit lists six chaplains of Engelthal during this period: Heinrich (1321-23); Friedrich (1322-25); Heinrich of Ekewint, a Dominican (1323); Conrad (1336); Ulrich der Feuchter (1336); and Conrad "the young chaplain" (1351-55).[28] None of them matches the identity of the brother with any certitude. Any one of them would have been literate and could have helped Christina to write her *Revelations*.

CHRISTINA EBNER

Christina Ebner came from a ministerial family that became a part of the patrician class when it moved to the city of Nuremberg. Christina was born on Good Friday (26 March 1277), the tenth child of Seyfried Ebner and his wife Elisabeth Kuhdorf. She entered the monastery of Engelthal at the age of twelve in 1289 and began a life of Dominican asceticism that led to the experience of visions and other mystical phenomena beginning in the year 1291. She served the monastery as author of the *Sister-Book of Engelthal* and undoubtedly as prioress for a time. In CEN the author refers explicitly to this office: "When she was prioress and was in great need . . . he [Christ] promised her that he would be prior and would not leave her in need."[29] Further, documentary evidence uncovered by Gustav Voit shows a prioress named Christina in 1338, who may be Christina Ebner. She also served the community in other practical ways as portress or in other community functions. Most importantly she was the author of *Revelations* and the primary source of information for her biography. Her fame as a mystic spread throughout Germany and elsewhere. A host of flagellants urged her to preach to them in 1349 as they passed by the monastery and listened to her attentively. King Charles (later Emperor Charles IV) with a retinue of nobles and ecclesiastics visited her in May 1350, seeking her advice and asking her blessing.

She corresponded with Henry of Nördlingen and through him was connected to the wide circle of the Friends of God, chiefly with Margaret Ebner but also with the numerous other Friends of God among whom were numbered Queen Agnes of Hungary and Rulman Merswin. Henry visited Christina Ebner for three weeks in 1351 and introduced her to the works of Tauler. She died on the feast of St. John the Evangelist (27 December) in 1356 and was buried in the chapel of Engelthal—such was her reputation for holiness. Most nuns were buried in the cloister walk, but those considered to be particularly holy were buried in the monastic church. This was also the case with Margaret Ebner, who had an entire chapel (formerly the chapter room) adjacent to the church for her resting place.

THE *REVELATIONS*: STRUCTURE

In the library catalogue of the monastery of Engelthal, two books in addition to the *Sister-Book* are listed as being by or about (*von*) Christina Ebner.[30] Although both of these texts, joined together in the Stuttgart manuscript, have Christina Ebner as their source, and although both texts are very important for the reconstruction of a complete biography, it is clear that the Nuremberg manuscript is closer to Christina as author. Even though portions of the Medingen manuscript may have been compiled during the years of tutelage under Conrad of Füssen, in its full form, as we have received it, it serves as a biography at some distance from Christina, gathered from diverse sources and compiled clearly for hagiographical purposes. The difference between the two manuscripts (CES and CEN) mirrors the difference between the basic kerygma about Christ that proclaimed his resurrection from the dead and exhorted hearers to believe in him and be baptized (Acts 3), and the progressively fuller account of Christ's life developed into the Gospel of Mark. Thereafter were added an account of Christ's teachings in the Gospel of Matthew, the birth narratives in the Gospel of Luke, and finally the high Christology in the Gospel of John beginning with the account of the preexistent Logos in the prologue and adding an extensive account of Christ's final discourse. So, too, manuscript CEN represents the core of the mystical life of Christina Ebner as recorded by herself. Manuscript CES takes some of that material and adds to it more details about her birth, her childhood, entry into the monastery, connections with others, and finally a report of her death.

If the above is true, then manuscript CEN takes on particular importance in interpreting the life, works, and spirituality of Christina Ebner. The basically chronological structure of the work covers the time from the vigil of Easter Sunday 1344 up to the feast of the Holy Trinity in 1351 or 1352. The chronology is not certain at the end of the document. Even though the final paragraphs (*191-193) are not explicitly dated by feasts and years, as many of the paragraphs are, it follows logically that these paragraphs take the reader into events from the year 1352 since the paragraphs prior to these reflect an explicit chronology beginning with paragraph 178, which gives the year as 1351. The following paragraphs progress through various feast days: St. Elizabeth (5 November), St. Cecilia (22 November), St. Andrew (30 November), St. Catherine (25 November), St. Nicholas (6 December), St. Lucy (13 December), St. John (27 December), and then paragraph 190 is dated Tuesday of Pentecost week. There is no indication in the text that this is a remembrance or a rehearsal of things past. The final paragraph (*193) is marked as Holy Trinity Day.

The chronology of the manuscript progresses from the Easter Vigil of 1344 up to St. Appolinaris Day celebrated on 23 July 1348 (*30). The next paragraph begins: "As one counts from the birth God thirteen-hundred years and after that forty-five . . ." (1345), and the strict chronology breaks down.[31] The year 1346 may begin with paragraph 35 and continues until paragraph 44, which is dated 1345. This chronology progresses up to paragraph 66, which mentions Christina's age as being seventy years old (1347), but paragraph 68 explicitly mentions the year 1346. Thereafter the progression is strictly chronological (*69-193). The chronology is broken into four distinct parts: (1) paragraphs 1-30 cover the years 1344-1348; (2) paragraphs 31-43 cover 1345-1346; (3) paragraphs 44-65 cover 1345-1347; and (4) paragraphs 68-193 cover 1346-1352. Three feast days are repeated in different parts of the text. New Year's Day 1346 is mentioned both in paragraph 35 and 72. Christina writes of events on Holy Thursday 1347 in paragraph 11 and again in paragraph 78. She also mentions the Feast of the Ascension 1347 in paragraphs 19 and 80. None of texts repeats the same events already reported. In each case, the paragraph repeating a previous date (*72, *78, *80) contains a considerably lengthier entry describing events, revelations, visions or dialogues on that day. If these paragraphs do indeed refer to the same day previously reported, which, because not every paragraph is dated by year, is not absolutely certain, then each of the second entries reports another remembrance of events on that day, which in retrospect may have taken on greater significance. Christina's memory may also have been jarred by conversations with her confessor or someone else. Unless there is some theological reason for the arrangement of the overlapping chronologies, then parts two and three may be simply more details added to an account previously written. Not enough of these events are repeated in CES to posit any kind of theory as to the arrangement of the texts.

THE *REVELATIONS*: TEXT

This text has an integrity of its own independent of the other manuscripts. The content is closer to the author-subject. The distinct paragraphs are more precisely dated by year and feast day. The contents of this manuscript show an immediacy of the author to the events reported, and these events represent the highpoint of Christina Ebner's mystical experience. Christina had already written the *Sister-Book of Engelthal* and had already begun to set down her spiritual experiences as early as the Advent of 1317. In this unique manuscript she relates for posterity the apex of her spiritual growth and the unbelievable extent to which Christ graces her with mystical experiences.

Significantly her *dike* into mystical experience occurs on the vigil of Easter, the greatest feast day of the Christian year and the feast day (especially as Triduum) that celebrates the core beliefs of the Christian message—the establishment of the Eucharist and priesthood, Christ's passion and his sacrifice on Calvary, and his rising from the dead with the promise of resurrection to those who believe in him. Christina immediately associates herself with the fundamental events and teachings of the Christian religion, identifying herself with Christ in his passion, death, and resurrection. In fact, every aspect of this experience forms a preamble or overture to her entire mystical experience. Christina is described as a "holy person who is well known in heaven and on earth" because of the grace she has received.[32] "The grace of God increased in her heart with such incomparable richness that the grace overflowed from her soul into her body and into all her members so that she was possessed by grace and made heavy with it just like a woman pregnant with child."[33] After matins "this holy person was enraptured in a spiritual light and led to Jerusalem. She saw how the three Marys were coming to the tomb and especially how St. Mary Magdalen lamented. This person went with them as one of those going to the tomb and she saw that of all the humans on earth it seemed to her that fifteen who were in the same degree of grace had come along."[34]

In these opening sentences Christina stresses the importance of grace, which makes her "heavy," a term not uncommon among fourteenth-century mystics. Similar to her contemporary, Margaret Ebner, Christina Ebner designates the heart as the source of change in her body and in all her limbs. The grace as given and received significantly feels like "possession," and in its flowing Christina is helpless. That she compares the experience of grace to that of a woman pregnant with child hints at the mystical birth of Christ in her soul and all the goodness that will occur because of her status as the Beloved of Christ. Also significant here is the introduction of a mystical vision, especially since in this vision Christina is numbered among the chosen and accompanies none other than Mary Magdalen, the patroness of the Dominican Order and "lover" of Christ, to the tomb. Christina is among the fifteen highest in grace on earth; thus she is numbered among a community of the select few. All of these features will be of immense importance for Christina's spirituality: the reception and power of grace, mystical experiences, the concept of being chosen and ranked at the highest levels of grace. Consequently these characteristics will be rehearsed innumerable times throughout the document. Underlying these themes are the free will, power, and love of Christ, all of which will be directed to Christina.

The revelation continues, emphasizing a quality of the highest level of perfection. Speaking of the select group in the vision composed of men and women, religious and secular persons, Christina shows them commiserating with Mary Magdalene, who more than anyone else laments and weeps uncontrollably over the death of Christ. Her weeping effects them all and brings forth compassion from them so that they are described in the vision as *mitleider und mitleiderin* ("fellow sufferers") with Mary Magdalen over the sufferings of Christ.

When Christina awakes from the mystical vision, she finds herself still lamenting, in part because she recognizes no one, especially none of her sisters, among the fifteen chosen ones. As a result of her lamentations and disappointment, she receives a revelation. This pattern will occur frequently throughout the *Revelations*. God/Christ will respond to her prayer, her petitions, her questions, and even her thoughts. Here it is revealed to her that God "wanted to have a special Love-Day (*minnetag*) with her and with the sisters of the monastery on Easter Day.[35] Not only does Christina receive this revelation, she is also given a task to fulfill. She is told that she should tell the sisters "to prepare themselves for it."[36] On Easter "they would have to come to Jerusalem to that upper room where our Lord Jesus Christ ate with his disciples and where he showed them their unbelief and the hardness of their hearts."[37] With this further revelation the sisters of the monastery are associated with the disciples at the Last Supper. Not only are they followers of Christ, but they also behave like the first followers—Judas betrayed Christ, while Peter professed his faithfulness and received the prediction of his triple denial. All the other disciples heard that they would abandon him. Christina's own disappointment over the absence of her sisters among the chosen leads the entire community to an encounter with personal conversion. The intent of the revelation and the *minnetag* is that the sisters "should ponder this with attentive hearts."[38] Christina learns that Christ will give to each one a special virtue. The motive for this special day and for the individual gifts is likewise the motive for the Crucifixion—love—but the particular love that brings about this showering of graces is Christ's love specifically for Christina. Emboldened by that love, she reveals to her sisters what she had received; as a result, they prepare themselves with desire and special prayers for the *minnetag*. Somewhat surprised at the positive and quick response of her sisters, Christina breaks into an ecstatic canticle. At this point the text changes dramatically into what amounts to Christina's own *Magnificat*. Similar to the reaction of the Virgin Mary, Christina, filled with ecstatic joy, cries out:

> O you friend in the inner recesses of my heart! How you know well those you have chosen forever and call to them so that they come quickly as soon as they hear your voice and follow after you. So was it also that the chosen children of this monastery received the news of God in full faith from their faithful mother.[39]

Christina emphasizes the role of Christ, who has chosen these nuns (and especially Christina), for he dwells in the inner recesses of her heart. By that union she has the power to draw her sisters by the sound of her and his voice so that the sisters will come ever closer to Christ. She is also portrayed here as their mother. Like Mary, the mother of Christ, she leads others to him. Like an *abbas* of the desert (desert mother) she leads her disciples. Her role as prioress may also come into play here, for as superior she would have been "mother" to all the nuns. Most importantly she functions in this way by the will of Christ and because he dwells in her heart.

With this reference to the indwelling, Christina is closely linked to the spiritual strain that emphasizes the presence of Christ within. Paul expressed it succinctly: "I have been crucified with Christ; it is no longer I who live, but Christ who lives in me; and the life I now live in the flesh I live by faith in the Son of God, who loved me and gave himself up for me" (Gal. 2:20). For Christina, much the same dynamic is at work here. Further confirmation of her special status occurs during the celebration of the Mass on Easter Day. When the priest elevates the consecrated host Christina perceives something unique: "And then . . . an oversweet fragrance arose within and about her the likes of which no other creature had and this strengthened her in body and in spirit so that she became stronger than before."[40] Christina describes this as a unique experience, and since the description lacks more specific details, the singular character of this experience must be granted despite prevalent reports of special fragrances or tastes experienced by other mystics. Clearly the reception of this unique fragrance serves as a key moment of conversion into mystical life. She reports immediately that it had a strong and lasting effect on her. "Also, the same delightful vision of the holy body of God which she saw bodily from the priest forced itself through her outer senses into her mind and there she saw the same vision frequently with the inner eye of her soul spiritually and with supernatural delight just like she had it in the presence of the body [the elevated host]."[41] Further, Christina reports that this experience draws her closer to the priest who celebrated the Mass and about whom she had also received instructions on the vigil of Easter. Christina's attachment to and fondness for priests, both in general and individually, marks her spirituality. Finally she reports another effect of this experience: "It also happened . . . that when she suffered bodily her spirit soared and wandered in friendly familiarity among the nine choirs of angels in incomparable joy just like that joy one has from great love when invited to a wedding feast."[42] This last description links Christina to a vision of herself as the beloved bride of Christ with whom she will celebrate joyous nuptials.

This initial paragraph (*1) concisely sets forth the important features of Christina's spiritual life and theological world view. These features are developed at various points in the manuscript, principally during visionary experiences associated with communion but not always. Significantly,

Christina enters into mystical ecstasy on three other occasions when she is transported to Jerusalem. In addition to these Jerusalem visions, the visions of heaven and an interrogation by some unknown woman present the major themes and teachings of Christina Ebner.

As already noted in the first vision of Jerusalem, Christina found herself in the upper room in which Christ celebrated the final Passover with his disciples. The vision produced reflections on the Eucharist itself as well as on the comparison between the disciples and the nuns of Engelthal; both groups must be shown their shortcomings. The second ecstatic vision in Jerusalem also occurs in the upper room. Here Christina witnesses "everything that God did there with his disciples and also with the other believers who were there."[43] The disciples split into two groups, the men following Peter, the women, among them the Mother of God, following Mary Magdalen. Both groups wept and lamented until the nuns of Engelthal arranged themselves behind Mary Magdalen. Dominican nuns identified with Mary Magdalen because she was the original patroness of the Dominican Order. They also identified with her as a penitent, beloved of Christ, who was the first to see Christ in a postresurrection experience. Significantly the two groups go to a mountain where they witness a theophany: "There they saw Our Lord Jesus Christ in great beauty and brilliance sitting on a marvelous throne decorated with gold and with precious gems and the craftsmanship of this throne was so masterfully done and so richly decorated that no tongue would be able to tell about it."[44] From the mouth of Christ enthroned in glory, Christina hears the words, "Audi filia et vide." Significantly, the verses of Psalm 45 immediately preceding this quote likewise describe a king enthroned in glory. Patristic and medieval interpretations of the psalms prefer to read them in terms of Christ so that the king celebrated in the psalm becomes Christ himself. Christina becomes the daughter to whom the speech is addressed. "Hear, O daughter, consider, and incline your ear; forget your people and your father's house; and the king will desire your beauty" (Ps. 45:10-11). This visionary experience marks Christina's call to mystical intimacy with Christ. The continuation of the vision designates the power that she will receive by virtue of her response to that call. On his left hand, Christina sees the great number of souls floating in the air who will enter heaven with Christ. As the vision continues they enter heaven amid gladness and rejoicing, singing a song in German praising the Trinity. Christina grows sad at this but receives a personal revelation echoing Zechariah 9:9 and the text of one of her favorite works, *The Song of the Daughter of Zion*: "Rejoice, you daughters of Zion! Love gives us great reward and therefore we should sing sweet songs."[45] In a vision reminiscent of the Book of Revelation the angels and saints fall down in worship before the Trinity, the members of which converse. Although Christ had to suffer, the Holy Spirit now gives love and joy. The vision concludes with the revelation from the Holy Spirit, "My ways are ways rich in grace and joy."[46] In this vision Christina is numbered among the elect who follow Christ, specifically with those who follow him like Mary Magdalen. Even beyond that election she receives a personal invitation to live in intimacy with Christ and the strong affirmation that the ways of God the Spirit bring joy and grace.

The third vision in Jerusalem takes place at the site of the coming of the Holy Spirit on Pentecost. In company with Martha and the saints, Christina sits enraptured from prime until the end of day. Here Christina does not remain passive but engages in dialogue compelled by the sad state of Christendom: "Much beloved Lord, what is the cause of the confusion and why so much complaining?"[47] Christ reveals to her that it has really always been so and will always be so: "From the beginning of the world many humans have set themselves against me and taken the counsels of the devil."[48] Christina begins to assume the role of intercessor before the Trinity for the welfare of others.

The fourth ecstatic vision of Jerusalem also takes place in the house in which the Holy Spirit descended upon the disciples. Christina witnesses the preaching of Peter and remarks on the change of heart of the audience. She quotes a portion of the biblical text in Latin and clearly has the entire text in mind. "Men of Israel, hear these words: Jesus of Nazareth, a man attested to you by God with mighty works and wonders and signs which God did through him in your midst, as you yourselves know . . . And Peter said to them, 'Repent, and be baptized every one of you in the name of Jesus Christ for the forgiveness of your sins; and you shall receive the gift of the Holy Spirit'" (Acts 2:14;38). Christina portrays the crowd as having hearts set afire by the preaching of Peter. Innumerable times in the *Revelations*, Christ promises her that he will make hearts burn through her.[49] Here Christina begins to model herself after Peter in the effect that her words will have on her sisters and on others.

While the visions of Jerusalem affirm Christian teachings, invite Christina into intimacy with Christ, and provide her with a mission in the world, they also show the glory of the world to come and affirm the basis of the Christian economy of salvation—love. In one of these visions Christina sees a beautiful virgin wearing a magnificent golden crown inlaid with precious gems. She is given to understand by a voice that this virgin is the Love about which St. John had written. The virgin Love bears the Christ Child in her arms and places him before the Father announcing, "I have brought this about and have brought him to the cross. I have brought all to completion."[50] At this all the angels and saints dance around the Child and sing with the sweetest voices the Christmas hymn "Resonet in laudibus."

Toward the conclusion of the *Revelations*, Christina has two other visions of heaven. When she is taken to heaven she observes Christ at the age of eighteen placing a crown upon his own head, being the only one worthy to do so. He speaks in a kingly manner promising that "of all those here today at Mass, none will ever be separated from me."[51] This vision also includes trinitarian dialogue. Christ proclaims, "Father, I stood on the holy cross until my soul went forth. Therefore I want to receive all of them into the arms of my mercy and I will give them the kiss of my love."[52] Once again the love motive features prominently as the basis for Christ's sacrifice and as the means by which his mercy will extend to the world. The kiss of love goes beyond mercy to all, for it invites those who have received mercy to share in the intimacy of Christ himself. This is evident from the reaction of the angels and the saints who prostrate themselves before his face and kiss his feet. And as part of this vision Christina is granted the privilege of sucking the wounds of Christ, a visionary metaphor rich in association. By drinking his blood she shares in his suffering; through this act she also receives the Holy Spirit, and because of both associations, Christina becomes a foundation of the Church.

Christina also enjoys a sublime vision of the heavenly court in a scene reminiscent of the images and imagery of the Book of Revelation.[53] She goes into mystical ecstasy on the vigil of Easter during the Mass. She sees the Father seated upon his throne with a great host of angels about him. Into this scene enters the Only Begotten Son bringing with him all those in Christian lands who have hearts burning with love and who experience jubilation. The hearts of all are opened as written in the book (of life). The Son professes his greatest interior quality in relation to the Father—his obedience, by which he opened the gates to heaven. At this point all the angels of common people fly before the Father, bringing him whatever good they have done. The angels make the venia before the Father and offer him thanks and praise. Next the Holy Spirit arrives in the form of a fiery dove bringing four gifts for the earth. He will not punish the greatest sinners as they deserve. He will prolong the lives of others so that they may improve. He will give just rewards to those who are good. He will set the hearts of others on fire with his burning love. These four gifts imitate the ever-recurring *Gnadenfrucht-Topos* in Engelthal literature in which the entire spectrum of believers is improved—sinners are converted, the tepid become strong in faith, the faithful are made perfect. Finally the singing of the angels and the playing of their harps focuses the action on the nuns of Engelthal, who are usually blessed in a special way on the vigil of Easter. Christina is entrusted with the task of giving the nuns something to drink as a sign of this grace. What she is to give is not specified, but that she must give them something to drink symbolizes the grace that flows from the heavenly scene down to the earthly convent. It is clear that the Father is the source of the grace, which comes by virtue of the Son and by the action of the Holy Spirit who gives gifts to all manner of people. Christina as visionary then takes on the role of giving the gifts already granted symbolically to the nuns in heaven on earth through the medium of some beverage. Christina completes the action begun in the Father.

Christina's theological acumen and pastoral sensitivity come through in a scene in which she is confronted by an angry woman at the gate who demands answers to her questions. This historical encounter has mystical significance. At the beginning of this encounter with the mysterious, unknown woman, Christina calls the words of St. Paul to mind: "I know only Jesus Christ and him crucified" (1 Cor. 2:2). The woman poses her first question: "Where is earth higher than heaven?" The koan-like question receives a clever and theologically astute response from Christina: "Where God's Body is transubstantiated." The woman asks her second question: "Is there any human on earth who can do without all creatures?" Christina begins by stating that the Scriptures do not answer that, thus indicating her knowledge of the sacred texts. She continues to relate the personal experiences of the Virgin and Joseph and even describes those who were able to do without any creatures for long periods of time. She recalls the story of Mary Magdalen, who, although she lived thirty years without anyone else, at her death still accepted the ministrations of Maximinius. Even Mary of Egypt received communion from Zosimus at the end of her solitary life of penance. The third question is: "What is the final step to heaven?" Christina asserts that the final step before heaven is a person who has never had enough suffering and who has endured all suffering patiently. The fourth question the woman poses is: "What is jubilation in the highest degree?" Christina answers that the highest jubilation is attained when a person loses all human senses and education as if he or she had never been born. The interrogation continues with the question: "What is the greatest grace that our Lord can give to a human on earth?" Christina's response is immediate and from her own experience: "That the person may be enraptured and taken to heaven." Finally, the woman asks, "Of what does love consist in the highest degree?" Christina, sounding exasperated, exclaims, "You ask me about such exalted things!" She then mentions a council of seventy masters who met to discuss this question without success. She then uses St. Augustine as her source: "St. Augustine has written that love is in the highest degree when it does not seek its own possession whether in heaven or on earth. It wants only to serve God." Undaunted the woman persists, "What is the final reward that God gives the soul?" Christina responds, "When the soul first sees God in heaven, what he gives to her, she has forever." The woman leaves as suddenly as she had arrived. This account concludes, "no one could ever find out who she was or where she came from."[54]

In this dialogue Christina shows herself to have knowledge of Scripture. She uses the quote from Paul as a leitmotif in her responses and as a guiding principle and a profession of humility. She also uses biblical texts as source material for her answers. Christina also shows herself as knowing legends of the saints, whose stories likewise become sources of inspiration and give her a method of analysis in answering the second question. Christina draws on the mystical teachings of her day in emphasizing the role of patient endurance of suffering as preparation for eternal life. In answering the question about jubilation, she really speaks about the highest level of contemplation and shows herself to be theologically learned and perhaps also mystically practiced in the highest form of prayer. That the woman was unknown to all and that she was able to pose theologically and mystically advanced questions implies some miraculous test of Christina's theology, or, more practically, attests to Christina's fame, which led people from afar to seek her wisdom. It certainly lends mystery to the encounter and shows Christina's wisdom and patience.

Not only in the account of her life offered by her anonymous biographer but also by her own words, Christina Ebner shows herself to be an extraordinary woman and nun. Educated and active in a literary way, she produced a reflective and theologically rich work on the foundation history of her monastery that also contained biographical sketches of the nuns who came before her. She also left her sisters and posterity a remarkably detailed account of her thoughts, prayers, visions, and other mystical experiences. The author of the biography augments Christina's work to include material from her family background, birth, childhood, and the time immediately before and after her death. The author wishes to emphasize Christina's holiness and heroic virtue to spread her fame, retain the memory of her life, and prepare for the initiation of the formal process of beatification. In a literary sense Christina served as a key figure in the formation of a sense of history among her sisters. She produced two works and was the subject of a third. No other nun or friar associated with the monastery did so much to promote the remembrance of the extraordinary lives of the members of the community. Conrad of Füssen may be credited with encouraging the community members to write, but Christina actually wrote and thereby encouraged others, such as Adelheid Langmann, to become active in writing. Christina's literary activity and the fact that she was a subject of a book comments upon the quality of her life. Conrad of Füssen, Adelheid Langmann, and the other nuns, friars, and priests saw in Christina a woman very close to God, spirit-filled and mystically graced.

THE *GNADEN-VITA* OF FRIEDRICH SUNDER, CHAPLAIN OF ENGELTHAL

Disciplina tua correxit me in finem
et disciplina tua ipsa me docebat.
Psalm 17:36 (Vulgata)

I INCLUDE THIS TEXT relating the life of a famous chaplain of the monastery of Engelthal because it reports the spiritual experiences of a man who served as priest and advisor and thus influenced a community of nuns for decades. Also, I believe the nuns would have considered him a real member of the extended community. While the nuns clearly understood the distinction between a cloistered community of women and the outside world, they also considered everyone associated with them a participant in the life of the community. This circle of associates includes not only the priests and brothers of the Dominican Order, but also secular priests, such as Friedrich Sunder, and all the lay people, among them villagers and peasants, attached to lands belonging to the monastery. This work is preserved along with other texts of Engelthal, and it shows the great extent to which Friedrich Sunder absorbed and adopted the Dominican spirituality of the nuns and their visiting friars.

THE MANUSCRIPT

Like the *Vita* of Gertrud of Engelthal, the text of Friedrich Sunder's *Gnaden-Vita, Chaplain of Engelthal* appears only in the *Codex Scotensis Vindobonensis* 308

(234), 174^v-227^r. However, this text appears to be based upon earlier versions and shows signs extensive revision.[1] Like the *Revelations* of Adelheid Langmann this text has undergone a *Legendarisierungsprozeß* developing original texts by Friedrich Sunder and augmenting them with textual commentary, criticism, a prologue, and a detailed account of Friedrich Sunder's death compiled from other sources and eyewitness accounts such as those of Christina Ebner. The number of sources demonstrates an abiding interest on the part of the writers of Engelthal in the life and spirituality of this humble priest.

THE AUTHOR

The authorship begins with Friedrich Sunder's personal account of his graced life which he was encouraged to record by the Dominican preacher, Conrad of Füssen, whose advice Friedrich had sought. After Friedrich's death, a redactor who knew the details of Friedrich's life compiled the edited text upon which the received text is based. The redactor also had extensive knowledge of theology and characterized the chaplain of Engelthal as a man graced with spiritual perfection as evidenced by certain events in his life— by the practice of monastic discipline even though he was not a monastic, by the exercise of virtues, by mystical experiences and revelations, and by his holy death. A second redactor added an introduction and may also have added editorial comments at various points in the manuscript. No evidence from the text allows a definite association of the various parts of the manuscript with any certainty as to whether a passage derives from the first or the second redactor, except, of course, the introductory paragraphs.

FRIEDRICH SUNDER

Friedrich Sunder was born in 1254, sometime between April and December.[2] Various Sunder families lived in villages around Engelthal, but none were from the nobility. Monastery documents contain various references to this surname from 1290-1437.[3] As stated in the *Gnaden-Vita*, his mother died when he was young.[4] One reference to his father shows only that Friedrich had outlived him.[5] Friedrich himself testifies that he had led a worldly life during his youth, something for which he repeatedly showed regret: "This guilt that he had not served God in his youth was always with him. He could not lament this enough."[6] After 1287, he entered religious life but was neither a pastor nor a member of a religious order, although he was greatly drawn to the Cistercians. He served as chaplain to the nuns of Engelthal for 40 years, a position that entailed ministering to the layfolk, whose churches were also serviced by the chaplains of Engelthal. Documentary evidence shows that there may have been as many as three chaplains serving simultaneously, so heavy were the ministerial duties to the populations under the care of the monastery. By his association with the nuns of Engelthal and with the various Dominican preachers who passed by, Friedrich learned to love the Dominican Order and to adopt many elements of Dominican spirituality into his own. He also seemed to have identified strongly with St. Dominic. Dominic featured prominently in his visionary life, and also influenced Friedrich's personal prayer. On the evening of 14 April 1328, he died at the age of 73 after an illness that had lasted three weeks. He was laid to rest at the monastery, but no monument exists to mark his grave.[7] Other writers from Engelthal describe him in their works. In her *Revelations*, Christina Ebner records events from his life in five places, and twice in her *Sister-Book of Engelthal*. Other documents belonging to the monastery also mention him.

Christina Ebner reports Friedrich Sunder's effective ministry to others as related in a vision around 1292 or 1293 of a former Cistercian abbot who had lived with a woman in the village for years before he died.[8] The abbot appeared completely engulfed in purgatorial flames and gave testimony that two things had saved him from the fires of hell: "When your chaplain came to me I became so contrite that I confessed to him as thoroughly as never before."[9] The second reason for his deliverance from damnation was the intercession of St. James and other saints. The abbot directed Christina to inform the chaplain, who could in turn testify to the truth of it. Having confessed his sins, he received absolution from Friedrich and was delivered from eternal damnation.

Writing sometime around the year 1297, Christina Ebner's biographer reports an incident in which Friedrich Sunder gave her advice: "When she was about twenty years old, the old chaplain told her that he would like it if our Lord were to give himself to her every day . . . and so she prepared herself every day as if she were going to receive our Lord because she had complete trust that this is what our Lord wished."[10] This has to do with receiving spiritual communion, since she did not actually receive holy communion every day. The practice at that time restricted the reception of communion to certain days only, even for nuns.[11] Friedrich's concern for Christina shows an appreciation for her spiritual welfare and offers a practical solution to a pastoral problem since she was unable to receive communion every day.

Christina's biography also reports a vision about Friedrich Sunder: "She saw brother Friedrich, the chaplain, in a vision as he was reading Mass at an altar and when it came to the time that he should consecrate Our Lord she heard a voice that said, 'That is your creator or mine.'"[12] After Christina, in ecstasy, had come to herself again, she reported that, "the previously named chaplain was saying Mass on the same morning at Offenhausen, when she saw him at the same time."[13] Christina Ebner, writing about events after 1328, relates what she heard about the death of Friedrich Sunder: "I was informed that the old chaplain went to heaven with immeasurable joy and that the saints, whom he had served with special devotion and special prayer, rejoiced because of him and according to the measure of the love he bore for them."[14] These saints, she writes, were later identified as being his mother, daughter, spouse, sister. They could have been his real mother or sister (if he had one), but they could not have been his daughter or wife, such relationships being not real but rather symbolic. Relationships between a mystic and the saints are designated by title of a blood tie or marriage bond to indicate their closeness. In other instances, mystics such as Adelheid Langmann had more than one spouse. These symbolic associations for relationships may have their basis in the saying of Jesus that it is they who hear his word and keep it who are his mother and sisters and brothers (Matt. 12:50). Christina also assures the reader that "no tongue could tell what honor, joy and gladness were given to him by God."[15]

Concerning Friedrich's quick death, Christina Ebner reports a personal revelation in which she learns that there were three things that displeased the Lord about the chaplain, one of which was his reluctance to give out communion, but that nonetheless our Lord had promised him that he would go to heaven without delay and that had to be brought about.[16]

In the *Sister-Book of Engelthal*, Christina writes about Friedrich twice. She reports a revelation about him with regard to the intention of the Mass.[17] She further describes the effectiveness of his ministry and also reports the events surrounding his death: "This holy chaplain was a godly man in all his activities. When he was with the people, he was so loving that it was truly a wonder. When he was at prayer, he was so on fire that it was beyond all measure. He was adorned with all virtues. Then when it came time that our Lord wished to reward him for all his work, he thanked our Lord with great fervor and said, 'Lord, be gracious to me and remember that to me even from the days of my childhood your works have always pleased me.' Then his companion, Heinrich, came over to him with great lamentation and said, 'Beloved father and faithful brother, I thank you for all the faithfulness that you have shown to me. And you should forgive me when you have been annoyed by me.' Then he said, 'I have never been annoyed by you. If you have sometimes been harsh with me, I surely deserved it . . .' and then he said, ' I have never been annoyed, I have always been made better by you.' They both agreed that for the forty years they were together that they never had any lack of love or dispute between them over night."[18] Christina continues with more details about Friedrich's death and concludes with a report: "It was made known to three persons, that he went into eternal joy without any delay."[19]

Aside from these hagiographical reports, public documents relating to the monastery of Engelthal also contain references to Friedrich Sunder from the years 1280 to 1323. The documents never contain the family name, Sunder, but refer to him variously as "brother Friedrich, the confessor to the nuns," or as "brother Friedrich of Engelthal" and often in combination with a brother Heinrich.[20] Siegfried Ringler also notes three instances in the literature of Engelthal that may refer to Friedrich Sunder. Christina Ebner refers to the illness of the "chaplain."[21] In the *Sister-Book*, St. Leuprecht appeared to "the chaplain."[22] In public documents of Engelthal dated 1310, a chaplain "Friedrich" is mentioned, but this may refer to Friedrich von Lauterhofen.[23] The various sources paint a portrait of the chaplain, that while demonstrating his human failings nonetheless shows him exerting a strong influence over the nuns and laity by the quality of his life, prayer, service, and the celebration of the mass in particular.

STRUCTURE OF THE *GNADEN-VITA*

The text relating to the life of Friedrich Sunder can be divided into 154 paragraphs. Certain divisions in the manuscript bear titles. Siegfried Ringler further divides the text into the following nine subdivisions: I. Prologue (FS *1-59); II. The Community as the Setting for the Life of Grace (FS *60-323); III. The Beginning of the Life of Grace (FS *324-397); IV. Extraordinary Manifestations of Grace (FS *398-678); V. Experiences of the Birth of God and Union with the Divine Child FS *679-958); VI. Insights about God, Mary, and the Souls (FS *959-1181); VII. Ecstatic Union of the Soul with God (FS *1182-1309); VIII. Phases of the Life of Grace (FS *1310-1756); IX. Death and Glorification (FS *1757-1905).[24] An overall view of the structure, whether divided according to the manuscript or according to Ringler, reveals an organized and theologically appropriate account of the life of a holy man. The text was written with the intention of being not only a true report of the events, primarily the mystical events, of Friedrich

Sunder's life but also a lesson book for the edification of the reader or hearer in order to teach about the ways of God in relation to Friedrich.

THE TEXT

The editor of the text clearly identifies the subject and the purpose of the book: "In the year of Our Lord 1325 a blessed and godly father, a secular priest, was living at a monastery of nuns of the Order of Preachers in the diocese of Eichstätt in Bavaria. May God be praised, who never ceases to perform wonders with his saints and who improves the devout readers."[25] The very purpose of writing about the life of this particular holy priest is to effect the spiritual improvement of the devout reader. This imitates the biblical writers who likewise recorded the life of Jesus so that "you might believe" (John 20:31).[26] Just as the life of Christ is worth knowing for the betterment of those who hear about it, so the life of someone who believes in Christ can help the reader or hearer believe more deeply in the figure who graced Friedrich in special ways. By learning about Friedrich's experiences and his relationship with God and the saints, the reader gains encouragement to live with the lively expectation that Christ and the saints may likewise enter into a personal relationship with him or herself. To introduce the exact nature of God's relationship with Friedrich the editor uses the etymology of Friedrich's name: "He had peace (frid) originally from the working of the Holy Spirit in him, and then in conveying that [peace] from himself as the image of God to his neighbor, and also in being directed to the goal of perfection in the riches (rich) of virtue by his God and Lord."[27] This opening paragraph shows the precise process whereby Friedrich was blessed by God for the good of others. He was set at peace by the indwelling of the Holy Spirit, which restored his soul to the image and likeness of God. This text resonates with the noble image of the human person presented in Genesis 1:27. Friedrich has been restored in the image of God that was intended for all human beings created in the image and likeness (Ebenbild) of God. This image, having been lost by original sin, can be restored only by the Holy Spirit after Christ's sacrificial death. Having received the "peace which the world cannot give," (Phil. 4:7) Friedrich was called to the mystical experience of God in its fullness, and was able to then act as a means of bringing peace to his neighbor. Further, Friedrich had been endowed with the plenitude of virtues leading him to spiritual perfection. From the example of his life and how God has acted powerfully in and through him, the devout reader should be encouraged to know that this has indeed happened to

Friedrich, and should likewise take heart in the knowledge that such activity on the part of God takes place far beyond biblical times and may even happen in the present time.

The editor carefully details the pertinent elements of Friedrich's character and notes his pious activities. Friedrich performs "such great works and practices by keeping vigil, by doing the venia, by fasting, by taking the discipline and by being in need."[28] He suffers illness and leads a hard life. The editor asserts that a trustworthy priest who lived with Friedrich for 38 years witnessed these events of his life and became the source of knowledge about them. This companion may be the Heinrich frequently mentioned in public documents in connection with Friedrich Sunder. Aside from Friedrich's sufferings, "he worked and strove, he prayed and was in jubilation."[29] The editor further characterizes Friedrich as having a "burning heart" and as "bearing the martyrdom of Christ in his mind."[30] He was also a great penitent, crying aloud to God because of his sins and asking for love, wearing a hair shirt and a belt of hair for many years, and eating no meat except under obedience, working diligently for the monastery in word and deed, performing all things in the church well, and spending the whole night and day in "burning devotions."[31] The characterization of the chaplain shows a devout man, faithful to his priestly duties which he performs well. He bears all the expected signs of leading a devout life of penance and discipline that mark the holy man. He is described as "burning at prayer" which signifies the quality of his prayer as being contemplative. The "prayer of fire" as described in Cassian's *Conferences* and perpetuated in the Nine Ways of Prayer of St. Dominic indicates the highest form of prayer.[32]

Beyond the contemplative nature of Friedrich's prayer is his experience of the mystical. God, Mary, and the angels speak with him as do the souls in purgatory who ask him for assistance by the power of his prayer.[33] He is concerned about sinners and prays for them. He loves the poor and comes to their aid. He befriends good people, remains peaceful in word and deed, serves God diligently by singing and reading. The editor describes his voice as being sweet and young as that of a schoolboy even at the age of 73 years, thus hinting at Friedrich's innocence, a theme that the author reiterates frequently.[34] The editor portrays Friedrich as being connected with holy personages and therefore being useful to others, both the living and the dead. Having described Friedrich in such glowing terms as a holy man who has mystical experiences, the editor asks, "What more can I say?"[35] He then proceeds to write that Friedrich was so friendly that when one spoke with him, time flew. When he prayed he was like a "vat filled with love." He contemplated, was reverent, true, loyal, and always regretted that he had not served God in his youth.[36] Lest the reader think Friedrich was always spiritually perfect, the editor includes this detail as a true element of his life but also as one that will help the reader identify with the experience of the subject. The description of Friedrich Sunder continues by cataloguing his practices at prayer. Every day during Advent, in Holy Week, Easter Week, and Pentecost Week, and in the octave of Our Lady (the Assumption) he made the venia 500 times. He took the discipline every Friday. Not even sickness deterred him from these practices. His whole mind was directed toward God. Modestly, when others spoke of the great things God did for him, he kept silent.[37] This very athletic regimen of prayer shows him to be utterly devoted to cultivating his relationship with God by being willing to pursue the outward disciplines he felt necessary to foster interior discipline. The venias demonstrate an attitude of adoration, humility, and penance. The discipline shows a desire to imitate Christ and to share in his passion, "to complete what is lacking in Christ's affliction for the sake of his body, that is, the church" (Col. 1:24). His single-mindedness shows awareness of his goal and the necessity of staying focused on it.

The final paragraph of the prologue invokes the reputation of a famous Dominican preacher named Conrad of Füssen who, after hearing Friedrich's confession, urges him to write down the experiences of his life to show others what graces God had given to him. Typically, Friedrich opposes this idea out of humility, until God reveals to him that he should follow Conrad's advice. Under obedience he records the wonders that God had done for him. The editor expands on this standard trope of obedience and humility by emphasizing that Friedrich preferred to be called "brother" out of humility rather than to be called "priest" or "lord."[38]

FRIEDRICH SUNDER AS IMITATOR OF ST. DOMINIC

Being associated with Dominican nuns and friars, Friedrich adopts many elements of Dominican spirituality and identifies himself particularly with the saintly founder of the Order of Preachers. Dominic also preferred to be called "brother" and intentionally founded an order of equals as signified by the original title of address. The title "abbot" was used only once in the history of the order for Matthew of Paris, who led the first group of friars to that city.[39]

Even more important than a preference for a title that signified humility, Friedrich Sunder imitates Dominic at prayer. The nuns of Engelthal almost certainly possessed a copy of Theodoric of Apoldia's *Life of*

Dominic to which was frequently appended a copy of Dominic's Nine Ways of Prayer. In this magnificent attachment a secret glimpse into Dominic's personal prayer is seen. Given the account of Friedrich Sunder's life, one might be tempted to believe that the following description of Dominic at prayer in the second of the Nine Ways could just as easily describe Friedrich Sunder at prayer:

> St. Dominic often used to pray by throwing himself on the ground, flat on his face, and then his heart would be pricked with compunction, and he would blush at himself and say, ". . . Lord be merciful to me, a sinner." . . . He would weep and groan passionately, and then say, "I am not worthy to look upon the height of heaven, because of the greatness of my sin; I have provoked your anger and done evil in you sight."[40]

This passage contains reference to the venia (prostration) as a prayer practice and also especially to compunction and the accompanying tears of sorrow, both of which were very important in Friedrich's expression of prayer.

Friedrich Sunder likewise imitates Dominic's third of the Nine Ways of Prayer by practicing the discipline. The taking of the discipline for Dominicans was an imitation of Dominic's personal prayer practice and also a constitutional requirement of the Dominican monastic regimen. Both nuns and friars were obliged by the Constitutions to practice the discipline. The intention in doing so had little to do with imitating the scourging of Christ at the pillar. The key to understanding the Dominican rationale is the psalm quote (Ps. 17:36) by Dominic in the Third Way of Prayer. "For this reason, rising up from the ground, he used to take the discipline with an iron chain, saying, 'Your discipline has set me straight towards my goal.'"[41] The meaning of the practice comes from the writings of John Cassian, particularly a passage in the *Institutes* that uses the same psalm verse in terms of the virtue of discretion. "And having thus secured discretion, strengthened with which we can cast down our enemies, let us cry aloud to God: 'Thy discipline has set me up unto the end, and thy discipline the same shall teach me.'"[42] The discipline was meant to "whip into shape" the nun or friar for the daily struggle against temptation by training him or her in the practice of moderation and therefore of virtue. Through this practice the monastic would be kept on the narrow path, the mean between two extremes, and thus be able to reach the ultimate goal without any delay or distraction. This concept is perpetuated in the Benedictine idea of moderation in all things so that the monk will achieve just the right amount of virtue. For example, the monk must be neither slothful nor overly zealous but must discipline himself to take the middle path between these two extremes. In order to accomplish the strenuous daily regimen of prayer, work, and study, he must discipline or pace himself accordingly.

Of the many associations of Friedrich Sunder and Dominic, the description of them praying in the highest form of prayer is the most important. Friedrich is described as being "on fire" or as "burning" in prayer. In the Ninth Way of Prayer, Dominic is likewise described: "So sometimes he went aside from his companions or went on ahead or, more often, lingered far behind; going on his own he would pray as he walked, and a fire was kindled in his meditation . . . The brethren thought that in this kind of prayer the saint acquired the fullness of sacred scripture and also a power and a boldness to preach fervently, and a hidden intimacy with the Holy Spirit to know hidden things."[43] This description of Dominic on fire while praying echoes the teachings of the Egyptian abbas as related by John Cassian. Speaking of the Lord, Abba Isaac said, "he taught us by the example of his withdrawal that, if we too wish to address God with purity and integrity of heart, we should likewise draw apart from all the turbulence and confusion of the crowd. Thus, while sojourning in this body, we shall in some fashion be able to prepare ourselves for the likeness as it were of that blessedness which is promised to the holy ones in the future, and God will be 'all in all' for us."[44] In the *Conferences*, the "prayer of fire" is described three times. The first of these shows how superior this type of prayer is to the standard four types of prayer mentioned in the *Conferences—obsecratio, oratio, postulatio, gratiarum actio*: "Yet sometimes the mind which advances to that true disposition of purity and has already begun to be rooted in it, conceiving all these at one and the same time and rushing through them all like a kind of ungraspable and devouring flame, pours out to God wordless prayers of the purest vigor. These the Spirit itself makes to God as it intervenes with unutterable groans, unbeknownst to us, conceiving at that moment and pouring forth in wordless prayers such great things that they not only—I would say—cannot pass through the mouth but are unable even to be remembered by the mind later on."[45] The prayer of fire transcends all human categories. "This prayer, then, although it seems to contain the utter fullness of perfection . . . nonetheless raises his familiars to that condition which we characterized previously as more sublime. It leads them by a higher stage to that fiery and, indeed, more properly speaking, wordless prayer which is known and experienced by very few."[46] Yet more detail is given to explain this form of prayer: "And so it is that our mind will arrive at that incorruptible prayer. . . . This is not only not laid hold of by the sight of some image, but it cannot be grasped by any word or phrase. Rather, once the mind's is attentiveness has been set ablaze, it is called forth in an unspeakable ecstasy of heart and with an insatiable gladness of spirit, and the mind, having transcended all feelings and visible matter, pours it out to God with unutterable groans and sighs."[47] The prayer of fire not only transcends the accepted four types of prayer, it also transcends the "perfect prayer," that is, the seven petitions of the Lord's Prayer and it also transcends the inspired psalms. The prayer of fire is always described as the summit of prayer incorporating yet transcending what has come before. Thus to describe Friedrich in terms of "burning at prayer" makes him not only an imitator of Dominic at prayer but shows him to be practiced in the highest forms of contemplative prayer.

In addition, Friedrich himself gives adequate testimony to the role that St. Dominic played in his prayer and mysticism. For Friedrich, the veneration of St. Dominic comes only after his devotion to the Blessed Virgin Mary.[48] As a preparation for the celebration of Mass Friedrich always prays a *Pater noster* and an *Ave Maria* "to praise and honor the Father so that he would give him preparedness and grace to complete the Mass in a way that would be praiseworthy and honorable to him. And he recited them also to the holy Son and to the Holy Spirit, and also to the Trinity, and a *Salve Regina* to Mary, the Queen, and a *Pater noster* to St. Dominic."[49] Friedrich's veneration of Dominic surpasses that of any other saint of the many mentioned in the *Gnaden-vita*.

Dominic also appears prominently in Friedrich's mystical experiences. One such occasion in 1318 Friedrich shows his scrupulous concern to thank God for graces given to him in the celebration of the Mass: "Lord, St. Dominic, I ask you to help me thank Our Lord for all his graces and mercy. I am one of the most serious of men living on earth in the service of God according to grace, which God gives me and has already given me . . . and yet I do not want to thank God."[50] St. Dominic responds to Friedrich's concern in the following way: "There are many saints in heaven, who have given up homeland and people, father and mother and the whole world for God and had great suffering and suffered a bitter death and know full well that he had not thanked God as he rightly should have done. And therefore give over your own will to the mercy of Our Lord, so that he himself may be thanked by you as he wishes."[51] This exchange happens at the beginning of his life of special grace. It shows his concern to be thankful, which is at the core of the celebration of the Eucharist in which the priest, standing in the place of Christ renders thanks to the Father for the work of salvation accomplished by Christ's sacrifice re-presented in each celebration of the Mass. Friedrich's own identity as a priest leads him to this special concern to celebrate the Mass as it is intended. He seeks assistance and advice from a heavenly priest—Dominic, who stresses the mercy of God and the divine ability to complete whatever may be lacking in Friedrich's rendering of thanks.

Dominic's care for Friedrich is emphasized also in the events of the celebration of Dominic's feast day: "One time on St. Dominic's Day after he had sung the Mass of St. Dominic, he asked him for the sake of this praise he offered for himself and for all of Christendom, even as he had also prayed in the evening and the morning, that Dominic help him to receive various graces so that his soul would rejoice in them and be consoled."[52] After having assured Friedrich that he had already done so on his behalf, Dominic proceeds to relate exactly what he had accomplished:

> Today I came before our Lord and asked him diligently for the sake of his mercy to give you various graces for my feast day. Then Our Lord said to me, "Now tell us first what graces you want to give her" [the soul/anima of Friedrich]. Then I went to Our Lady and asked her to advise me as to what grace I should give. Our Lady said, "Go into my workroom. There you will find his rich crown of roses and lilies made by Cecilia, the brother's little mother, and by Agatha, his wife, and bring it here to see how it will please Our Lord." When Our Lord saw the crown, it pleased him very well and he said, "If only we had the soul here to see if it fits her." And he said to St. Dominic and to his soul's angel, "Go and bring her to me!" Then St. Dominic said, "Lord, she may not come now because the body is presently awake and is going into his room to recite his prayer." Our Lord said, "Well, go anyway and make him sit down and when he falls asleep bring me his soul here." That happened. Our Lord received her lovingly and with honor and placed the crown on her head. It fit her just right. And he pressed her lovingly against himself and said, "Now be clothed today with my divinity because of the feast of St. Dominic."[53]

It is the occasion of Dominic's feast day and the intercession of Dominic himself that acquires the gift of a share in the divinity for Friedrich. Narration of this event ushers in the section of the text concerning extraordinary mystical occurrences. That his soul was pressed against the Lord is a powerful symbol of affection, and hints even at union of the two. The gift given is mystically significant, for a share in the divine life sets Friedrich's soul at a higher level of association and intimacy with the Godhead. It symbolizes the beginning of his mystical life and foreshadows its climax of union described later in much more erotic terms. Dominic therefore shows himself to be Friedrich's special and powerful intercessor, and it is through his influence that Friedrich enters into the mystical realms in association with divinity. That Dominic plays such an important role underscores the importance of Friedrich's constant association with Dominicans, both the nuns of Engelthal and the itinerant Friars Preachers.

These mystical events are then revealed to the sleeping Friedrich. Because of the importance of this event, Dominic admonishes Friedrich to write more about this. He has evidently been lax in recording the graces given to him. With this Dominic becomes the heavenly source for Friedrich's own record of these events, just as previously Conrad of Füssen had been the earthly impetus in writing down such important revelations.

The importance of the Dominican Order for Friedrich is symbolically represented also by the heavenly assistants at Friedrich's masses. Two apostles, St. Andrew as deacon and his brother St. Peter as subdeacon, serve Friedrich's Mass assisted by two acolytes—St. Dominic and St. Peter Martyr. Thus in the celebrations of his masses, Friedrich is surrounded by apostles and Dominicans. Dominic founded the Order, and Peter of Verona (d. 1252) was its first martyr.

Dominic also consoles Friedrich in the years 1326-1327: "After that on the next Wednesday before St. Peter's Day in Lent Our Lady sent grace again to the brother by St. Dominic. He had lacked grace since Easter and was therefore disappointed and had prayed to Our Lord and Our Lady often about this."[54] In the work Dominic is consistently portrayed as Friedrich's constant friend and helper.

These connections presented above may also suggest that the second editor was a Dominican who consciously strove to portray Friedrich in the image of Dominic. Dominic preferred the title "brother" and founded an order of "brothers" (friars). Certain elements from Dominic's Nine Ways of Prayer appear as part of Friedrich's portrait—the venia, the discipline and the reason for taking the discipline, the emphasis on contemplation and conversation with God or about God, the stress on singing. That Friedrich is so completely drawn into a Dominican form of spirituality with its veneration and visions of Dominican saints and the above-mentioned prayer practices shows the powerful influence of the example of the nuns and the friars.

THE *GNADEN-VITA* AS A DOCUMENTARY OF CONVERSION

The editor of the *Gnaden-vita* has already cast the life of Friedrich Sunder in terms of conversion through the etymology of his name and through a detailed description of his prayer life, priestly ministry, virtues and mysticism.[55] This editorial introduction operates as a grand thesis of Friedrich's conversion, the details of which form the rest of the document on his life. The narrator, "I," whether Friedrich himself or, more likely, his companion Heinrich, the chaplain, describes Friedrich as a "sinful priest," for he had committed all kinds of sins before he was a priest and even afterward.[56] Further, Friedrich prays especially to Our Lady from his childhood up to his death with a special prayer about the seven joys of Our Lady, asking her to help him turn from sin to lead a good life. The editor, narrator, and presumably the original text by Friedrich stress the need for his conversion of life.

Many factors contribute to the ongoing conversion of the chaplain. Aside from his own realization that he needs to grow in goodness and his prayerful desire to do so, he also receives help from human sources. The narrative continues immediately with a detailed description of Friedrich's meeting and friendship with Gertrud of Engelthal.[57] They met in the church at Entenberg, one of the churches nearby served by the chaplains of Engelthal.[58] He served as her confessor and he took part in the wonders given her by God.[59] The narrator carefully notes that the "chaplain grew to love her and she him in God."[60] Their relationship as described begins with a profession of loyalty. Gertrud, presumably having been disappointed by others in the past, pointedly asks Friedrich, "Tell me, dear Sir, what is your loyalty to me? That I would like to know from you."[61] Friedrich assures Gertrud of his loyalty to her: "Every good thing I receive or ever will receive from God I will give to you . . ."[62] Gertrud is greatly pleased by his answer and professes her own loyalty to him. "I will show the same loyalty to your soul as long as I live. And not only your soul, but also to your body whenever you are in need. If anyone wants to take your foot or hand or eye or a whole member I always want to offer my own instead."[63] They profess their mutual fidelity in a church before an angel, who in turn takes them before the face of God and confirms their fidelity there. The narrator comments that "they were true to each other always. And they share whatever God gave to each one.[64] In conclusion the narrator assures the reader that the priest increased in grace ever more and more. This spiritual marriage, a pledge of loyalty unto death between a man and a woman, and witnessed by an angel before God, strengthens the priest as any husband should be strengthened through the goodness of his wife. In turn, Gertrud receives many graces and witnesses many wonders from the priest.[65] The narrator portrays the mutual friendship of Gertrud and Friedrich in terms of a marriage ceremony and relationship that will benefit both "bride" and "groom" in spiritual progress. Later in the narrative, Gertrud jealously refuses to greet St. Agatha, who has been given to Friedrich by Christ as a heavenly bride. When Gertrud protests that Agatha has stolen her spouse, the saint responds, "My dear, it does you no harm. Do good things for him and remain faithful to him and I will do the same in heaven."[66] The image of the bond of marriage represents the importance, intensity, and intimacy of two friends, whether on earth or in heaven. The purpose of this "union" is to assist each other in growth in holiness, something that Gertrud shows herself ready to do. In conversation with St. Caritas, Gertrud learns of her role in Friedrich's continual conversion. Gertrud believes that someone wishes to murder Friedrich. Caritas reassures her and gives her instruction on how to help him: "You are very worried about your friend. Now listen well for I want to teach you and him something that will help you and him if you do it. For three days you should recite five *Pater nosters* and *Ave Marias* for the five words Our Lord spoke and with these bless the three days. Recite a *Pater noster* and an *Ave Maria* for the words our Lord said to Peter: 'You should not forgive seven times but seventy times seven times" so that our Lord will forgive the priest his sins and will protect him in body and soul."[67] In the context of the passage, the directive admonishes Friedrich to forgive whoever intends to take his life. It also suggests a history of conflict, and elsewhere the narrator mentions that Friedrich could be irascible. This reality also accords with the need for the Lord to forgive the priest. Apparently Friedrich bears some of the blame in this unexplained situation. Caritas further directs Gertrud: "For the second recite the words which our Lord asked his Father to deliver him from his passion so that he will deliver the priest from all suffering."[68] By the efficacy of Christ's sufferings, Friedrich will be delivered from his present and even future suffering through the intercessory prayer of Gertrud. Caritas continues her discourse: "The third to the words with which our Lord commended his Mother to St. John so that the priest may be commended by our Lord to St. John."[69] Given Friedrich's close attachment and devotion to Mary, this explanation seems surprising. One would expect Friedrich to stand in the place of John and be commended to Mary. However, Caritas clearly directs otherwise. Gender reversal occurs several times in the *Gnaden-vita*, most particularly at the mystical climax of the life. In this passage John takes Friedrich into his care, and by extension Friedrich becomes a "beloved disciple" whose intimacy with Christ parallels that of John. Just as John wrote eloquently of Christ in the Fourth Gospel, in the Book of Revelation, and in his epistles, all of which a medieval thinker would have considered authentically identified with the Beloved Disciple, so in his own written account Friedrich will record the love story between himself and Christ. Just as John's

authority to reveal a fuller picture of Christ rests upon their unique relationship, so Friedrich enjoys a singular relationship to Christ and therefore can
write authoritatively about him, because Christ continues to reveal himself
in history. Caritas continues her directives to Gertrud: "The fourth to the
words with which our Lord prayed to the Father for those who crucified him
to forgive them so that he will also forgive the priest his sins."[70] This fourth
set of prayers indicates the forgiveness that Friedrich Sunder will receive
from Christ, for Friedrich, like Christ's crucifiers, knows not what he is
doing. Despite the statement that Gertrud worries about a possible threat
on Friedrich's life, these five prayers may simply be a *topos* to indicate the
effectiveness and power of Gertrud's intercession. This may very will be,
since all the directives have to do with Friedrich being forgiven, and only
by analogy would the teaching be extended to the "murderer." Finally,
Caritas pronounces the fifth intention: "The fifth prayer to the words with
which our Lord on the cross commended his spirit to the heavenly Father,
so that the priest may be commended to him."[71] Here Friedrich is identified
with Christ in his passion and, given the conclusion of the *Gnaden-vita*,
prophecies Friedrich's holy death. It is also significant, despite the fact that
Caritas is portrayed as a real saint, rather than a virtue, that Love (Caritas)
directs Gertrud to engage in such intercessory prayer and to make this
known to Friedrich.[72] The motive for Christ's salvific passion and death was
love for human beings and the will to save them. Here, Love directs Friedrich
in such a way that he will be saved and eventually will live up to the
etymology of his name offered in the prologue, thus becoming an instrument
of Christ's continuing work in the world to save all people.

Gertrud offers earthly companionship to Friedrich, but he also
receives numerous heavenly friends. Agatha becomes his heavenly spouse.
The narrator devotes much time to this idea: "Because the brother had no
father or mother on earth who could do his soul some good after his death,
our Lord gave him many heavenly friends who gave him much. As a father
he gave him the apostle St. Andrew who obtained much grace for him on
earth. He gave him the twelve apostles as brothers. From among the martyrs
he gave him many sons and friends. Our Lord asked many saints to join his
company and some even asked for this themselves."[73] He received five other
saints as his sons and numerous others from among the martyrs as his
children. From the confessors he received many friends, principally St.
Dominic. Likewise he received friends from among the virgins. Cecilia
became his mother, Agatha his spouse, Martha his fiancée. Numbered
among his daughters were Caritas, Fides, Spes, and many others, all of whom
wanted to be his mother or wife rather than his daughter.[74] Further, the

Virgin Mary gave him 100 virgins in heaven to pray for him, among whom were Ursula and her companions, Mary Magdalen in whom he had great hope, and Elizabeth who became his wife. This spiritual polygamy and the presence of numerous spiritual family members underscore the closeness of the relationship that Friedrich would have with these saints. They are bound to him with unbreakable bonds.

In both cases, his relationship with Gertrud and with various saints, the importance of the indissoluble bond between Friedrich and the others points out his special status, something that will be reiterated repeatedly in many ways throughout the *Gnaden-vita*. The pattern of relationships follows the standard classifications of saints: apostles, martyrs, confessors, and virgins.

The weaving of the bonds of spiritual family and friends is augmented by the various titles and roles that Friedrich will receive that indicate his status and importance in a wider context. In a revelation about his position in heaven, Friedrich learns that he will be like a pope in heaven. In this vision of hierarchy, Friedrich also has twelve cardinals, three each from the most important orders: Dominicans, Franciscans, Cistercians, and Augustinians.[75] Further, connections were made with two hermits and their respective coteries of devotees.[76] From the Virgin he received 1,000 human beings, was spiritually affiliated with the Cistercians, and consequently became especially dear to St. Bernard.[77]

Finally, Friedrich relates to the nuns and also to the souls in purgatory through the celebration of Mass and the distribution of Holy Communion. His priestly character and identity mark his relationship with the people whom he serves immediately. In addition his priestly intercession aids those in purgatory.

FRIEDRICH'S MYSTICISM

Siegfried Ringler makes no judgment as to Friedrich Sunder's classification as a mystic. He is a mystic in a deeply theological sense, even aside from any reports of visions, auditions, out-of-body experiences and other such happenings popularly associated with the life of a mystic. His mystical identity depends upon his union with God, a union assured through words of promise and symbolic actions.

Further, a constant theme in the *Gnaden-vita* is Friedrich's desire to die in order to be with the Lord. At one point when he is ill he prays to be taken.[78] When he does not die he is disappointed and wants an explanation.

In response the Lord tells him: "I will tell you why it has not happened. Your convent has prayed so diligently for you and other people as well to maintain you in life because they receive such great consolation from your life. And the souls in purgatory cried out and complained when they heard from the angels that you should die. They cried out, 'Lord, merciful God, what are you doing to us? Do you want to take away the one from whom we receive so much consolation every day, since we have so few on earth who can console us? No, oh God, for the sake of your passion and death, let him live longer.' See, my beloved, the lamentable cries of the souls and the prayers of the people have convinced me that you must and will live longer."[79] The Lord continues by asking Friedrich to give over his will to that of the Lord, who has listened to the cries of mercy. Like St. Paul, who also wished to go to the Lord but remained living for the sake of his mission to preach salvation to others (Phil. 1:21-24), Friedrich is likewise asked to forego his own desire to be with Christ in heaven for the sake of the salvation of souls. The importance of giving over his will to God is a constant subtext in the *Gnaden-vita*. In a revelation about this Friedrich asserts: "The Lord himself made known to me once that I could not give anything more dear to him than my own will . . ."[80]

Friedrich's mystical progress in conversion of life is indicated by special revelations in connection with the celebration of his daily Mass. The editor makes it clear that this begins to happen only after having lived in grace for twenty years. Directly after the consecration Friedrich hears these words directed to him: "I, who have taken all evil from you, have come and will always be with you forever in my heavenly kingdom. I am there, as you are here, and I will never leave you in body and soul and never want to leave you. And this is a loving game to your soul. You are mine and I am yours and this should always be between me and you in my heavenly kingdom."[81] This lyrical section, rhymed in the original German, asserts the union of Friedrich and God according to will and full personhood. Despite the separation in space (heaven and earth), they are one and will be most completely one in heaven. The pledge of mutual possession echoes famous love lyrics of the Middle Ages:

> Du bist min, ich bin din:
> des wolt du gewis sin.
> Du bist beslozzen in minem herzen:
> verloren ist daz slüzzelin:
> du muost immer drinne sin.[82]

The manuscript version corresponds textually to the poem: *"Du bist min, so bin ich din."*[83] It also corresponds thematically indicating the sort of union that will occur not only in the will but in the heart as well.

Other markers of conversion have to do with the appropriation of titles and offices of both ecclesiastical and civil importance. The editor reports: "Our Lord gave him much power before his holy face and told him he would be a pope in heaven and through him Our Lord wanted to be gracious to many people who would be improved through him."[84] And like a pope on earth he receives twelve cardinals, three each from the Dominicans, Franciscans, Cistercians, and Augustinians. To be a pope in heaven must bear an analogy to being pope on earth. The primary power given to Friedrich by the conferring of the highest ecclesiastical title in the church is the power to improve the lives of other people so that they will grow in holiness. Friedrich receives this honorific title as a reward for what God is able to accomplish through his mediation on earth. No hint of temporal power taints the revelation. Friedrich's symbolic power remains spiritual and appropriate to any successor of St. Peter. Like St. Peter, Friedrich would also have the power of the keys through his priestly ministry. This is evident in a later revelation through the Virgin, who tells him that when he goes to heaven he will be ranked in the sixth choir of angels, among the *Potestates* or Powers. In response to Friedrich's question as to why he belongs in that choir, the Virgin rehearses the earlier revelation about the granting of the title "pope."[85] The activity of hearing confessions and giving absolution features prominently in his ministry. Nowhere in any of the documents does any writer or editor speak of any sacraments in association with Friedrich except the celebrating of Mass and the hearing of confessions. At an advanced age while very ill, Friedrich is willing to rise from his sickbed to hear confessions for the sake of the reward promised him for the souls in purgatory as well as for the benefit of the penitents.[86] Friedrich scrupulously performs these duties properly and sometimes worries about his authority to hear the confessions of people from other places and whether they have the permission of their pastor to confess to him. "Now Our Lady removed the fear from him that he had of hearing the confessions of the people and she made known to him from our Lord the power that he had given him to hear the confession of any human being and forgive sins."[87] With this revelation Friedrich receives faculties that extend far beyond his position as chaplain at Engelthal. Such a chaplain would have had the faculties to hear the confessions of the lay people in his ministerial care—people associated with the monastery and also those attached to the churches serviced by the chaplains. Normally he would not have the jurisdiction to hear the confessions of the nuns or people coming from other places. As "pope," he seems also to have the power to forgive sins to any degree. The forgiveness and absolution for some sins are reserved to the Pope alone. As a "pope in heaven," Friedrich exercises full authority to forgive any sin of anyone at any time. He possesses the "power of the keys" to the highest degree.

The second important title conferred on Friedrich is revealed on the feast of St. Louis, king of France, to whom Friedrich prayed daily.[88] After Mass Friedrich makes his thanksgiving to the Father, Son, Spirit, Virgin, and St. Dominic, and it is revealed to him by St. Dominic that:

> Our Lord has asked me to make known to you the grace which St. Louis has obtained for you today. This is so great that you will always praise and honor him as long as you live. Now listen well. Early today St. Louis knelt before the holy Father in heaven and prayed to him diligently for you because you have honored him every day, so that you will enjoy his feast day. Then the Father said, "Louis, my much beloved son, what do you want me to do to this brother or to his soul?"—"Lord, Father God, know well that he has had great temptations and has struggled with the three enemies and that he has triumphed over them by your help and mercy so that he will never more be separated from you, Lord Father, if you will it. The three enemies are his flesh, the deceptive world, and the evil spirit." And St. Louis said to our Lord, "Lord, out of your mercy I want you to make him a king ever to serve you before your divine face." The holy Father said, "Louis, you know well the customs of worldly lords. When they want to choose a king or confirm him, so they, who wish it, must be present and also the one who is to be chosen so that one may see whether he lacks anything." Then the holy Father said to St. Dominic and to the brother's angel, "Go forth and bring us the brother's soul! He is sleeping now." When he was brought, he received the soul happily and lovingly and laid before the Son and the Holy Spirit the prayer of St. Louis, who had prayed to him on behalf of the brother. Then he asked them whether it be their will that he should be a king in heaven. Then God the Son and the Holy Spirit spoke, "Much beloved Father, the more honor and grace you give him, the more we like it." Then the Father placed the soul in front of him and said, "You should be king forever in heaven in the name of the holy Father and the Son and of the Holy Spirit. And I will give you strength and power so that you will overcome your flesh and serve me as long as I will." Then the Holy Son said, "I will give you sense and wisdom, so that you can defend yourself against the false world and also against whatever is thrown at the people." Then the Holy

Spirit said, "I will give you goodness and patience and love of all virtues so that you will conquer the temptations of all evil spirits." After that Our Lady came with a beautiful glorious crown and asked the Holy Father to crown the soul as a testimony that it is now king in heaven. When St. Louis saw the great honor and grace given to the brother and to his soul and that the Father had heard his prayer for him, he thanked the Holy Father, Son, and Holy Spirit diligently and also the Queen, Mary.[89]

This magnificent coronation scene mirrors the practice of German medieval ceremonial for the election of the king. The candidate (Friedrich) is made known to the electors (Father, Son, and Holy Spirit) who acclaim and proclaim him king after which he is formally crowned.[90] Interesting as such details may be, the primary reasons for this coronation are spiritual rather than temporal. It is noteworthy that Friedrich is presented by St. Louis, the very model of Christian kingship in that he ruled the people with justice and protected and promoted the church. The model for Friedrich as king in heaven is an analogy to Louis, who is both king and saint on earth. Louis as king on earth fought against the enemies of the state and the church. As king in heaven, Friedrich must fight against the enemies of body and soul. From the Father, Friedrich is given the power to overcome the first enemy—the flesh. His ability to do so rests upon his union with the Father. This personal enemy must be vanquished if King Friedrich is to act justly and offer protection to his people. This is the particularly saintly aspect of his kingship and is based upon the belief in integrity of character. Friedrich would never be a good king unless he has power over himself. The Son grants him knowledge and wisdom, perhaps an allusion to the model of kingship in the Old Testament—King Solomon. These gifts are given so that he may fight against the forces of the world and defend the people from all worldly allurements. In his just rule, he must constantly remind his people of the reality of the spiritual realm and protect them from embroilment in purely worldly concerns and promote them in spiritual affairs. The Holy Spirit grants Friedrich the gifts of goodness, patience, and love of virtue in view of the battle with evil spirits. These gifts are both personal and useful to him as leader of the people. Only a king endowed with goodness, patience, and all virtues can share these with others and show by the example of his life how one should live correctly. The coronation of Friedrich is not only a reward but primarily a calling to serve. These three enemies—the flesh, the world, and the devil—represent the standard formulation of the primary temptations in the fourteenth century.

The high point of Friedrich's mystical experience occurs significantly on Christmas. In this extended passage so many themes and significant details are included that it is worth an extensive treatment. The editor begins by setting the context of the significant events that will occur. The wider context is the Christmas season with a special focus on the three Masses of Christmas and on the Mass on the Feast of the Epiphany.

> One Christmas, when the priests sing and read three masses, this brother also did that. Before the mass he asked Our Lord as the Holy Babe and Our Lady, the holy queen and the holy child's mother that due to the joy the whole world receives from his holy birth, they should also give many graces to poor people and then his poor soul will be consoled and made glad. Then Our Lady said she would gladly do this.[91]

Unselfishly Friedrich prays for the benefit of poor people. In the prayer he recognizes the power of Christ and the Virgin to grant his petition, but this power is given specifically in view of the power of the incarnation by which God takes on human flesh and becomes human in every way, uniting in Christ both divinity and humanity. As God/Man, Christ mediates all graces to the people. By this union, Christ's experiential sympathy and compassion for the human condition produces abundant graces for all. Ultimately this compassionate love revealed at Bethlehem will take action on the hill of Calvary. In Catholic and medieval theology this sacrifice of love continues in the celebration of the Mass, the particular setting of this mystical event.

The editor continues with the description of events during the Mass at night—*Dominus dixit ad me: Filius meus es tu.* The title of the Mass already hints at the mystic event for in being united to the Son of God, Friedrich becomes a son of God—*filiolus in filio.* "When he [Friedrich] came to the canon of the Mass, the little holy Child came to the brother's soul and divinized (*vergottet*) it with himself and united himself with it in total joy and they stayed united as long as the Mass continued."[92] Presumably this event occurs at the consecration of the elements. The appearance of the Christ Child at that moment is a frequent occurrence in the mystic literature of the fourteenth century and especially in the literature of Engelthal. The straight-forward and unambigiuous description of this mystic event leaves no doubt as to what is intended. The word *vergottet*—to be made into God—could not possibly be expressed in more forceful and direct terms. Friedrich's soul and the Child Jesus are made one. The Word becomes flesh, not only in the historical birth of the Son of God, but now in its union with Friedrich. This union produces joy but lasts only as long as the length of time the Mass is celebrated. "When the Mass was finished one thousand angels were present and led the tender Child before the Father who received him and the angels with the greatest joy and because of this all the angels rejoiced in heaven. And Our Lady called the same Mass a divine Mass because the Holy Father, the Holy Spirit and all the angels were present."[93] In Trinitarian theology, whatever happens to one member of the Trinity happens to all. All three are present at the union, although it is Christ who is united with Friedrich. This union imagery continues and intensifies in the second Mass of Christmas at dawn *(Lux fulgebit)*. "When he [Friedrich] received the true body of Christ, the Holy Child united himself with his soul in the cradle of his heart and played with the brother's soul until he wanted to begin the third Mass. And the same Mass Our Lady called a special Mass since all his friends on earth were consoled and nourished by it and many thousands of souls were freed from purgatory."[94] Whereas the angels in heaven rejoiced at the first union of Christ and Friedrich, now people on earth and souls in purgatory rejoice as a benefit of this mystical union at the reception of communion. Once again Christ and Friedrich unite symbolically in the Eucharist in order to benefit others. Christ came to save, and now through his union with the mystical Christ, Friedrich becomes an agent of salvation for the living and the dead. This continues in a revelation to Friedrich after celebrating the third Mass of Christmas during the day *(Puer natus est nobis)*.

> When he [Friedrich] had finished the third Mass, our Lady made known to him that one thousand souls were freed from purgatory by it and as many sinners from their sins and as many good people were confirmed in faith and increased in leading a good life. And the same Mass Our Lady called a common Mass because with it one sings in the daytime and to it come both the good and the bad, young and old, by which Our Lord is praised.[95]

The Mass was common not only because common people came to hear it but because it was celebrated during the day. Mystical events occur in the night or at dawn. Notice that there is no description of the communion or of the union of Friedrich and Christ, only a revelation about the fruits of the Mass.

Friedrich prays for union with Christ on a frequent basis. In answer to his prayer on the feast of St. Damasius (11 December), Friedrich hears from the Child, "I have come to unite myself with your soul now spiritually and later during the Mass bodily. And to this my Holy Father is my witness and the Holy Spirit is the master worker and Mary, my Mother, a maintainer of the work between you and me so that we will never be separated from each other."[96] Once again the Trinity plays a role in the uniting of Friedrich and Christ, but the Virgin also plays a very important part in maintaining the union.

The imagery used to speak of union up to this point has centered on a union in the heart. However, there are other images employed to convey the same meaning. In answer to Friedrich's prayer, the Christ Child says to him, "Now I have come and am now spiritually born from you. Now I have two mothers: Mary who is my bodily mother, and you, my beloved soul, are my spiritual mother. I have nourished you with myself, now you should nourish me spiritually. Give me, lord, your right breast so that I can suck from it and be fed spiritually."[97] The imagery of union switches to birth, drawing an analogy between the historical birth of Christ and the mystical birth in the soul of Friedrich Sunder. In giving birth to Christ, Friedrich becomes his mother and performs the maternal function of nourishing the newborn from himself even as a mother. Friedrich's soul (*anima*) performs these maternal acts. These powerful and strange images for union receive an explanation in the text. The Child speaks to Friedrich's soul. "My much beloved soul, the works which have happened between you and me are miraculous and are a sign that we should love each other and that I will accomplish much through you today according to my dearest will as long as you live because you hold me dear and love me above all things." Once again the union of love is asserted along with the dynamic that this will result in great benefit to others. Later in the same revelation the Virgin reveals once again that because of this there is great rejoicing in both heaven and earth.

The most striking image of union used in the *Gnaden-vita* occurs immediately after the previously mentioned revelation. This new episode is likewise placed within the context of receiving communion. In it the Child Jesus addresses his mother. "Dearest little mother make a very joyous bed for me and for my much beloved spouse since I and my much beloved wish to take pleasure together."[98] This request is followed by a description of the pleasurable union. "When the little bed was made with many beautiful flowers which were noble virtues, the little Jesus lay himself down on the bed and Mary, his holy mother, united the holy soul with Jesus. And they had such loving joy and pleasure with one another by embracing and kissing, by laughing and with taking divine pleasure so that the angels and the saints who were present wondered that such a human being was still alive on earth in body and soul with whom Our Lord did such wonders."[99] Such bridal imagery in speaking of a relationship of union between a nun and Jesus surprises no one in the fourteenth century, but to use such powerfully erotic imagery with reference to a man, even with the cautious use of the feminine *anima* (soul), is quite striking. Perhaps in association with the women mystics of Engelthal, Friedrich (or the editor, who may have been a woman) employs highly eroticized imagery in an attempt to describe the power, mystery, and depth of emotion connected with any moment of union with the divine. The union as described in some ways includes both the bridal imagery and Friedrich's identification as king. The union of Jesus and Friedrich is consummated as any marriage is expected to be consummated, but it takes place in a richly decorated bed in the sight of the "court"—Mary the queen, and all the angels and saints, just as if an heir to the throne were on display before the royal court so that they could witness the consummation of his marriage.

The eroticism continues after the consummation/union. "When the little Jesus had taken his pleasure with the soul as he wished, he said to the angels and the saints who were there, 'Now strike up the instruments, violins, *rotte* and harp with all the pleasure that you find from the wedding that I have had with my much beloved spouse. And you should know that from this wedding that has happened between me and the soul, many people will be made glad and especially those he has in the monastery and elsewhere. And the souls who are in purgatory are all consoled and many are freed from their pain.'"[100] In explicit terms, Jesus calls Friedrich his "spouse" and speaks of the "wedding" and its "consummation," which all present have "witnessed." He reiterates the same dynamic that this union will benefit others, who are then specifically named, among whom are the nuns of the monastery, who would be expected to understand the imagery as signifying union. Jeffrey Hamburger writes of this passage, "Sunder's biographer describes the chaplain's experience of union in terms both so explicit and bizarre that one must forcibly remind oneself that the passage relies on a *topos*."[101] A modern interpreter may see in this *"topos"* a clear signification of homoeroticism, but the author, scribe, and monastic audience would have interpreted this as an image of spiritual union expressed in physical terms. The biographer or perhaps a later editor of Friedrich Sunder also comments on such mystical events in reference to an earlier passage. "What the sucking of the two breasts means—one must show this to our senses with bodily things because we cannot comprehend how this is accomplished between God and the soul with the inexpressible inflowing and outflowing of divine sweetness which he has granted to the soul, and also her desire, body and all her strength has been pulled into him."[102] Siegfried Ringler believes this passage is unique in the text of the *Gnaden-vita* in its use of explicitly acceptable mystical terminology and probably stems from a later editor.[103] Jeffrey Hamburger further states his belief that this editor may have been "troubled by the overt eroticism of the imagery."[104] It seems evident from the passages that homoeroticism is not the basis of these passages even though the imagery would suggest it. It seems more likely that Friedrich more closely identifies himself in feminine categories when relating to Christ. Friedrich gives birth to Christ spiritually as Mary gave birth physically. He is the bride of Christ as the bride in the Song of Solomon is the Beloved of the Bridegroom (Christ). However eroticized these passages may be, they simply attempt to express the reality of the imagery as a poor and insufficient means to convey the inexpressible. It seems that even Friedrich Sunder had difficulties with such texts. Immediately after these mystical events of union, the Virgin comes to Friedrich and says, "My Child and your Child has bade you to be greeted fervently."[105] Friedrich protests that Christ is not his Child but his Lord and God, but Mary responds, "He is your Child spiritually and mine corporeally. He was born to you three times on Christmas once at each Mass. And from each Mass one thousand souls were freed from purgatory and as many sinners were converted and as many good people increased in grace and especially those who belong to the monastery . . ."[106] As is so often the case, the mystic must have what he experiences revealed or explained to him. Given Friedrich's character and zeal for the salvation of souls, he would accept any revelation with the promise that souls would be saved, sinners converted, and good people made fervent.

However one reacts to the imagery, it does seek to express the union between Friedrich Sunder and Christ, from which many others will benefit. This, in brief, represents the entire dynamic of Christian, spiritual, and mystical life—union with Christ in whatever way deemed possible and useful. And from this union, others are helped to draw closer to Christ, who is salvation. Souls in purgatory are freed from their punishment, now to enjoy the presence of Christ in the heavenly kingdom. Sinners turn from evil to do good. Lukewarm people become fervent in faith. This progression in spiritual growth should continue then into the experience of mystical union that will help others. Many more examples from the text could be given to show the intensity of the relationship between Christ and Friedrich.

The received text recounts events, prayers, and mystical occurrences from the life of this extraordinary chaplain. The redactor clearly shows Friedrich as a faithful priest in a very traditional sense but does not hesitate to use remarkable imagery to convey Friedrich's high spiritual status despite his humble position in the world. The author does not shrink from employing stark, surprising, and striking images to strengthen belief in the possibility of spiritual growth; in the victory over the world, the flesh, and the devil; and in mystical union expressed in spousal and maternal images. In so doing the writer links Friedrich with the rare breed of mystic men who shared in distinctly feminine categories being portrayed as brides and mothers of Christ.

PART TWO

THE SPIRITUALITY
OF ENGELTHAL

THE LITERARY SOURCES: SCRIPTURE

THE WRITERS OF ENGELTHAL show in their works great familiarity with a wide variety of scriptural texts ranging from the Book of Genesis, various prophets such as Hosea, Ezekiel, and Isaiah; the Book of Psalms; and the Song of Solomon to the four Gospels; the letters of Paul; and the Book of Revelation. Their knowledge of scripture comes from many sources: the practice of *lectio divina*, the chanting of the divine office, readings in refectory, personal study, liturgical texts, and other spiritual texts such as *The Song of the Daughter of Zion*.

Frequently the writers of Engelthal quote directly from the Latin vulgate.[1] For example, Christina Ebner uses a scriptural verse in Latin at a crucial moment of decision. When she hears a voice that tells her that what was said in the Gospel will be accomplished through her, she quotes, "Cum turba irruerent in eum, et audirent verbum Dei" (Luke 5:1 Vulgate).[2] In the Gospel this passage introduces a string of events that concludes with the miraculous catch of fish and Christ's promise to make Peter a "fisher of men." For Christina this passage validates the same conclusion, for she must also go forth at that time to preach to the flagellants who had come to the monastery asking to hear her talk. She had resisted, but with reference to this passage about Christ, Christina follows in his way, goes to the cloister door, and speaks to them.[3] The authors of Friedrich Sunder's biography quote Galatians 4:19 twice, and the Virgin Mary quotes St. Paul in a passage in which she seeks to console Friedrich: "Filioli mei quos iterum parturio donec formetur Cristus in vobis."[4] This quote is personalized and applied to Friedrich, and it is easy to see why it might come from the mouth of the Mother who cares for her children. This same quote appears in a vision of the Christ Child somewhat later in which Christ asks Mary whether she has made this possible.[5]

Christina also quotes from a German version of the Bible. For example, in an extended revelation about Christ the Son, Christina quotes a passage from a German source. The Father says, "Dirr ist mein liber sun in dem ich mich selber wol gevalle . . ."[6] Of the four scriptural passages possible, this text corresponds to Matthew's version of the Baptism in the Jordan (Matt. 3:17) or to his version of the Transfiguration (Matt. 17:5) or Peter's version of the Transfiguration (2 Pet. 1:17), each of which has the Father describe Christ in identical words: "This is my beloved Son, in whom I am well pleased." Christina also paraphrases Matthew 11:25 (or its parallel passage, Luke 10:21) twice in reference to herself as being numbered among the "babes" to whom Christ has revealed his mysteries: "At that time Jesus declared, 'I thank thee, Father, Lord of heaven and earth, that thou hast hidden these things from the wise and understanding and revealed them to babes.'" This reference to Scripture is used to emphasize Christ's free will, his choice of Christina and the miracle he is able to work through her.[7] This is made even clearer in the second use of the passage: "These three things I have hidden from many great saints, as I have already said in the holy Gospel, that I thank my heavenly Father, that he has hidden from the wise, what he revealed to children and to the simple."[8]

Frequently the authors of the Engelthal texts paraphrase scripture in German. In the *Sister-Book*, Christina writes about Anna Vorchtel of Nuremberg and alludes to Matthew 11:29-30. "Whoever carries God's yoke, he makes it sweet and light."[9] Many other passages in the literature of Engelthal paraphrase Scripture verses in German.[10] Among the most important of these from a thematic standpoint are three references made by Christina Ebner to 2 Corinthians 12:9: "Let my grace suffice for you."[11] Each time that she uses this paraphrase, Christ assures her of his care and the power of his grace, and Christina's special status in relation to him.[12]

The writers of Engelthal also show knowledge of biblical passages and personages from both the Old and the New Testaments. Gertrud of Engelthal receives directions from Caritas to recite prayers honoring the five words of Christ.[13] The five words of Christ given to Gertrud refer to the following passages: 1) "Jesus said, 'I do not say to you seven times, but seventy times seven'"(Matt. 18:22); 2) "Father, if thou art willing, remove this cup from me; nevertheless not my will, but thine, be done" (Luke 22:42) or parallel passages: (Matt. 26:42; Mark 14:36); 3) "And when Jesus saw his mother, and the disciple whom he loved, standing near he said to his mother, 'Woman, behold your son!' Then he said to the disciple, 'Behold your mother!' And from that hour the disciple took her to his own home" (John 19:26-27); 4) "And Jesus said, 'Father forgive them; for they know not what they do'" (Luke 23:34); 5) "Then Jesus crying out with a loud voice said, 'Father, into thy hands I commit my spirit!' And having said this he breathed his last" (Luke 23:46). Later, the authors of the *Gnaden-vita of Friedrich Sunder, Chaplain of Engelthal* repeat the reference to Matthew 18:22.[14] Christina Ebner, in the *Sister-Book*, alludes to Luke 24:40 and 2:46, Deuteronomy 30:6, and John 1:1. In her autobiography she makes reference to the Upper Room, the Transfiguration, Christ's agony in the Garden, and numerous psalms (6, 21, 50, 66, 68, 85, 116, 118, 129, 139). She mentions biblical persons such as Abraham, Moses, David, Solomon, the Queen of Sheba, and Paul. She alludes to the "Book of Life" from Revelation and to Cyprian wine from the Song of Solomon. She mentions the parable of the vineyard, the root of Jesse, and the lepers being made clean and the blind receiving sight. Such references are too numerous to cite. Their number shows to what extent the writers of Engelthal were immersed in a biblical world view and naturally used scriptural quotes, paraphrases, and allusions throughout their texts. They interjected themselves into the biblical texts and, in turn, interpreted their lives in biblical modes.

Another important means of becoming familiar with scriptural sources and ecclesial and mystical interpretation of them comes through the use of Scripture in liturgical texts such as antiphons, responses, hymns, and sequences as well as through Scripture texts embedded in influential spiritual works such as *The Song of the Daughter of Zion*, the sermons of Bernard of Clairvaux, and other sources. Among these are some of the most important quotes as markers of spiritual progress and initiation into the mystic life. The text sung by Hailrat, the first chantress of Engelthal, marks the beginning of the mystical life of the community and helps the nuns to define themselves and their relationship to God. The verse as recorded by Christina is placed within a liturgical context. "Then they came to the fourth Sunday in Advent and when they were singing Matins and came to the fifth response 'Virgo Israel' and to the verse 'In caritate perpetua,' then she sang in German and sang so wonderfully that one thought she sang with the voice of an angel. The verse goes like this: 'I have loved you with an eternal love and therefore I have drawn you to myself with my mercy.'"[15] Christina's further comments about this event mention that they have these words through the prophets. This remark, no doubt, led Schröder to comment that Christina had an insufficient knowledge of Latin, for the text was drawn from Isaiah 11:1: "Haec dicit Dominus Deus: Egredietur virga de radice Jesse, et flos de radice ejus ascendat." This was the reading for the fourth Sunday of Advent.[16] Actually the important text was the response that derives from Jeremiah 31:3: "Et in charitate perpetua dilexi te; ideo attraxi te, miserans." Christina used the liturgical text of the response rather than the scriptural version upon which it was based.

One example of the use of Scripture through a literary source would be the fascination that the writers had with their identification with the daughters of Zion. In the *Sister-Book*, a Sister Alheit began to sing as she lay dying:

> Rejoice O Daughter Zion,
> beautiful news is coming to you.
> You should sing sweet tones
> according to the great desire of your heart.'
> You have become God's shrine,
> therefore you should be happy
> and should not suffer heartpain.
> Join the line which beautiful children want to see.
> Jubilation, meditation,
> Jubilation, contemplation,
> Jubilation, speculation,
> Jubilation, harmony.[17]

While based on Zechariah 9:9, it was embellished in the *Song of the Daughter of Zion* as Schröder has shown.[18] The mystics of Engelthal number themselves among the "daughters of Zion." This identification is based not on race, descent, or location but on their identification as Christians (the New Israel) and as nuns (daughters) in a monastery (Zion—the dwelling place of God).

The *Revelations* of Adelheid Langmann is a text particularly rich in demonstrating the use of Scripture as sketched above. Along with her contemporaries, Adelheid Langmann showed certain and familiar knowledge of scriptural passages in her *Prayer* and in her *Revelations*. The entire *Prayer* focused on events from the life of Christ taken from the Gospels and elsewhere. She quotes from the Gospel of Luke, the epistles of Paul, and the Song of Solomon. Her knowledge of Scripture comes not from academic study but from monastic immersion in the story of Jesus. The Song of Solomon and the Book of Revelation seem to have had the greatest impact on Adelheid's thought and visionary imagination.

There is no way to exaggerate the importance of the Song of Solomon for mystics of the fourteenth century. This book or numerous texts based on it had circulated throughout the monasteries of Europe. In German-speaking areas the *Hohelied* of Williram of Ebersberg from 1063 made a paraphrase available to German speakers.[19] *The St. Trutperter Hohelied* written in the twelfth century continued to make the text available. The biblical text was also available in the German language, as evidenced by the extant *Wenzelbibel* (1389-1400). The nuns sang and heard portions of this biblical text in antiphons and other liturgical texts, especially from the Little Office of the Blessed Virgin, which they recited every day. They also listened to readings from the Song of Solomon in refectory. The nuns of St. Katharina's monastery, a daughter house of Engelthal, listened to chapters of the Song of Solomon read in refectory fourteen times during the year. They heard chapters one and two during Advent, chapter six on Christmas Eve, chapters three and four on Pentecost, and chapter five on Corpus Christi.[20]

Correlations between the Song of Solomon and Adelheid Langmann's *Revelations* occur through paraphrase, terms of address, the motif of lovesickness, and the use of garden imagery. In a revelation from the Lord during Mass on the summer solstice she hears, "My Beloved, your mouth is sweeter than pure honey. Honey and milk are under your tongue."[21] This is directly reminiscent of the Song of Solomon 4:11: "Your lips distil nectar, my bride; honey and milk are under your tongue." On the octave of the Dedication of the Church, she is addressed in a similar way, "My Beloved, my Tender One, my Beautiful One, my love-sweet dear One, under your tongue is honey."[22] This revelation follows immediately upon the interrogation with the high-ranking preacher who confirmed the rightness of Adelheid's thought and experience and commanded her to write it all down. It serves as a divine affirmation of Adelheid's experience and a confirmation that she must speak sweetly of the Lord's mystical marriage to her. That Adelheid paraphrases texts from the Song of Solomon 4 demonstrates the importance of that chapter for her imagery and understanding of her relationship to Christ, the Beloved. Further, the Lord himself preached to her in terms very close to those used in chapter four of the Song of Solomon. "Your mouth smells of roses and your body of violets. You are altogether beautiful for nothing is lacking in you."[23] The comparison of the Beloved with lovely things is characteristic of the terms of address in the Song of Solomon, but more important here is the idea of perfection: "You are all fair, my love, there is no flaw in you" (Song of Sol. 4:7). The Bridegroom echoes this theme when he addresses the Bride, "My dove, my perfect one . . ." (Song of Sol. 6:9). In her own Prayer Adelheid makes this ideal of perfection an important element in her theological world view. Speaking of the Virgin Mary, she prays, "I remind you, Lord that the angel found her perfect in holiness and that you had sanctified her so that she was without sin because she was always overflowing with all grace. And so I ask you to bring me to all perfection and fill me up with all graces so that nothing will be lacking in me and you will find me ready at all times when you come."[24] The heavenly personages proceed to shower gifts upon Adelheid. the Holy Spirit promises her, "I will make you so perfect with my divine goodness that nothing will be lacking in you."[25] The Virgin Mary addresses God asking for a gift for Adelheid. "Lord, you who bring about all good things, and have also made me perfect in all things, give me something out of your goodness for this person today."[26] The Holy Spirit also promises, "I will never cease from granting her my goodness until she becomes the most perfect of all human beings."[27] Christ himself chastises her for doubting his perfection, asserting, "There is nothing lacking in me."[28] Adelheid responds immediately, "Lord, I see nothing lacking in you."[29] The idea of perfection in holiness—nothing lacking—identifies Adelheid not only with Mary but with Christ himself. Adelheid's prayer for perfection, and the Holy Spirit's promise assures her position among the elect, the Christ-like, whose first member was Mary.

Terms of address used by Adelheid in her *Revelations* echo those found in the Song of Solomon. As the Bridegroom addresses the Bride, so does Christ address Adelheid. On the Feast of the Epiphany Christ promises to make Adelheid his bride: "I will make you my bride today so that I will never be separated from you. I will show you all the loyalty that a lover gives to the Beloved. I marry you today so that I will always remain with you and I will do everything that you wish."[30] He continues using this bridal vocabulary, saying, "Every bridegroom gives a wedding band, so I have married you by giving you my body."[31] He addresses her as "Beloved" or "Love."[32] He also uses extended terms of address reminiscent of the Song of Solomon: "My Love, my Tender One, my Spouse" (*32), "My Darling, my Tender One, my Spouse and my Sister and my Child" (*35), "My Beloved, my Tender One, my Betrothed, and my dear Spouse and my dear Child" (*37), "My Beloved, my Tender One, my Beautiful One, my love-sweet dear One" (*41), "My Beloved, sweet as sugar or honey, my Tender One, my Pure One" (*63), "My Beloved, my Love and my Tender One" (*81). Such terms of endearment frequently occur in the Song of Solomon: "Behold, you are beautiful, my love; behold, you are beautiful" (Song of Sol. 1:15, 4:1); "Arise my love, my fair one" (Song of Sol. 2:10); "my sister, my bride" (Song of Sol. 4:9,10,12; 5:1); "my sister, my love, my dove, my perfect one" (5:2); "My dove, my perfect one" (Song of Sol. 6:9). These expressions of affection link the two texts both in content and intent. Adelheid consciously imitates the expressions in the Song of Solomon and thereby shows that the same loving relationship exhibited between the Bride and Bridegroom exists between Adelheid and Christ.

Adelheid also uses the motif of lovesickness found in the Song of Solomon. The Bride in the Song of Solomon professes, "I am sick with love" (Song of Sol. 2:5). Later, unable to find her beloved, she asks the daughters of Jerusalem, "if you find my beloved . . . tell him I am sick with love" (Song of Sol. 5:8). Adelheid mentions an undisclosed sickness several times. In her *Prayer*, while meditating upon the Three Kings she implores the Lord to guide her with love "and not with suffering" since he knows all about her sickness.[33] However, Adelheid speaks of her lovesickness while relating the episode of being guided on a lengthy and arduous journey by Spes and Caritas to meet her Beloved. After Adelheid has been weakened considerably by the rigors of the journey, Spes and Caritas ask her, "Lady, what is wrong with you that you are so sick? What are you yearning for?" To this question Adelheid responds, "I am yearning for him who is Lord of all lords and God of all gods, for my only beloved Love Jesus Christ. If he does not come to me I must die . . . I must die of painful longing for him."[34] Her lovesickness derives from her fear of abandonment. In the *Revelations* Christ constantly affirms that they would "never be separated" (*5, *14, *19, *46, *50), or asserts that "Just as little as I can ever be separated from my Father, so little will I ever be separated from you."[35] Yet Adelheid also believes that Christ often plays at abandoning her, and she has to be reassured by Ulrich, the prior of Kaisheim, that this was simply *minnespil*, a game of love. "Often he [Christ] will act as if to play at betraying you and wanting to abandon you or to drive you away. Pay no heed. Believe me, it is his intention for you to act more tenderly and kindly."[36]

The *Revelations* (*42) and the Song of Solomon (Song of Sol. 4, 5, 7) also share the imagery of an enclosed space—a lady's chamber (*kemenate*) and a garden. The Bridegroom compares his Beloved to a garden: "A garden locked is my sister, my bride, a garden locked, a fountain sealed" (Song of Sol. 4:12); "a garden fountain, a well of living water, and flowing streams from Lebanon" (Song of Sol. 4:15). He professes, "I will come to my garden, my sister, my bride" (Song of Sol. 5:1) and will knock at the gate saying, "Open to me, my sister, my love, my dove, my perfect one . . ." (Song of Sol. 5:2). In a similar space, a vineyard, the Bridegroom promises, "There I will give you my love" (Song of Sol. 7:12). Adelheid also uses the imagery of an enclosed space when writing about a revelation she had while listening to preaching. After telling Adelheid that she was all beautiful for there was "nothing lacking" in her, Christ goes on to describe their relationship, echoing the Song of Solomon. Speaking to Adelheid, he says, "You have captured me, just like a maiden who holds a young man captive in a lady's chamber and who knows well that if his friends were aware of it they would kill her and him."[37] The entrapment seems mutual, for when asked what had forced Christ to enter the enclosed space, he responds, "Your beauty has drawn me."[38] In turn he asks why he has been permitted to enter. She answers, "It is the great love that I bear for you." Just as the Bride in the Song of Solomon is compared to a garden, so Adelheid becomes this enclosed space and she alone has the key to allow or forbid entrance. Christ says to her, "See, thus have you captured me in the lady's chamber of your heart . . . your conscience holds the key."[39] He also warns her to guard against letting anyone else into her heart.

In both paragraph 42 of the *Revelations* and principally in chapter four of the Song of Solomon, the Bride (Adelheid) and the Bridegroom (Christ) meet in her locked and enclosed space where they can be alone together, safe from any intrusion, for she possesses the key. In each scene, love is professed. In each, a fountain wells up in the midst of the garden as a symbol of life and of new life in Christ—that is, divine indwelling. Adelheid concludes her encounter with Christ in the garden professing the all-importance of Christ and ends with a quote: "Lord, heaven is nothing to me, earth is too weak for me, the consolation of angels I count as nothing and I do not want the consolation of humans. Lord if you have any love for me and care for me, then come to me yourself and send no messenger and kiss me with the kiss of your mouth" (Song of Sol. 1:2)[40]. This emotionally charged encounter underscores the love shared between the two. In concluding with the scriptural passage, Adelheid tempers the eroticism of the meeting by placing it on a higher and more acceptable spiritual level.

Adelheid never directly quotes from the Book of Revelation, but her use of images often suggests an active knowledge of it. This is especially so when she images Christ as the Lamb. While the nuns sang the *Sanctus* during Mass (a text already suggestive of the Book of Revelation 4:8) Adelheid hears the words, "Greetings from the Highest Lamb!"[41] She wishes to know who that is and inquires, "I recognize from your words that it is you who is speaking to me. Who is the highest Lamb?"[42] She receives assurance that it is Christ himself. Christ proceeds to explain why Adelheid has to suffer, stating, "Often I send you suffering so that I can praise you in heaven."[43] The sentiment expressed in this same dialogue is reminiscent of Revelations 3:1): "Those whom I love, I reprove and chasten; so be zealous and repent."

Bridal imagery also relates to the Wedding Feast of the Lamb in the Book of Revelation: "'Hallelujah! For the Lord our God the Almighty reigns. Let us rejoice and exult and give him the glory, for the marriage of the Lamb has come, and his Bride has made herself ready; it was granted her to be clothed with fine linen, bright and pure'—for the fine linen is the righteous deeds of the saints" (Rev. 19:6-8). Adelheid experiences three episodes of mystical marriage with the Lamb. On the feast of the Three Kings during Mass while the choir chants the *Agnus Dei* ("Lamb of God, who takes away the sins of the world, have mercy on us"), Christ speaks to Adelheid after she has obeyed his command and showed herself to be conscious of the feelings of the other sisters: "I will make you my bride today so that I will never be separated from you. I will show you all the loyalty that a lover gives the Beloved. I marry you so that I will always remain with you and I will do everything you wish."[44] One year later Christ reminds Adelheid of this marriage and notes the detail that he had led her through the nine choirs of angels on that occasion and that the entire heavenly host of angels and saints had found her pleasing, and all showered her with wedding gifts.[45] On St. Matthias's Day Christ "consummates" the marriage: "I will give you myself, because I can show you no more love with anything other than myself."[46] Again he leads her through the nine choirs of angels and promises Adelheid: "Then you will be crowned with the purity of your heart" and "I will be yours forever."[47]

The imagery of the city that Adelheid describes after she has been led by Spes and Caritas on an arduous journey reminds one of the New Jerusalem in the Book of Revelation. Adelheid's description:

> When she [Adelheid] heard about his beauty, she became powerfully strong and in joy she came to the place where the Lord, her Beloved lived. All the gates were opened to them. With joy they entered the city. It was so wide that she could not see to its end. All the paths in the city were of pure gold. It was so high that they could see no roof above. The city was bathed in bright sunlight which was its roof."[48]

John the Evangelist describes the New Jerusalem in similar language and uses like images: "And I saw the holy city, new Jerusalem, coming down out of heaven from God, prepared as a bride adorned for her husband" (Rev. 21:2). Adelheid herself identifies with this image in her journey to the meeting place with her Beloved—she is the bride who was prepared and has to be accompanied to the bridal bed with the encouragement of Spes and Caritas. One of the seven angels showed John the "Bride, the wife of the

Lamb" (Rev. 21:9) who was likewise the new Jerusalem, the "dwelling of God" (Rev. 21:3). The association of the city as dwelling place of God and the constant refrain in the *Revelations* that God dwells within link Adelheid (the Bride) and the city. When Adelheid asks Christ to show himself to her, he responds: "Look into your own heart!"[49] In a revelation Christ also admits to Adelheid, "See, thus have you captured me in the lady's chamber of your heart."[50] He also professes to her, "Your heart is mine. I want to be in your heart."[51] The City, the Bride, and the meeting place of Love exist within Adelheid. She has thoroughly internalized the scriptural texts and their developing mystical interpretations. She is, in a mystical and therefore very real sense, the dwelling place of God, the sharer of his love.

The description of the City in both works appears similar. The New Jerusalem contains the "glory of God, its radiance like a most rare jewel, like a jasper, clear as crystal" (Rev. 21:11). It has "a great, high wall" (Rev. 21:13) built from precious stones, and each side has gates. However, the New Jerusalem has no temple, "for its temple is the Lord God the Almighty and the Lamb" (Rev. 21:22) and "the glory of God is its light, and its lamp is the Lamb" (Rev. 21:23). Only those whose names "are written in the Lamb's book of life" (Rev. 21:27) may enter it. The City contains the tree of life and its fruits (Rev. 22:2). Also, "the throne of God and the Lamb shall be in it, and his servants shall worship him; they shall see his face"(Rev. 22:3-4). Adelheid's description is precisely the sort of imitation of imagery and themes that one who had heard these readings but never actually studied them might produce. After describing a place similar to that recorded by John, Adelheid embellishes the setting, making it a place of loving union and using erotic terms to emphasize the indwelling: "The Lord now approached the bed. In all his joyous beauty he knelt down before the bed and his face was turned toward mine. I looked up and gazed at him. He was so beautiful that I could not bear it and it seemed to me that my soul would dissolve from true love. He said, 'My Beloved!' With the same word that so sweetly came out from his mouth he drew my poor, sinful soul into his Godhead."[52] This passage is in every sense the climax of Adelheid's mystical experience. It shows a union of the two lovers initiated by Christ and consummated in the breathing of Christ, a liturgical action that confers the presence of the divine, and by the absorption of Adelheid into the Godhead after which she can remember nothing. The union is not of equals; it is begun and completed by Christ, and its effect on Adelheid remains mysterious to her and cannot be conveyed in writing.

Adelheid mentions specifically "the book of life," which is found seven times in the Bible—once in Philippians (4:3), where Paul wrote of his fellow workers whose names were in the book of life, and six times in the Book of Revelation, where the names written therein would not be blotted out (Rev. 3:5). Those whose names were not written in the Lamb's book of life would not be admitted (Rev. 21:27) but would be "thrown into the fire" (Rev. 20:15) because they had been judged by their deeds (Rev. 20:12) since they had worshiped the beast (Rev.13:8; 17:8). Adelheid's source was certainly the text from the Book of Revelation, for she uses the "book of life" especially in the context of Revelation 3:5. Christ announces to her on a Saturday at the beginning of Advent: "I want to write your name in the book of life so that it will never be erased from it."[53] Adelheid wishes to know what is meant by this "book of life." Christ explains, "It is my divine heart that is the book of life. Whoever has been written down there can never be erased."[54] Adelheid also uses this inscribing of the heart to apply to herself. "Lord, inscribe your name in my heart so that it will never be erased."[55] Just as her name is never to be removed from his heart (the book of life), so his name is never to be effaced from hers. This inscribing of the heart occurs at other times as well.[56] Its significance is primarily as an image of union and salvation, but it also links Christ and Adelheid as authors. He is the Word made flesh as revealed in the Word of God (the Bible), while she makes not only his Word (as enfleshed in her) but her own words available through her writings.

Adelheid also alludes to certain experiences of St. Paul. She reports that on Candlemas she has to be led away from the table, being unaware that she is in the world. A flame shoots out from her mouth and she exclaims, "Lord God, have mercy on me!"[57] Immediately thereafter, alone in her cell she asks the Lord where she had been. He tells her, "Your soul was taken home to heaven and I cared for it and showed it to my mother."[58] Paul likewise describes a similar incident. "I know a man in Christ who . . . was caught up to the third heaven—whether in the body or out of the body I do not know, God knows. And I know that this man was caught up into Paradise—whether in the body or out of the body, I do not know, God knows. And he heard things that cannot be told . . ."(2 Cor. 12:2-4). Also Adelheid, like Paul, has the choice of remaining on earth or going to heaven. Paul exclaims, "I am hard-pressed between the two. My desire is to depart and be with Christ for that is far better" (Phil. 1:23). Once when Adelheid is gravely ill, Christ says to her, "If you wish to die now, I will grant you entrance into heaven, but you will have to relinquish the great reward that you could still gain."[59] Like Paul, who concluded, "to remain in the flesh is more necessary on your account" (Phil. 1:24), Adelheid chooses to remain among the living for the good that she could gain for others.

In her *Prayer*, Adelheid quotes directly from the Gospel of Luke in German. In the *Prayer* she rehearses events from the life of Christ and makes reference to the incidents contained in Scripture, but she quotes directly three times from the scene of the Annunciation and once, in Latin, from Christ's baptism in the Jordan, "Hic est filius meus dilectus in quo mihi bene complacui."[60] Since her *Prayer* rehearses the major and often minor events from Christ's life, it alludes to all the Gospels and even to Pseudo-Gospels.

Adelheid's use of Scripture, as representative of the other writers of Engelthal, shows familiarity with the Gospels, St. Paul's letters, the Song of Solomon, and the Book of Revelation, but basically her knowledge of Scripture was absorbed rather than practiced. Her knowledge depended upon what would be learned in singing the liturgical texts, and listening to refectory readings and sermons rather than upon careful study and use of biblical texts. Adelheid absorbed the images from and sometimes texts of Scripture into her visionary and imaginative faculties and used them to describe her spiritual progress.

LITERARY INFLUENCES

IN ADDITION TO BEING FORMED BY THE BIBLICAL AND LITURGICAL TEXTS in which they were immersed every day through the Mass and especially the celebration of the Liturgy of the Hours, the writers of Engelthal were also greatly influenced by important nonscriptural texts. This chapter will treat the most significant of these: the *St. Trutperter Song of Songs*, the *Sermones super Cantica Canticorum* of Bernard of Clairvaux, the *Flowing Light of the Godhead* by Mechthild of Magdeburg, and the various version of *The Song of the Daughter of Zion*. The *St. Trutperter Song of Songs* provided the nuns and priests at Engelthal with Williram of Ebersberg's translation of the scriptural Song of Solomon into German along with a spiritual interpretation of the Scriptures formulated by two abbesses in the twelfth century. It is apparent that the writers of Engelthal were also greatly influenced by Bernard of Clairvaux's *Sermones super Cantica Canticorum*, undoubtedly one of the most significant collections of sermons in the Middle Ages. This is not surprising given the high regard in which these sermons were held and their use in mystical writings. Also, the close ties of the Dominicans of Engelthal with the Cistercians of Kaisheim suggest a source of enrichment in Cistercian spirituality for the Dominicans, especially for Adelheid Langmann. Mechthild of Magdeburg's *The Flowing Light of the Godhead* greatly influenced all the writers of Engelthal. Their source for this text was Henry of Nördlingen, probably the greatest contact-person among the Friends of God. Also important for Christina Ebner and Adelheid Langmann in particular was some version of *The Song of the Daughter of Zion*. In this chapter each of these four texts will be presented to show how the writers of Engelthal made use of the themes, images, vocabulary, and ideas expressed by their august literary and spiritual predecessors.

THE *ST. TRUTPERTER SONG OF SONGS (HOHELIED)*

In the now outdated critical edition of Adelheid Langmann's *Revelations* produced in 1878, Philipp Strauch referred to several literary influences, among them *Das Hohelied* (ed. J. Haupt) in which he noted five paraphrases or images that connected with portions of Adelheid Langmann's *Revelations*. This *Hohelied*, published in 1864 in Vienna, contains the first German translation of the Song of Solomon, Williram of Ebersberg's *Hohelied* which was written around 1060, and an extensive exegesis interpreting the scriptural text, written in the middle of the twelfth century by two abbesses of Hohenburg in Alsace—Rilindis and Herrat. The correlations between this interpreted text, known as the *St. Trutperter Song of Songs*, and the *Revelations* of Adelheid Langmann occur not in the translated passages but in their corresponding interpretations. According to Strauch, the monks of Kaisheim, who frequently lent texts to the nuns of Engelthal, possessed a copy of Williram's *Hohelied*.[1] Whether this text corresponded to the Vienna manuscript (Ms. 2719) upon which Haupt based his edition remains uncertain. Nonetheless the textual correspondences suggest that Adelheid had the St. Trutperter text available to her in some form.

The interpretation offered by the abbesses assumes various perspectives at different points in the text, beginning with a mariological interpretation but at other times interpreting the dialogue between bride and groom as a conversation between the Church and the Synagogue. The abbesses also emphasize the role of the Holy Spirit, which later would also form an important element in the spirituality of Adelheid Langmann. Oddly enough the translation superscribed with the Latin scripture quote began with "Quia meliora sunt ubera tua uino flagrantia [*sic*] unguentis optimis" (Song of Sol. 1:1b-2a: "For your love is better than wine, your anointing oils are fragrant.") rather than with the famous opening line of the Song of Solomon used by Adelheid, "Osculetur me osculo oris sui!" (Song of Sol. 1:1a: "O that you would kiss me with the kisses of your mouth!"). However, prior to the beginning of the actual translation the abbesses wrote at length on the kiss, describing the kiss between Virgin and Child:

> By the Son was never a soul so lovingly kissed. The mouth with which she kissed you was her will and her love. . . . [T]he mouth was kissed so much that he began to speak. He had kissed her before ever he spoke. He was the one who kissed, she the one who loved. She was the one kissed, he, the one loved.[2]

In their mariological interpretation, Rilindis and Herrat also saw the kiss as a metaphor for the incarnation. The kissing of the bride and groom symbolized Christ coming down from on high and taking on flesh from the humble Virgin.[3] Also through this kiss (by becoming man) Christ kissed not only the Virgin but kisses all human beings and offers them grace.[4]

Strauch saw an influence of Haupt 51:12f. on AL 85:26f. with regard to the mystical meaning of the gifts offered by the Three Kings to the Christ Child. Both interpret the incense as the prayers of the pure in heart. The use of the terms "drunkenness" and "Cyprian wine" to describe spiritual intoxication appear both in Adelheid and in Haupt.[5] The most important connection noticed by Strauch concerns a quote identified in the St. Trutperter Song of Songs with St. Augustine. The text of the Hohelied appears under the commentary on the Song of Solomon 5:1b: "Eat, O friends, and drink: drink deeply, O lovers!"[6] The significant text in the Hohelied reads: "wahs unde iz mich, nicht daz ich in dich verwandelot wurde also das ezzen des libes, sundir diu solt in mich verwandelot werden."[7] In the Revelations Adelheid records a similar passage in which Christ says to her: "'ich wil nit gewandelt werden in dich, sunder du solt gewandelt werden in mich.'"[8] This sentence clearly echoes the text in the St. Trutperter Song of Songs that is attributed to St. Augustine. The greatest love is to eat the Lord (receive communion). "Those who eat God are his friends," and his best friends are drunk on the immeasurable sweetness that they have with God.[9] Through the reception of communion, Adelheid will take in the body of Christ and be transformed into being like him.

Other connections between the two texts beyond those mentioned by Strauch require a brief survey. The following passages may well have helped to form Adelheid's creative world view, since the images, vocabulary, and spiritual perspective they contain coincide with hers. The most important element to note concerns the role of the Holy Spirit. The St. Trutperter Song of Songs seems almost a commentary on the Holy Spirit, for it begins, "We want to tell of the highest love, the greatest grace and the most fragrant sweetness: this is the Holy Spirit."[10] Throughout the commentary on the Song of Solomon, the Holy Spirit plays a large role and receives extensive treatment, especially at the conclusion of the work. Adelheid also stressed the importance of the Holy Spirit in the Revelations, more so than do her contemporaries such as Margaret Ebner. Since many of her visions and dreams were Trinitarian, the Holy Spirit naturally played a role in them.[11] In a vision on the Feast of St. Peter the Preacher, the Holy Spirit promised to bring Adelheid to perfection.[12] In a similar but later vision, the Holy Spirit promises: "I will never cease from granting her my goodness until she becomes the most perfect of all human beings."[13] In a subsequent vision the Spirit also promises: "I give you all the virtues and I will confirm them in you."[14] On the Feast of the Chair of St. Peter, the promise was even more detailed: "I will make you so perfect with my divine goodness so that nothing will be lacking in you."[15] Adelheid prayed, "May you, Lord Holy Spirit, inflame me with the fire of your love so that my heart must burst more from love than from the pain of death."[16] For Adelheid, the Holy Spirit was the driving force in the perfection of the soul in goodness and love.

Other elements that suggest Adelheid's use of the *St. Trutperter Song of Songs* have to do with vocabulary, symbols, and the imaging of Adelheid's own history. Both texts utilize the term "martyrdom" of Christ to signify his passion.[17] Symbolic adornment in which the colors or parts of vesture receive symbolic meaning appears in both works.[18] The symbolism of trees occurs in both works.[19] Adelheid may also have read her own history into the text of the *St. Trutperter Song of Songs* and used it in imaging her relationship with Christ. In the commentary on Song of Solomon 8:6, "Set me as a seal upon your heart, as a seal upon your arm; for love is strong as death, jealousy is cruel as the grave. Its flashes are flashes of fire," Christ rehearses what he has done for the soul. He has created and saved it by his death, but more importantly he unites himself with the soul. Speaking to the soul, he says that he "drew you . . . against your will into my chamber (*kemenate*) onto the bed of spiritual suffering . . . so that you would love me above all things."[20] This passage is part of the abbesses' commentary on Song of Sol. 8:6: "Set me as a seal upon your heart, as a seal upon your arm; for love is strong as death, jealousy as cruel as the grave."[21] In this Adelheid may have read her own story, for she had entered the monastery against her will and had to be induced to make profession.[22] Adelheid specifically uses the same word (*kemenate*) to signify the meeting place of the lovers, of herself and Christ.[23] Christ tells her that he gives her suffering so that she will be his alone.[24] Love and suffering are inextricably bound together.

THE *SERMONES SUPER CANTICA CANTICORUM* OF BERNARD OF CLAIRVAUX

The importance of Bernard of Clairvaux as a figure in his own time, important as he was in political and religious affairs, is overshadowed by the lasting influence of his writings to which the spread of numerous copies of manuscripts produced all over Europe gives evidence. His influence extended not only to the wide circle of Cistercian and Benedictine monasticism but to other monastics as well. As an example of the lived experience of the mystical life in Christ and through his eloquent descriptions of the mystical life, he gained a lasting place in the hearts and minds of the Dominican nuns of the fourteenth century. For Adelheid Langmann his influence lies principally in his image as a practical mystic as expressed in his famous *Sermons on the Song of Songs.* Bernard wrote from the abundance of his meditation in *lectio divina* but also from his experience, as he himself claimed: "I myself, however wretched I may be, have been occasionally privileged to sit at the feet of the Lord Jesus."[25] His inclusion of personal experience shows a new approach in interpretation.[26] Although the biblical quotes and allusions that Adelheid employs might just as easily be said to have come directly from the Song of Solomon, the spirit of their use and their interpretive context match Bernard's thought expressed in his sermons.

Bernard of Clairvaux completed 86 sermons on the Song of Solomon covering merely the first two of the eight chapters of the biblical text. He departed from earlier interpretations that saw the Song of Solomon variously as a marriage song between Solomon and his bride, a conversation between the Church and the Synagogue, or a love song between Christ and his Bride, the Church. In his series of sermons, Bernard personalized the text by interpreting it as a love song between Christ as bridegroom and the believer as bride. Every Christian soul, whether male or female, may enter into a bridal love relationship with Christ. In reference to the bride, Bernard posed the question, "Now who is this 'she'?" "She" is "the soul thirsting for God."[27] When a monastic heard the Song of Solomon or used it for *lectio divina*, the interpretation and understanding of the text was at once personalized. Adelheid reads her own relationship with Christ in the text. She is the bride of Christ in a mystical and not simply metaphorical sense. What is true of the relationship and the progress of the biblical Bride applies also to Adelheid. Like the Bride, Adelheid is chosen by the Bridegroom, undergoes trials of her love, and is adorned with virtues so that she will become perfect and share the marriage bed of the Beloved.

The social conventions of the writing of the Song of Solomon made it necessary to assume that the Bride had been chosen by the Bridegroom. Adelheid, however, resists Christ's choosing her to enter into a special relationship with him. Although when she was a young girl everyone said that she certainly belonged in a monastery, Adelheid refuses to enter a cloister despite the revelations given to some other spiritual person about her and despite the assurances of others. Not until she has to deal personally with Christ's wish for her to enter the monastery of Engelthal does she reveal her apprehensions and ultimately acquiesce to the call. In her resistance to Christ she shows considerable theological acumen, if not actual casuistry, when she thinks she will promise Christ whatever he wishes but be released from the vow by the priest because she would have made the promise under duress. Ultimately Adelheid relents, convinced of the good will of Christ for her and assured of his assistance. Later she learns that her profession day had actually been a "wedding day" as are the profession days of all the nuns.[28] Again and again Christ assures her that he will never abandon her and will never be separated from her, comparing their union with his immutable union with the Father.[29] That Christ writes Adelheid's name in the "book of life" assures her status as one of the elect.[30] Explicitly Christ refers to her as his Bride and gives her gifts for the wedding. She could find Christ in her heart just as she could be found in his.[31] Adelheid's status surpasses that of all others, even Christina Ebner, and Christ speaks to her professing his love.[32] His affections intensify, "I will be yours forever . . ." he proclaims.[33] He reveals to her, "I have chosen your heart for me . . ."[34] Finally, using *minnesang* vocabulary, Christ professes, "You are mine and I am yours. We are united and shall remain united forever."[35] He has chosen her to be one with him.

As the biblical Bride was tested by the Bridegroom (Song of Sol. 3:1-2; 5:6-8) so Adelheid suffers tests of her love for Christ on several occasions. Aside from the initial disagreement over her vocation to become a Dominican nun, Adelheid has to be taught the nature of the love that she must have for her Bridegroom. She has to give up her earthly family but receives the reward of membership in Christ's heavenly family.[36] She has to learn the purpose and the motive of suffering.[37] Even though Adelheid undergoes temptation by the devil, she also has assurance that she will grow in holiness.[38] Christ tells her that he sends her suffering so that he can praise her in heaven.[39] Making an analogy between Adelheid and the growth of a fruit tree, Christ teachers her that she has a mission to help others. On the feast of the Three Kings she proves both her obedience to Christ and her sensitivity to others, which prompts Christ to celebrate their marriage.[40] On occasion Christ seems disappointed in Adelheid's lack of response or disloyal behavior. He wants to know if she is ashamed of him.[41] Christ asks her to "gladly bear suffering for my sake" and reminds her of his own suffering for her.[42] Testing Adelheid's will to obey, Christ commands her to leave the infirmary although she is ill, requests that she eat the rotten vegetables no matter how repulsive they seem to her, allows her to be frightened by snakes and vipers so that she will learn that "no one has received such great grace so as not to be on guard at all times against the wiles of the devil."[43] Adelheid also suffers from her own doubts, believing that the Lord will be unfaithful to her even as others have been unfaithful and thinking that no one will do any good for her.[44] Her doubts call forth reassurance and advice from Christ. Adelheid also learns of the exclusivity of her relationship with her Beloved when he upbraids her for her budding relationship with a Dominican preacher.[45] She must come to Christ for advice and consolation, not to the preacher. After Adelheid has doubted the reality of a vision on Christmas, Christ explains: "How little you believe and how much it takes to make you believe."[46] Further, he warns her, "I will not be changed into you, rather you should be changed into me."[47] Adelheid must also give gifts—her soul and body, and all human beings whom she has ever met.[48] Her final test has to do with Christ's plan to betroth Adelheid to St. John the Evangelist. Despite her feeling of rejection, she proves that she will do Christ's will.[49]

Just as the biblical Bride was adorned with ornaments, jewels, and gold, so Adelheid is adorned with virtues so that she will grow in holiness (Song of Sol. 1:9-11). Throughout the Song of Solomon the Bride's anatomy, vesture, and raiment are described. Any anagogical or allegorical interpretation of the biblical text would attach symbolic significance to the description of the Bride whose physical beauty and rich attire reveal the inner beauty of the soul and its adornment with Christian virtues. This imagery connecting virtues with garments or crowns occurs often in Bernard's sermons and appears in Adelheid's writings as well. Writing of the Bride, Bernard notes the "splendor of her adornment" as far surpassing the raiment of Solomon.[50] She is "graced with the jewels of consummate virtue," which are "more brilliant than the sun."[51] The Bride's beauty consists of virtues: love, justice, patience, voluntary poverty, humility, holy fear, prudence, temperance, and fortitude. This virtue/clothing symbolism finds a use in Adelheid's *Revelations*. On the feast of the Holy Trinity, Christ gives her three garments and explains their symbolism. When Adelheid asks what the white dress signifies, he responds: "It symbolizes true purity since I have purified you of all your sins. The red dress signifies the burning love that you have for me. The green dress signifies my divinity for I am within you."[52] He then places a crown upon her head that should be decorated with her good deeds. Christ restores the garment of innocence to her and professes that she is dearer to him than any other human being on earth.[53] He promises to do whatever she wishes and on numerous occasions professes that he will never be parted from her.[54] Much to Adelheid's chagrin, Christ "robs" a virtue from every sister in the monastery and gives them to her instead.[55] Despite her sense of the unfairness of her benefice, she consents to it because it is Christ's will. When Adelheid finally demonstrates that her will is in total accord with

Christ's, she receives promises and gifts from God the Father, the Holy Spirit, the Virgin Mary, and the archangel Gabriel.[56] On a second occasion through the intercession of the Virgin Mary, the members of the heavenly company make promises to her. From God the Father she receives divine power to resist all vices. Christ grants her divine wisdom. The Holy Spirit promises to make her perfect by giving her all the virtues.[57] Ultimately Christ confers upon Adelheid what amounts to a new baptism:

> My Love, it is necessary for me to wash you all over. First, your eyes so that they will look at me alone and also your ears so that they will hear my teaching and the teachings of my teachers so that you will keep them; and your nose so that it will detect the falsehood of the world and know that faithfulness is found in no one, but me alone. Your heart should belong to me alone and have no one except me. Your tongue should speak the truth for it should rightly be that those who do not speak the truth should have their tongues ripped out. Your mouth should praise me at all times. Your hands should do my works. Your feet should walk in my ways. You should gladly come to me. All the strength of your limbs should be consumed in my service. I have purchased heaven for you by my death. You must serve me . . . I have given my life for your sake and am dead for you and you must give your strength for the kingdom of heaven . . .[58]

This text rehearses the blessings at baptism with the sanctification of various body parts that are anointed or blessed—the forehead, the breast, the hands, the lips, and the ears (ephphetha). In poetic language Christ promises to give Adelheid a share in the love of the patriarchs, the confessors, and the virgins.[59]

As the biblical Bride was perfected by association with the Bridegroom, so Christ frequently promises that he will make Adelheid perfect (Song of Sol.8:5-7). Ultimately the biblical Bride is led into the wilderness of her Beloved and sealed with love that is as strong as death. These three verses represent the climax of the entire poem and can be interpreted to symbolize union and therefore perfection in love between the Bride and the Beloved. About Adelheid the Holy Spirit also states, "She cannot reach perfection without me. I want to bring her to perfection."[60] Christ rehearses what he has done for Adelheid and promises, "I shall never let up with my divine power until you have become a perfect human being."[61] On another occasion the Spirit promises, "I will never cease from granting her my goodness until she becomes the most perfect of all human beings."[62] This promise is repeated later: "I will make you so perfect with my divine goodness that nothing will be lacking in you."[63]

Although Adelheid's marriage to Christ is mentioned on several occasions with reference to her profession and to her marriage ceremony on the octave of the Dedication of the Church, it is in Christ's bedchamber, to which she is led by Spes and Caritas that Adelheid experiences the ecstatic consummation of union.[64] For Bernard, "the bedroom [represents] the mystery of divine contemplation."[65] There in the bedroom of contemplation God "is neither fearsome nor awe-inspiring, he wills to be found there in the guise of love, calm and peaceful, gracious and meek, filled with mercy for all who gaze on him."[66] Adelheid prays to be united with Christ: "Lord, unite yourself to me and me to you so that our union will last forever without any separation."[67] The amazing revelations during the sermon of the unnamed Dominican preacher provide a passionate foreshadowing of the consummation of the marriage with Christ in that the lovers both profess their love in unmistakable terms.[68] Christ speaks to her in loving words: "My Beloved, sweet as sugar or honey, my Tender One, my Pure One, you are mine and I am yours."[69] And when she prays for the lord of Hohenstein, Christ reveals to her, "With this man I will let you know how much I really love you."[70] By her advice and prayers the knight becomes a Cistercian. The climax of her bridal relationship with Christ occurs in the vision in which she is led by Spes and Caritas to the wedding bed.

> The Lord now approached the bed. In all his joyous beauty he knelt down before the bed and his face was turned toward mine. I looked up and gazed at him. He was so beautiful that I could not bear it and it seemed to me that my soul would dissolve from true love. He said, "Beloved!" With the same word that so sweetly came out from his mouth he drew my poor, sinful soul into his Godhead and I can say nothing about this vision except to say that it began when they had begun to sing compline and continued until the next day as Mass was being sung.[71]

Adelheid writes specifically about the "kiss of the mouth" in response to the incredible blessings she receives in the revelation during the preaching of the Dominican:

> Lord, heaven is nothing to me, earth is too weak for me, the consolation of angels I count as nothing and I do not want the consolation of humans. Lord, if you have any love for me and care for me, then come

to me yourself and send no messenger and kiss me with the kiss of your mouth.[72]

This concluding request finds an echo in Bernard's sermons: ". . . if he has genuine regard for me, let him kiss me with the kiss of his mouth."[73] To understand the fullness of meaning behind that expression one must know the depth of significance given to it by Bernard of Clairvaux. He devoted three sermons (2,3,4) to an interpretation of "O that you would kiss me with the kisses of your mouth" (Song of Sol. 1:2). He differentiated between three types of kiss: on the feet, on the hands, and on the mouth of Christ. The kissing of the feet was a sign of genuine conversion of life. When describing this kiss he wrote of the penitence and love of Mary Magdalen: "It is up to you, wretched sinner, to humble yourself as this happy penitent [Mary Magdalen] did so that you may be rid of your wretchedness. Prostrate yourself on the ground, take hold of his feet, soothe them with kisses, sprinkle them with your tears and so wash not them but yourself."[74] As a symbol of reconciliation, the kissing of the feet is also a sign of peace, as are all the kisses.[75] When Adelheid describes the kiss of the feet, she treats each foot separately. From the right foot she draws out divine faithfulness and from the left, divine purity and protection from evil.[76] These correspond to Bernard's "genuine conversion of life" in that both faith and purity are required for conversion. Mary Magdalen had turned away from a life of sin and put her faith in Jesus. Adelheid follows her example of conversion leading to love.

Bernard's "kiss of the hands" was given to those who are making spiritual progress. The kissing of the hands represented the reception of the grace necessary for perseverance and conversion.[77] Adelheid again separates the kiss, giving one to each hand. From the right hand she draws divine mercy and from the left, obedience.[78] For her, these are the tools of perseverance. She has to learn to obey Christ's commands to her and to conform her will to his under all circumstances. To do this she begs for God's grace and mercy, especially in her own *Prayer*.

Adelheid also mentions the kiss of the side of Christ from which she receives the abundance of the divinity and humanity of Christ.[79] Although she prays to receive the "kiss of the mouth" explicitly in her *Revelations*, she does not treat it using those terms. However, this kiss of the side of Christ bears some of the meaning attributed to the kiss of the mouth by Bernard, for his "kiss of the mouth" was "no other than the Mediator between God and man, himself a man, Christ Jesus, who with the Father and Holy Spirit lives and reigns as God for ever and ever. Amen."[80] Both Christ's humanity and divinity are contained in each kiss. Bernard further described the "kiss of the mouth" in Trinitarian terms:

> Listen if you will know what the kiss of the mouth is: "The Father and I are one;" and again: "I am in the Father and the Father is in me." This is a kiss from mouth to mouth, beyond the claim of any creature. It is a kiss of love and peace, but of the love which is beyond all knowledge, and that peace which is so much greater than we can understand. The truth is that the things that no eye has seen, and no ear heard, things beyond the mind of man, were revealed to Paul by God through his Spirit, that is, through him who is the kiss of his mouth.[81]

Bernard quoted or paraphrased verses from Scripture here: "The Father and I are one" (John 10:30); "I am in the Father and the Father is in me" (John 14:10); "love which is beyond all knowledge" (Eph. 3:10); "peace which is greater than we can understand" (Phil. 4:7); and "no eye has seen" (1 Cor. 2:9).

In imitating Bernard, Adelheid is greatly influenced by a Trinitarian spirituality. In her major visions, the Trinity of Persons plays an important role.[82] Adelheid desires the kiss of the mouth, for it symbolizes union with Christ and, in fact, with the whole Trinity through him. She describes this union in her vision of Christ's bedchamber in which their union is consummated. Bernard also described the kiss in Trinitarian terms: "If, as is properly understood, the Father is he who kisses, the Son he who is kissed, then it cannot be wrong to see in the kiss the Holy Spirit, for he is the imperturbable peace of the Father and the Son, their unshakable bond, their undivided love, their indivisible unity."[83] As previously noted, Christ often promises Adelheid that just as little as he could be separated from his Father, would he be separated from her. It seems that Adelheid expands on Bernard's teaching on the kisses by increasing their number and by adding to their symbolic significance. But for both Bernard and Adelheid the various kisses all represent the spiritual progress of the soul in connection with ever-increasing intimacy with Christ in his passion and in his love.

There are also numerous correspondences of texts that suggest the influence of Bernard on Adelheid. These correspondences range from descriptive detail of angels to statements concerning the virtues of the bride or the bride's capability to behold the beauty of heaven. Although these correspondences occur frequently throughout the text of the *Revelations* and in Adelheid's *Prayer*, I shall mention only a few of the more pertinent parallels.

On one occasion Adelheid, having been roused from ecstasy, desires to know where she has been. It seems puzzling to her to learn from Christ that she has visited heaven but can remember nothing. Wishing to remember what heaven is like, she asks him, "Lord, why did you not let me know it?" and he responds, "You are not yet worthy of it, but it will happen to you soon."[84] The Bride in Bernard's sermon heard similar words explaining why she could not see heaven. "The vision that you ask for, Bride of mine, is above your capacity, you are not yet able to gaze upon that sublime noontide brightness that is my dwelling place."[85] In the same sermon the Bridegroom consoled the Bride using words from the biblical text that occur frequently in Adelheid's *Revelations*. "The time will come when I shall reveal myself and your beauty will be complete, just as my beauty is complete you will be so like me that you will see me as I am. Then you will be told: 'You are all fair my love, there is no flaw in you.'"[86] The Holy Spirit promises Adelheid, "I will make you so perfect with my divine goodness that nothing will be lacking in you."[87] In her prayer Adelheid makes a petition to that same end: "And so I ask you to bring me to all perfection and fill me up with all graces so that nothing will be lacking in me and you will find me ready at all times when you come."[88] The same phrase applies to Christ when he makes the same claim for himself, "There is nothing lacking in me."[89] Adelheid's thought matches the teaching of Bernard. Just as Christ is perfect ("nothing lacking",) so Adelheid will be made perfect, but for now, still in a state of imperfection, she is not able to take in and remember her vision of heaven.

The unity in love between Bride and Bridegroom, Adelheid and Christ, is expressed in similar words in the *Revelations* and in the *Sermons on the Song of Songs*. Bernard's Bride exclaims, "My Beloved is mine and I am his!"[90] Christ likewise uses this formula to express his love for Adelheid: "You are mine and I am yours!"[91]

THE DIVINE INDWELLING

Bernard's comments on the indwelling of Christ in the heart find a reflection in Adelheid's *Revelations*. Bernard teaches that Christ dwells in the virtuous as in heaven.[92] His supporting Scripture also suggests Adelheid's experience. The quote: "Christ dwells by faith in our hearts" (Eph. 3:17) corresponds to Adelheid's relation of how Christ told her to look into her own heart to find him.[93] In this regard Bernard also quotes from the Gospel of John: "I and the Father will come to him and make our dwelling with him" (John 14:23).[94] Also the mutuality of the indwelling mentioned briefly by Bernard finds a powerful resonance in Adelheid. Bernard expresses this mutual union in the following way: "Therefore, when God and man cleave wholly to each other—it is when they are incorporated into each other by mutual love that they cleave wholly to each other—I would say beyond all doubt that God is in man and man in God."[95] Adelheid uses "pressing" instead of Bernard's "cleaving" to express the same reality. Christ promises Adelheid, "I will press your soul to my divinity so that you will be as like me as is possible."[96] Later, he "stretched out his arms, embraced her and pressed her against his divine heart so that she thought she clung to him like wax to a seal."[97] Friedrich Sunder and Christina Ebner use the same word, press, to describe similar experiences. The writing of Jesus' name in her heart also symbolizes union, but even more importantly, Christ wishes to write his name on her heart as a testimony of mutual love and the coincidence of wills.[98] The unity occurs for Bernard and for Adelheid in the unity of wills. Bernard writes, "But that unity is caused not so much by the identity of essences as by the concurrence of wills."[99] As we have seen, Adelheid has to be trained to unite her will with that of Christ.

MECHTHILD OF MAGDEBURG'S
THE FLOWING LIGHT OF THE GODHEAD

In her autobiographical sketches, Christina Ebner, the most prolific of the writers of Engelthal, writes about Mechthild of Magdeburg's *The Flowing Light of the Godhead*. During Easter week of 1345, Christina receives a revelation from Christ in which he explains why he has given her Mechthild's book. "I have given you the book so that your spiritual joy may be greater."[100] Christina explains what this means by immediately writing, "And he meant the book that is called an outflowing light of the Godhead."[101] In a more detailed revelation written in 1346 or sometime afterward, Christ reveals more of his motives for giving the book to Christina: "My eternal love, I have sent you the book that is called an outflowing light of the Godhead before your death so that you will be more knowledgeable in graces, not just from your own experiences. You should speak about this as long as you live so that others will believe because of the grace I give you."[102] Unlike her references to *The Song of the Daughter of Zion*, here Christina mentions no specific details about the text but does assert its importance and the reason for her own reading of the text. As with Margaret Ebner, the text should help Christina better understand her own experience so that she will be able to tell others about the wonders she has received from Christ. Mechthild's text had been called by Henry of Nördlingen "the best book on divine love in the German language."[103] Henry had sent the book to Maria Medingen and it may have been Henry who sent it to Engelthal. He had either translated or had others translate the text of Mechthild's work into a High German that the nuns of Southern Germany would understand.[104] This is the only extant version—the original written in Low German dialect presumably no longer exists.

If Margarete Weinhandl's claim that Mechthild of Magdeburg influenced the thought, images, and vocabulary of all Middle and South German mystics rings true, then this certainly applies to the mystic writers of Engelthal.[105] In 1878, Philipp Strauch noted five instances of concurrence in narrative detail, imagery, and vocabulary between Mechthild's *The Flowing Light of the Godhead* and Adelheid's *Revelations*. More recently, in 1980 Siegfried Ringler has also emphasized the importance of the mystic of Magdeburg on the spirituality of the monastery at Engelthal, especially with regard to Christina Ebner, Friedrich Sunder, and Adelheid Langmann. The bridge between Mechthild and the nuns of Engelthal was Henry of Nördlingen. Speaking for himself and for his collaborators at Basel, Henry wrote, "It [the manuscript] was given to us in a very strange kind of German so that we had to spend two years of sweat and effort before we could put it into our German."[106] Mechthild's book survives only in Henry's translation.[107] As translator, Henry was so thoroughly familiar with the text that when he corresponded with Margaret Ebner he interspersed "lengthy quotes from Mechthild of Magdeburg's *The Flowing Light of the Godhead*" without identifying his source.[108] From his self-imposed exile in Basel, Henry also sent the nuns of Maria Medingen a copy of Mechthild's book and highly recommending the text to Margaret and also wishing a copy to be sent to the nuns of Engelthal.[109] Using Mechthild's text, Margaret would find help in understanding her mystical experiences. Henry also mentioned this book as belonging to the monastery of Kaisheim, the prior of which conducted correspondence with Adelheid Langmann.[110] It is known that he also corresponded with Christina Ebner of Engelthal.[111] Acquaintance and correspondence among various nuns, including Christina and Margaret Ebner, seems evident, since Henry mentioned friendship between them and directed Margaret to write to Christina, although no letter between them is extant.[112] Henry visited Engelthal for at least three weeks in 1351, as Christina's own words record.[113] He probably had the same kind of connection with that monastery as he had with Maria Medingen, being well known throughout southern Germany for his preaching and spiritual direction.[114] According to this external evidence, Mechthild of Magdeburg's *The Flowing Light of the Godhead* influenced writers of Engelthal through the connection with Henry of Nördlingen, Ulrich of Kaisheim, the nuns of Maria Medingen, and the Friends of God in Basel.

Internal textual evidence likewise supports the claim that such influence existed. Christina Ebner explicitly mentions Mechthild's work by title.[115] Further evidence consists principally in various common episodes, imagery, and vocabulary. Strauch pointed out a connection with regard to Adelheid's vision of the Christ Child and the host during the celebration of Mass and similar accounts in Christina Ebner's *Revelations* and Mechthild's book.[116] Adelheid reports her vision:

> [D]uring the Gospel Our Lord appeared on the altar in the form of a little child. He jumped down and ran over to all his friends and consoled them. When the priest began the preface, the child jumped back upon the altar and as the priest elevated the host, the child was changed into the host, but when he should receive the host, the host changed back into a child who resisted with his hands and feet. But when he received the host, his heart became as bright as the sun and the child played within him. When the priest gave the blessing, the child leapt over to the sister and grew larger to about the age of four and embraced her and kissed her and then ran over to the altar and back again and embraced and kissed her once again.[117]

Mechthild reports a similar incident when a priest was celebrating Mass: "When he took the white host into his hands, the same lamb which had been standing on the altar arose and, when he said the words and made the gestures it changed into the host and the host became the lamb, so that I no longer saw the host, but only a bleeding lamb hanging from a bloody cross."[118] Visions of the Child Jesus in the host at Mass are probably the most frequent type of vision in the Sister-Books. However, no such vision is reported in the *Sister-Book of Engelthal*. In the *Gnaden-vita of Friedrich Sunder, Chaplain of Engelthal*, such a eucharistic vision occurs only once in the passages about Gertrud of Engelthal, not about Friedrich himself.[119] Christina Ebner also has visions of the Child Jesus: "She saw Brother Friedrich, the chaplain, saying Mass at the altar . . . and when he had consecrated . . . he [the Christ Child] appeared to her in the form of a child and he was unutterably beautiful."[120] She had this vision even though Friedrich was celebrating Mass not at Engelthal but in a filial chapel at Offenhausen. In 1344, Christina records a similar vision: "That same year on St. Remigius Day during the Mass the same sister was sitting in the back of the choir and when the preface was begun Our Lord appeared to her like a little child and ran toward the front and out of the choir to her and stood before the bench and sat on it."[121] Eventually he lies down in her lap until the consecration. Christina also reports a vision of the Child elsewhere: "On Monday in Passion Week a Preacher was saying Mass in the choir. When the priest elevated the host in his hands, she saw His loving face and then He changed Himself into the form of a little child and was wrapped in a white towel . . . She often saw this vision in the sacrament."[122]

Such visions are common to Mechthild, Christina, Adelheid, and Gertrud of Engelthal. Although this is such a frequent occurrence in the mystical literature of the late Middle Ages, it does not necessarily prove any dependence; it does show, however, that all of them shared a common belief in the true presence of Christ in the Eucharist and that they shared similar mystical visions attendant upon that belief.

Strauch also noted that according to Dionysius the Carthusian in his *Colloquium sive Dialogus de partuclari iudicio animarum post morten* (1614), Mechthild of Magdeburg shared in the belief that there were souls in purgatory who had completed their penance but who nonetheless remained in purgatory. Mechthild wrote of three heavens, the second of which may correspond to Adelheid's experience: "There she [Adelheid] was also led to those souls who had already done penance for everything but still did not yet see God. . . . They had no other pain except that they could not yet see God.[123] Mechthild reports a similar set of circumstances: "The second heaven is made from the holy longing of the senses and from the first degree of love. In this heaven there is no light, and the soul cannot see God. She tastes an ineffable sweetness which flows through all parts of her body."[124] Margarete Weinhandl also compares Adelheid's vision of purgatory with that of Mechthild's.[125] Adelheid's is less descriptive, concerned only with the uppermost part of that place of punishment, where souls had already done penance but were denied the sight of God. Adelheid experiences their pain and describes it as an unquenchable thirst for God, for the vision of God and for the one Hail Mary necessary to deliver these souls into God's presence. With Mechthild this description is more detailed: "After that, with help and patient endurance of suffering, they overcome all need, that is, they come so near to Heaven that they have all joys. Only three kinds of joy do they not yet possess: they cannot yet see God, they have not yet received their glory, and have not yet been crowned.[126]

Strauch notes as well the formulaic use of a phrase from the anonymous poem "Du bist min, ich bin din" ('You are mine, I am yours'). Adelheid writes, ". . . you are mine and I am yours. We are united and shall remain united forever."[127] Mechthild expresses the same sentiments when she writes, "I am in you and you are in Me."[128] This same formula occurs in the

Gnaden-vita of Friedrich Sunder in a rhymed passage: "You are mine, as I am yours: and that should always be between you and me in my heavenly kingdom."[129]

Similar expressions for the computation of time appear in Mechthild and in the writings of Engelthal. Both Mechthild and Adelheid measure time according the length of a prayer. "Truly I cannot bear to think about it for as long as it takes to recite the Hail Mary."[130] Adelheid spoke of a period of silence lasting the length of 50 *Ave Marias*.[131]

Other passages from Mechthild, not previously noted by scholars, also find a resonance in Adelheid's autobiography. Book three, chapter one of *The Flowing Light of the Godhead* bears a striking similarity in some details to the episode Adelheid describes when she is accompanied by Spes and Caritas to meet Christ on the bridal bed of mystical union. In Mechthild two angels accompany the soul to bring her home. Despite still being "clothed with the dark earth," she [the soul] wishes to ascend to her love.[132] The two angels "take the soul between them and lead her joyfully away."[133] When she arrives in the land of the angels, her Beloved, "looked into her face. Note how she was kissed there. With this kiss she was raised to the highest heights above all the choirs of angels."[134] In Adelheid's vision, illness weighs her down when the two virgins/virtues, Spes and Caritas, come to her and ask why she is so ill. Like Mechthild's "soul," she yearns for her Beloved but fears that he will not come to her because of the heaviness of her sins.[135] The two virgins/virtues sing the praises of Christ's merciful love and encourage Adelheid to make the journey to meet the Beloved. After she falters twice, the virtues entice her by asking her to meditate upon the beauty of the face of her Beloved. They conclude their argument by saying, "All that is beautiful in heaven and on earth is nothing when compared to his beauty. Joy beyond all joys have those who look upon him forever."[136] Finally they bring her to the dwelling place of the Beloved, described in terms similar to those used to describe the heavenly Jerusalem. The Beloved approaches her bed. His beautiful face gazes into hers so that it seems to her that her "soul would dissolve from true love."[137] The high point of the visionary encounter shows Christ gazing into Adelheid's eyes and this meeting of the eyes transforms her.

Mechthild and the writers of Engelthal give prominence to the role of the Trinity in their works, more so than most of their contemporaries. Ringler has already noted instances in which the Trinity plays an important role in the *Sister-Book* and the three persons often combine into one.[138] Similar passages also occur in Adelheid Langmann.[139] Christina Ebner presents the same process in terms of three lights being united into one.[140] With regard to the characteristics and activities of God, there are also correspondences between Mechthild, Adelheid, and Christina. In Book three, chapter one of *The Flowing Light of the Godhead*, Mechthild describes the union of the three persons in the following passage: "Above on the throne one sees the mirror of the divinity, the image of the humanity, the light of the Holy Spirit and confesses how the three are one God and how they fit into one.[141] Adelheid also includes passages concerning the relations of the Trinity: "I, the Father, love you and so does the Son, who proceeded from my heart and yet remains forever with me, and also the Holy Spirit, who flowed out from both of us and who remains eternally in us."[142] Also after having a vision of Christ in a tree, Adelheid receives the following interpretation from Christ: "'The tree that you saw is the Father in heaven and that you saw me in the tree means that I am in the Father and he is in me. The fire that you saw that encircled all the branches of the tree means that the Holy Spirit is in both of us. However that may be: no mind on earth can grasp or ponder that.'"[143] Friedrich Sunder also writes of the Trinitarian relations in regard to the soul while praying in his usual way: "'Father, you are the source of all graces, that you give to me and have given to me. For that reason I praise you eternally.' Then the Father said, 'Yes, that is true. I am the source. But from me flow two others into the valley of your heart. By which you also have received consolation and grace every day . . .'"[144] The Father goes on to explain: "'See the two . . . that flow from me are my holy Son and my Holy Spirit.'"[145] These quotations show a concern to explain and understand the doctrine of the Trinity and to clarify the relations among the persons with regard to humans and the process of conversion. They do not show concretely any explicit borrowing from Mechthild's writings, but they do demonstrate a common concern about the workings of the Trinity within and *ad extra* for the benefit of the human person.

Sharing a common spiritual world view, Mechthild and the writers of Engelthal make use of the same images and vocabulary to express various aspects of the relationship between God and an individual human being. Margot Schmidt lists seven metaphors for the *unio mystica* in Mechthild's writings, five of which also find expression in the writings from Engelthal: sweet sleep, wine imagery, dance, music and *jubilus*.[146] Among these are the importance of the wine cellar as a mystic symbol and the corresponding description of the drunkenness of Christ or the Bride to indicate an intense spiritual experience that finds expression in the works.[147] In Mechthild, "the bride is made drunk by seeing the noble face."[148] Christina Ebner also employs this vocabulary in similar circumstances: "On the Epiphany when she received Our Lord, he said, 'My great love has set yours on fire. From my outflow you have become drunk.'"[149]

Many other points of similarity between Mechthild and the Engelthal writers, especially Adelheid and Christina, need to be investigated further. Both Adelheid and Mechthild use clothing symbolism connecting various virtues with colored garments, crowns, or jewels. Adelheid, Mechthild, and Christina write frequently of the nine choirs of angels.[150] A more detailed research into the similarities between Mechthild and Adelheid's works also includes the image of flowing from the Trinity, lovesickness, flower/tree symbolism, the wounds of Christ, the kiss, and the *Gnadenfrucht topos*, in which the mystic is promised deliverance of a certain number of souls from purgatory or strengthening in faith for lukewarm souls or confirmation in faith for those who already believe strongly.

THE SONG OF THE DAUGHTER OF ZION

The source of the many texts that bear this name is a brief Latin prose original entitled *Filia Syon*.[151] Many medieval German versions of an original Latin text from the early thirteenth century circulated among mystics and monastics in the fourteenth century.[152] Lamprecht of Regensburg composed a lengthier text in German verse, using the Latin text as a source, but creatively adding more details to the storyline and inserting interpretations into the text.[153] A further German rhymed version known as the "alemannic" enjoyed popularity in southern Germany.[154] Still other German prose versions complicate the matter of which version influenced the writers of Engelthal.[155] The Library Catalogue of Engelthal does not help in this matter, for it simply lists a work entitled "A Little Book about the Daughter of Zion" (*Ein puchlein von der tochter von Syon*).[156] The term *puchlein* may indicate one of the shorter prose versions, since Lamprecht's version extends to over 4,000 lines, considerably longer than the *Filia Syon* and texts such as the *Tochter von Syon* (Cgm 29).

The theme of all the versions of the of *The Song of the Daughter of Zion* is the union of the soul with God even in an earthly state. The text is allegorical, not personal, and seeks to show the reader the important elements that prepare for the union of the soul with God as well as to portray the union in bridal mystical images. With some variations among the three principle versions, the basic storyline follows this pattern: the soul is portrayed as suffering through longing for God. To the soul come allegorical figures, among whom are Fides, Spes, Caritas, Sapientia, and Oratio. Each figure personifies a virtue (faith, hope, love), a gift (wisdom), or an activity (prayer). Fides and Spes awake the soul from her slumber. These virtues draw the soul onward to the goal of meeting and being united with the beloved. Without them no progress would be made, for the soul would simply pine away with lovesickness. Fides and Spes summon Sapientia, who in turn calls Caritas, who is accompanied by Oratio. These hunt the King of Glory and wound him with their darts of love. They bring four drops of his blood to the soul: With the first drop (*gratiae infusio*) the soul receives infused grace as a free gift which makes it possible for the soul to progress with proper will and desire toward the goal. The second drop (*Dei cognitio*) gives the soul knowledge of God and therefore knowledge of the goal to which she must direct herself. The third drop (*coeleste desiderium*) brings the soul yearning for heaven and the things of heaven. The fourth drop of blood (*spirituale gaudium*) transforms the soul with spiritual joy, making her ready for her nuptials. Prayer (Oratio) feels drunk from the accompanying sweetness and no longer knows whether she remains in her body or ascends into ecstasy. Under these conditions, the Bridegroom arrives as he promised to hold his Bride in the embrace of love, the ultimate symbol of union in love.

Scholars offer differing opinions as to which version influenced the writers at Engelthal. Karl Weinhold concludes that it is impossible to tell whether Lamprecht's version or the "alemmanic" version influenced Adelheid Langmann and Christina Ebner, since both versions include mirrors (mentioned by Christina Ebner) and the allegorical figures Fides and Spes (mentioned by Adelheid Langmann).[157] Philipp Strauch asserts that Lamprecht's text influenced Adelheid Langmann.[158] L. Wolff also concludes that Adelheid read Lamprecht's version while Christina relied on the "alemannic" because in it each of the virtues carries a mirror.[159] However, with regard to the writings about Friedrich Sunder, Siegfried Ringler asserts that there is no certainly identifiable influence of the "alemannic" *Tochter Syon* on Friedrich Sunder.[160] However, he also argues that there are concrete connections between Friedrich Sunder and Lamprecht's *Tochter Syon*.[161]

Some version of this text assuredly played an important role in the imaginative visionary world of the writers of Engelthal. It need not necessarily have been merely one version, despite the fact that the Library Catalogue of Engelthal of 1444 lists just one copy without specifying the author. It is listed among the German texts, noting only that there were other Latin texts in the monastery.[162] Theoretically the nuns could also have possessed a Latin version, but it is unlikely. The evidence that the writers of Engelthal knew Lamprecht's *Tochter Syon* is compelling. Ringler claims that there are four definite connections between Lamprecht and the book on Friedrich Sunder. The first of these is the appearance of the powers of the soul: *memoria, intelligentia, and voluntas* against the three enemies: *caro, mundus,* and *daemon*.[163] These sets of three are also associated with the persons of the Trinity. In a revelation to Friedrich Sunder, each person of the Trinity grants him gifts:

> "And I [the Father] will give you strength and power so that you will conquer your flesh and serve me as long as I wish." Then the holy Son said, "I will give you good sense and wisdom, so that you will be able to protect yourself from the false world . . ." Then the Holy spirit said: "I will give you goodness and patience and love and all virtues so that you will be victorious over all temptations from the evil spirit."[164]

The text from Lamprecht uses the Augustinian formulation applying *memoria, intelligentia,* and *voluntas* as powers of the Daughter of Zion to fight against the flesh, the world, and the devil.[165]

The second connection that Ringler sees has to do with the juxtaposition of the story of Jacob wrestling with the angel with the motif of *amor ligans et vulnerans*.[166] In the passage from the *Gnaden-vita*, Friedrich Sunder's soul wrestles with the Christ Child:

> "Often one sees how strongly you win out so that it seems there is no one who can match your strength. Now I want to see if I can overcome you." Then he fell upon the divine child and quickly pressed him against himself and said: "Non dimmittam te nisi benedixeris michi." Then the child said to his mother: "Mommy mine, help me for the soul has bound me fast to itself by its darts of love and will not let me go."[167]

Ultimately Friedrich's soul compels the Christ child to bless Friedrich, meaning in the context that he will take great delight in the Eucharist. A similar passage occurs in the text by Lamprecht: "She [Caritas] acted like Jacob who wrestled with an angel."[168] Caritas fought with God and compelled him to take on flesh and be born, to be crucified, to be buried, to be raised from the dead, and to ascend to heaven.[169] This image forcefully portrays the power of love to exert force over even God, a theme that will appear in Adelheid Langmann's *Revelations*, in which the motive of every act of God/Christ is love.[170] The compelling force of love also "imprisons" Christ so that he must do whatever the mystic wishes. To Christina Ebner, Christ proclaims, "out of love I am your prisoner and come willingly to you. I will crown you with my mercy and I am a conqueror of your senses."[171] Christ also sees himself in the role of captive in a revelation to Adelheid: "'You have captured me, just like a maiden who holds a young man captive in a lady's chamber and who knows well that if his friends were aware of it they would kill her and him.' And then the maiden said to him, 'Who has forced you to come in here?' So he answers, 'Your beauty has drawn me, maiden. And what has moved you to permit me to enter?' Then she said, 'It is the great love that I bear for you.' 'See, thus divine love and love for you compels me at all times.'"[172] A letter from Ulrich of Kaisheim shows the currency of such imagery when he writes to Adelheid giving advice:

> He lets you be hunted and driven toward him so that you will serve him more fervently. Just as without shame a bride falls upon her bridegroom, caresses his neck, embraces him, kisses him and presses against him—see, that is his intention. He adorns you and arrays you with flowers according to the delight of his own good pleasure. He plays a game of love with you yet never has enough.[173]

The third connection Ringler makes between Lamprecht's *Tochter Syon* and Friedrich Sunder has to do with a quote from Scripture that opens up an entire image system. "See, dear soul, when God your Lord comes to you, take him tenderly and lovingly in your arms and say to him, 'Veniat dilectus meus in ortum suum ut comedat fructus pomorum suorum.' Then he will embrace you and say, 'Ego veniam et cibabo te.'"[174] These same quotes occur in Lamprecht.[175] They derive from the Song of Solomon, 5:1: "Veniat dilectus meus in hortum suum, et comedat fructum pomorum suorum." This text also occurs in the *Filia Syon*: "Surgite, camus hinc et veniat dilectus meus in ortum suum ut pascatur in deliciis, donec aspiret dies gloriae et inclinientur umbrae miseriae."[176] It likewise appears in Cgm 29, but there it is the Daughter of Zion who is speaking and asking for what has previously been described as pertaining to Christ the Beloved:

> From her heartfelt meditations this was often said: "Come to me in the garden of my soul, my faithful one, my dearly beloved, creator of all the world, through whom my heart is wounded. Be pleased with this and make my reason to green and from your graciousness let all kinds of flowers grow, especially violets and lilies and fragrant roses: that is humility, purity and divine love. And stay within until I accomplish the goal of my life by destroying the shadow of this world totally so that afterward the eternal light, Jesus Christ, the spouse of every believing soul, will shine on me.[177]

This image shows up in all the versions of the *Tochter Syon* and in Friedrich Sunder and Adelheid Langmann. In one account Adelheid employs the same images and vocabulary from the perspective of Christ, who says to her: "I will lead my Love into the garden of love and will show her the fruit on my love and will make her a wreath of white lilies from my divine and human purity and will crown my Love and set upon her head a crown of diverse fruits. This means I will give you a share in the love of the patriarchs, the prophets, the twelve apostles, the martyrs, the confessors and the virgins."[178] The flower imagery also appears in Christ's address to her: "Your mouth smells of roses and your body of violets. You are altogether beautiful for nothing is lacking in you."[179] The use of such images suggests a familiarity with a complexus of texts—The Song of Solomon, the various versions of *The Song of the Daughter of Zion*, the writings of Mechthild, and the sermons of Bernard of Clairvaux.

It is not surprising to find similar references in the works of and about Christina Ebner. In her autobiography she specifically mentions reading the book *Tochter von Syon* and consulting it to help her understand a revelation about mirrors.[180]

The fourth connection Ringler shows is the use of the personifications of Fides, Spes, and Caritas. He is concerned primarily with their use in the *Gnaden-vita of Friedrich Sunder*. In this work Fides, Spes, and Caritas appear not as allegorical figures but as visions of actual saints. A holy virgin appears to Sister Gertrud and complains that while Gertrud reveres many virgins, she does not revere the virgin in this apparition. Gertrud has no idea who she is and asks her name. "I was the daughter of king on earth and I was called Caritas and I suffered a great martyrdom at the hands of my own people because I did not want to return to the world."[181] In the course of the account of Sister Gertrud's experiences, Fides and Spes also appear. All three virgins are presented as authentic martyrs with assigned feast days. Only at the conclusion is there any hint of a symbolic meaning attached to these three figures: "Whoever praises and honors the three virgins and their names, takes on the three virtues: love, faith and hope."[182] These three saints were venerated in the Middle Ages, especially in Alsace.[183] In the literature of Engelthal these three figures do not seem to be the same as the three saints Fides, Caritas, and Spes in the *Legenda aurea*, an observation that leads Ringler to conclude that that text was unknown to the writers at Engelthal.[184] Ringler also concludes that the use of these three names in both Friedrich Sunder and in Adelheid Langmann's *Revelations* suggests a common source, which he sees as Lamprecht's *Tochter Syon*.[185]

Far more compelling is Adelheid's use of Fides, Spes, and Caritas, for she uses them in the same explicitly allegorical sense in which they appear in the three versions of the *Daughter of Zion*. A comparison of the texts makes it clear that Adelheid knew at least one version and incorporated its teachings, imagery, and plot into her own personalized account via her creative, imaginative visionary experience. Adelheid does not produce a new version of the *Daughter of Zion*, but she does show the reader her appropriation of the text into personal mystical experiences, as, for example, in her account of her *unio mystica*.

Adelheid reports her experience during Advent, when she was so filled with sweetness and grace that she has to be helped to her cell by her sisters. She records: "And when they had laid her down there she went into ecstasy and it was so painful because of her yearning for her beloved dear Jesus Christ, it seemed that her heart would burst into pieces because of true love for him."[186] Adelheid does not suffer in the same way as the Daughter of Zion. The Daughter yearns to find someone worthy of her love, whereas Adelheid already knows who the object of her love is. Both yearn for love, but only Adelheid specifies the object of love. Both the Daughter and Adelheid are in distress, sick from love and shocked into an inability to do anything. Precisely at that moment, two virgins—Spes and Caritas—come to Adelheid's aid, while Faith and Hope visit the Daughter. In the *Filia Syon* and in Lamprecht's version, Fides and Spes come to the Daughter's assistance. The Daughter is drawn to know the King of Glory by Faith and Hope because she does not yet know to whom she should offer the love of her heart. Adelheid (unlike Gertrud) recognizes the two virgins. She is already yearning for her Beloved, Jesus Christ, and has no need of Faith's ministrations. She will be guided by Hope and especially by Love, which should be no surprise given Adelheid's firm conviction that love is the motive for every act of God and Christ. Both sets of virgins ask why Adelheid or the Daughter is sick. Adelheid responds,

> "I am yearning for him who is Lord of all lords and God of all gods, for my only beloved Love, Jesus Christ. If he does not come to me I must die. I am afraid that he will not come to me and that he does not desire me for his wife because I have angered him much all my days. My sins are so great because I have never been concerned for one hour with his praise, and my heart and my soul desire him and call out to him when I fear he does not want to come to me. Therefore I must die of painful longing for him.[187]

The Daughter does not possess the self-awareness or the spiritual maturity exhibited by Adelheid. Faith and Hope instruct the Daughter, admonishing her to raise up the desire of her heart. After hearing their instructions to the Daughter, the author says of her: "When this lady, the Daughter of Zion . . . comprehended that there was nothing in the heavens or on earth in which her heart could find a home in burning love, she said yearningly with tears as if she had been just awakened from a dream, 'O dear virgins, who gives me wings as the dove that I may come up to the heights of heaven and recognize the Eternal and sink my heart into it?"[188] The virgins Fides and Spes give her Sapientia. Wisdom will be the wings of the dove to bear her up. She will instruct the Daughter in the right path. In response to Adelheid's speech, Caritas admonishes her not to think ill of herself but to think rather about her Beloved. Caritas then discourses at length about Love: "Think how rich, how high, how noble he is and how full of love he is."[189] Caritas rehearses every moment of salvation history under the motivation of divine love and concludes, "Love him and trust him and you will see him."[190] Hearing such speech, Adelheid becomes strong and can lift herself up from the bed to set off on her journey. To the Daughter, Sapientia discourses about Wisdom as the motivating force in creation and throughout salvation history. However, Sapientia also begins to speak of love:

> Since you have thought what you wish to love so you should know, it is an eternal one to whom no one is equal. He is already rich and mild, powerful and mighty above all children of men. Would you like to have him in the love of your heart? He is much more than you, but him you should acknowledge and love, because he loved you so much that he shed his blood for your sake and thereby purified you of all impurity.[191]

Sapientia sends for Caritas, and when she arrives there is silence for almost a half hour out of reverence for the queen of all virtues. In both accounts Love has enormous power over the Daughter/Adelheid as well as over God and Christ. In both it is Love who has the power to accomplish the union of the Lover and the Beloved.

At this point in all the accounts, the two virgins support the Daughter or Adelheid physically to set off on the journey of union. Adelheid is amazed at the great number of people who have gone before her on this journey.[192] In the *Tochter Syon* the Daughter faints three times from weariness. Here in *Revelations* Adelheid faints as well. Spes and Caritas remind Adelheid of the strength of her Beloved:

> No dear Lady, stand up straight and carry on. Remember the strength of the Lord to whom we want to lead you. He is so strong that

everything that lives in heaven and on earth has its strength, possessions and life from him. He is so powerful that no one is able to defy
his might. In a brief time he created the heavens and also the earth. He
is so wise that his wisdom ordered all things wisely. He is so good that
he lowers himself to many great sinners out of his goodness. He is so
rich that all in heaven and on earth is his. Therefore conduct yourself
well and stand up straight. There is nothing lacking in the Lord. To
him we wish to lead you so that you will look upon him as your
Beloved."[193]

The virgins appeal to the strength of the Beloved in order to strengthen
Adelheid and sustain her on the difficult journey to meet him. The Daughter
of Zion likewise receives assistance from the one whom she loves; however,
she receives this help by the actions and aggression of Love (Caritas) and
Contemplative Prayer (Oratio), who shoot arrows at the King of Glory,
wounding him in the heart. They return to the Daughter to strengthen her
with the four drops of blood from the side of the King: divine grace, godly
knowledge, heavenly desire, and divine joy.[194] In both cases the source of
strength and the power to carry on come from the Beloved with the help of
the virgins.

When the virgins conduct Adelheid to the place where the Lord
dwells, she loses her strength once again and begins to doubt Caritas and
Spes. This time they seek to revive her by dwelling on the beauty of the
Beloved.

Think of the beauty of his face. His face is a thousand times more
beautiful than the sun. Just as lighting comes down from the sky so rays
of light shine forth from his face. His beauty is beyond all human beauty
. . . Joy beyond all joys have all those who look upon him forever.[195]

This passage resembles portions of the text from Lamprecht's *Tochter Syon*,
in which Minne describes the Beloved as "brilliantly shining" with a "face
that is full of graces" so that he is described as the "Eternal Light."[196] When
the virgins return to the Daughter (Cgm 29), they describe the Beloved in
very similar terms but in less detail. Caritas tells her that he has the "brilliance
of eternal Light" and his gaze is "full of all graces." That description and the
four drops of blood strengthen the Daughter and prepare her for the final
phase of her journey. For her, all fear and desire for earthly things are
dispelled. When she reaches him, she kisses him on the mouth and her heart
is set afire with his love. She cries out, "My soul, my heart should be with

you in eternal nuptials until I am completely united with my beloved spouse."[197] As described above, the Daughter is so transformed that she is detached from all earthly things, ponders nothing passable, becomes pure, and has a clean conscience. Her love is expressed in terms from the Song of Solomon, for her Beloved is to come into the garden of her heart, wound her with his love, and give her humility, purity, and divine love as symbolized by violets, lilies, and roses. The Eternal Light is to shine in her. In Lamprecht's *Tochter Syon*, the virgins encourage the Daughter toward union until she too loses all fear, approaches her Bridegroom, embraces him and presses him against her heart, and kisses him again and again.[198]

Meanwhile, Adelheid approaches the city of the Beloved and describes the city in magnificent detail, making it the new and heavenly Jerusalem where the Lord dwells and by his brightness lights up the entire city. Adelheid dwells on the Lord's retinue and comments on those who are still so far away from him. Unlike the Daughter of Zion who advances toward the Bridegroom, here the Lord approaches Adelheid's bed in all his joyous beauty and pronounces, "My Beloved!" Adelheid describes her reaction:

> "With that same word that so sweetly came out from his mouth he drew my poor, sinful soul into his Godhead and I can say nothing about this vision except to say that it began when they had begun to sing compline and continued until the next day as Mass was being sung. And when I had come to myself I was not able to pray a single *Ave Maria* because of the love in my heart.[199]

This passage bears a striking resemblance to several verses in Lamprecht. After writing of the "kiss," Lamprecht continues: "The spirit draws the breath through the mouth, that is well known. Whoever then draws close to God, his spirit takes the breath that comes forth from his mouth . . ."[200]

It becomes clear with the analysis of these documents that we can speak of some important links of the texts of Engelthal with other key source texts. The analysis shows definite interdependence of the texts, not only those written at Engelthal but also their source material coming from Scripture, the liturgy, the *St. Trutperter Song of Songs*, Bernard's sermons, Mechthild's *The Flowing Light of the Godhead*, and the various versions of *The Song of the Daughter of Zion*. Such a complexus of interdependent texts along the lines of vocabulary, images, themes, and theological perspective is the hallmark of a monastic rather than scholastic approach to spirituality. One could argue that each of these texts reflects the revelation of God to an individual and that God has chosen to be revealed in different times and place in ways so similar that the texts discussed are all bound together by that common revelation. It would be reasonable then to expect the texts to be similar in theme, mode of expression, and other details. On the other hand, the writers of Engelthal did know these many literary source texts, and to notice similarities among the texts would reflect a common spiritual outlook produced by dependence upon similar received sources. In either case, what we have is a common and consistent teaching on spirituality—the relationship between God/Christ and the mystic—that seeks to express the inexpressible by resorting to bridal mystic imagery and vocabulary to convey what happens when the human experiences the divine immediately.

THE ELEMENTS
OF ENGELTHAL SPIRITUALITY

THE ELEMENTS OF A SPIRITUALITY of Engelthal are derived from the six texts produced at Engelthal along with the various sources that formed those texts: the Bible, the Dominican Constitutions, the liturgical texts, the interpretations of the mystical life such as the *St. Trutperter Song of Songs,* the sermons of Bernard of Clairvaux, Mechthild's *The Flowing Light of the Godhead,* and the several versions of *The Song of the Daughter of Zion.* The most important elements of the spirituality express a theology of salvation history, for the writers of Engelthal stress the role and importance of the Trinity; the images of Christ as Child, Lover and Lord; the progressive levels of "being chosen" by God; the importance of the eucharist and the teaching on the divine indwelling. The omnipresence of the Three Persons of the Trinity in relation to each other and in relation to their roles in the sanctification and perfection of the mystic takes a prominent position in the writings and the spirituality of Engelthal. Unlike the popular devotion of their contemporaries who so stressed the role of Christ in his image as crucified Savior suffering for the sins of the world, the mystics and writers of Engelthal, while not ignoring the passion of Christ, understand it as only one part of salvation history and as one action of one person. The inner life of the Trinity fascinates the mystics of Engelthal and forms their visionary imagination to see how the Triune God comes into immediate contact with a chosen human being. The author of the union between God and the nun is Christ, who is portrayed in his roles as Child, Lover, and powerful Lord. At times the mystic is drawn to contemplate and relate to Christ as a child, at other times as a Lover who comes to console or as mighty Lord, the Lord of time and all history. The mystics understand themselves to be called into a special relationship with Christ regardless of how that relationship is imaged. Just as Christ fulfills the Old Testament prophecies, so mystics of the New Testament see themselves as "fulfilling" the great men and women of the past and even surpassing them in Divine favor. The mystics of Engelthal surpass Moses, Esther, the apostles, and Paul. Divine favor draws the mystic into union with the Trinity by being united with Christ. Such moments of union are variously conceived in starkly erotic images. The divine indwelling takes prominence over other, more conventional, images used to express the abiding presence of Christ in the soul. Finally the *Gnadenfrucht Topos* is central to an understanding of the call to mission necessarily entailed by the act of being chosen and united to Christ.

These elements help to define the spirituality of Engelthal as expressing a mysticism of human perfection leading to union with the divine for the benefit of not only the mystic but for others whom the mystic helps by her intercessory power. These characteristics define the basis of the spirituality of Engelthal but do not exhaust its description.

THE TRINITY

"In the Name of the Father and of the Son and of the Holy Spirit," Adelheid Langmann begins her *Revelations*. Numerous other formulaic references to the Trinity occur frequently throughout the writings of Engelthal. One of the most remarkable aspects of the spirituality expressed in them is the predominance of the Trinity in the revelations and imagery. This emphasis on the central dogma of the Christian faith came into the spirituality and the writings of the mystics of Engelthal from the liturgy, but its meaning depends upon their connection with Dominican teachings, especially with those of St. Thomas Aquinas. This claim remains speculative in the absence of any direct quote or reference either internally or externally to the teachings of Aquinas. However, it seems likely that the emphasis on the Trinity developed through contact with Dominican Preachers inspired by the teachings on the Trinity found particularly in Aquinas's *Summa Theologiae* and *Summa contra Gentes*, among other works. The friars certainly studied these texts and the *Summa Theologiæ* was available to the nuns in German translation.[1] Writing about the text of Friedrich Sunder, Siegfried Ringler makes the claim that although it is clear that Friedrich knew about the important areas of speculation with regard to the Trinity, such as the ideas of emanation and the inner Trinitarian relations, he is not really interested in them.[2] None of the texts produced at Engelthal were intended to teach any theological point. The writers intended no textbook on theology; nevertheless, they produced texts rich in theological import. In all probability the training in preaching and teaching of the friars included the teachings of Thomas as a primary source, and the nuns would have received teachings and listened to homilies colored by Thomistic thought.

Certain themes common to the teachings of St. Thomas and the mystical experiences reported by the writers of Engelthal can be noted. In reading other portions of this book (*The Mystics of Engelthal: Writings from a Medieval Monastery*), it becomes clear that many doctrines discussed elsewhere in the writings of Engelthal coincide with teachings passed on by Thomas Aquinas. Among these is the belief that the human and divine may be united and that the Trinity can indwell in the souls of the just. In his treatment of the missions of the Trinity, Aquinas teaches that "The gift of grace, therefore, empowers the intelligent being not only to have this created gift at his ready disposal, but also for loving union with the divine person."[3] And further he explains that "grace prepares the soul to possess the divine person."[4] Writing on this very issue, T. C. O'Brien asserts that for Aquinas, "the exaltedness of grace is that it brings about an unmediated union with the divine."[5] This teaching Aquinas also uses in his *Commentary on the Sentences*: "By grace we are conjoined to God himself and not merely through the mediacy of some creature."[6] The strength of this tradition and the belief in the indwelling made a lasting impression on the mystics of Engelthal; it is believed by all the writers, and their mystic experiences bear out the reality of the belief.

From whatever sources the writers of Engelthal took their theology and imagery for the Trinity, they refer to the Trinity more frequently than other nonscholastic writers in the fourteenth century. The nuns invoked the Trinity in liturgical formulae used every day, such as that of Adelheid Langmann above. They employ Trinitarian hymns such as the *Te Deum laudamus* as inspiring texts. Adelheid Langmann refers to the antiphon to the Magnificat for the Feast of the Holy Trinity: *Te Deum Patrem ingenitum, te Filium unigenitum, te Spiritus Sanctum paraclitum, sanctam et individuum Trinitatem, toto corde et ore confitemur, lausdamus atque benedicimus: tibi gloria in saecula.*[7] Christina Ebner writes that she loves the Mass of the Holy Trinity, which the nuns seem to have celebrated on days other than the feast day.[8] Ceremonial references to the Trinity are too numerous to cite. The writers also record Trinitarian visions associated with the Feast of the Holy Trinity. Their visions sometimes reflect the artistic representations of the Trinity prevalent in their day. Christina records a vision whose basis may be in artwork prevalent at the time:

Then she saw in the vision of God the heavenly Father sitting resplen-
dent in majesty and she saw a white dove lying on the Father's chest
and it had spread wide its wings. Thus it covered over his heart and
breast and clung to him. After that the dove disappeared and a clear-
burning fire appeared in the same size and manner as the dove before
and it covered the same place—his heart and chest as the dove had
covered before. She saw the Only Begotten Son was sitting at the
Father's right attired in purple dress and she saw his five wounds
transfigured on him.[9]

Certain images appear in the writings that reflect the belief in the
mystery of monotheism with a God of Three Persons. About Anna Vorchtel
of Nuremberg, Christina Ebner writes:

. . . three lords appeared to her and around the three was but one
heavenly garment so that they appeared as one person. With this he
[Christ] showed her his Trinity and poured into her the flow of divine
sweetness that lasted for thirty days in her heart.[10]

Anna of Weitersdorf also reports a vision of the Trinity in similar terms:
"When Bishop Nicholas of Regensburg wanted to give us Our Lord, I saw
that at the door leading into choir, three lords entered before him and then
the three became one lord."[11] Anna explains her understanding of this
vision as an illustration and assertion of belief in the Threeness and
Oneness of God.[12] That yet a third account of this type of vision appears
in the *Sister-Book* underscores its importance. Christina writes that the
principle characteristic of Sister Liutgard of Berg is her devotion to the
Trinity. "She read about the Holy Trinity every day during the times for
prayer.[13] Liutgard's devotion to the Trinity shows itself also at the moment
of her death. "At her dying, she revealed to her sisters: 'The Holy Trinity
appeared to me as three beautiful lords. They were so alike that if one [of
them] went away one would not be able to tell which it was.'"[14] Christina
confirms this in her concluding comments about Liutgard's final vision of
the Three Persons. "But she knew them well and pointed to each one
present to her at the moment of her death."[15]
    In other visions Christina learns the identity, roles, or functions of
each person. During the Mass of the Holy Trinity, Christina receives a
revelation that the Father is the basis of security, the Son is the advocate,
and the Spirit supports and upholds all.[16] In a vision associated with the
Church festival at Engelthal, Christina identifies the Father with power. He

will give power and strength to all those attending the festival either now or at their time of death. The Son gives wisdom to each participant. The Holy Spirit offers each one loving kindness by promising to give sweetness and consolation to mortal sinners and to believers alike.[17] And in a similar vision Christina witnesses Christ performing his role as advocate. She sees him standing before the Father with his arms outstretched in the form of a cross saying to the Father, "I remind you that I opened my arms on the cross in holy obedience and I ask you to give grace to all who come to this monastery today."[18] In response to this request, the Father promises all graces, for "my mercy compels me to do this."[19] The identity of each Person is linked to a function and a gift, each of which has the purpose of saving men and women.

The Trinity is portrayed also in reference to the mystic. For example all three Persons of the Trinity attend Friedrich Sunder's Mass. "Whenever there was a great feast, the Holy Father came with his heavenly host, the Holy Son came with his and the Holy Spirit with his."[20] When, in a vision, St. Dominic and St. Louis wish to obtain good things for Friedrich, the Trinity holds council and each Person provides a gift to him:

> Then the Father placed the soul before him and said, "You will be an eternal king in heaven, in the Name of the Father and of the Son and of the Holy Spirit. And I will give you strength and power to overcome the flesh and to serve me as long as I wish." Then the Holy Son said, "And I will give you good sense and wisdom so that you will be able to protect yourself from the false world and against as many arrows as the people shoot." Then the Holy Sprit said, "I will give you goodness, patience, love and all virtues so that you will be able to conquer the temptations of all the evil spirits."[21]

Friedrich asks the Virgin Mary to intercede for him before the Trinity because he has sinned. The Persons of the Trinity each agree to have Mary as the judge in what quickly resembles a trial scene. Each Person complains about Friedrich in turn. Ultimately he must throw himself on the mercy of Mary before the accusations of the Trinity.[22] Mary intercedes for him yet again in 1326.[23] In 1328, the Father arranges a "spiritual Mardi gras" for Friedrich to which the three Persons and Mary come playing different roles.[24] The Persons of the Trinity in turn offer gifts to Christina Ebner. These gifts for the benefit of the mystic spring from the identity of each person. "The Father upholds you. The Son makes you glad. The Holy Spirit teaches you."[25] Christina reflects on the Trinity and concludes that the

Father has the power to make the impossible possible. To the Son he gives
this gift because the Son was obedient in his perfect life on earth. The Father
gives the Spirit his gifts because the Spirit is loving and mild. And these same
gifts, all that is impossible, the Father gives to his beloved on earth to make
what is impossible possible. Christina learns that she is one of those on earth
to whom the Father grants this gift.[26]

From the beginning Adelheid Langmann's spirituality was stamped
with a Trinitarian seal. Early in her monastic life she has a vision: "One time
on the Feast of the Holy Trinity during the *Agnus Dei* this sister prayed
fervently that Our Lord would come to her. Then Our Lord came and said,
'Peace be with you! I, the Father in heaven, love you.' Then the Son said, 'I
love you too!' And the Holy Spirit, "I, the true Godhead, love you!"' This
encounter with the Triune God shows to Adelheid the identity of the
persons and also their attitude of love for her. The vision is an invitation into
greater intimacy with God, an invitation that Adelheid will accept.

The image that conveys the Trinity to the believer, each of the Three
Divine Persons and the mystic, is the image of "flowing." All of creation flows
from the Father's heart. The Only Begotten Son proceeds from the Father
and their love flows out as the Holy Spirit. Christ as Word made Flesh and
in his presence in the Eucharist is the means by which grace flows into the
mystic and transforms her or him by the power of his grace. All of reality
receives the stamp of the Trinity. Christina Ebner receives a revelation in
which she learns that the Trinity operates in a "Trinitarian way."[27] All of
reality is based on the identity of God as Triune.

Two further visions illustrate the identity and mission of the Trinity.
Christina Ebner became ill but was made strong again by this vision:

> To the Father, Christ says, "From true love I said to you to send the
> Holy Spirit, the Consoler, to those whom I have won for you." Then
> the Eternal Father said to his Beloved Son, "What does the Holy Spirit
> say about it?" Then she [Christina] heard the voice of the Holy Spirit
> who said, "I go willingly . . . my ways are rich in grace and joy." And
> then the glory of these true revelations came to an end.[28]

Christ as advocate functions as the pivotal figure in this divine
council of the Three Persons. He has followed the Father's will and won
many souls for him. The motive for all his actions is love and precisely out
of love does he wish to have the Spirit, the Consoler, sent to the people.
The process of the indwelling on the part of the divine initiative is
explained here in terms of Thomistic doctrine. A stronger example of this

occurs in another vision of Christina in which the Three Persons are speaking about the Virgin Mary:

> Then, in my Fatherly heart, I formed the most beautiful image that has ever been and ever will be. And I asked my Only Begotten Son, without any coercion, whether he would want to born from her [Mary]. Then he answered me, "Beloved, faithful Father, I will gladly be born from her." Then I asked what the Holy Spirit had to say to that. Then the Holy Spirit answered me, "I will give her my seven gifts more than I have ever given them since I created heaven and earth or ever will give them to any human being. Then I saw that my works were good, but this is the best.[29]

Here everything in creation flows from the heart of the Father (*exitus*) and proceeds by divine providence and plan. The Father consults with the Son and the Spirit to further the plan with regard to Mary, but also with regard to all of salvation history. From the Spirit, Mary receives the seven gifts in their perfect form so that the perfect image created in the mind of the Father would be perfected in the flesh of the Virgin. With this vision Christina writes an icon of the operation of the Triune God in the life of the Virgin and in history. By analogy this icon and its teaching extend to the lives of all believers who are made in the image of God and who, by virtue of Christ's obedience, sacrifice and intercession, are able to receive the gifts of the Spirit and indeed the Spirit himself as a gift by the divine indwelling in the soul. The icon represents the reality of this teaching and proclaims its possibility for all.

IMAGES OF CHRIST: CHILD, LOVER, AND LORD

Diemut Ebner of Nuremberg meditates on the passion of Christ every day, and in her mystical visions of Christ his wounds are transformed into part of his glory rather than remaining real and horrible wounds.[30] In her vision of heaven, the wounds of Christ reveal the Trinity and are a source of joy to the heavenly hosts. Diemut's experience mirrors the dynamic of the writers and mystics of Engelthal, for while they read about, pondered, and celebrated liturgically the passion of Christ, their imaginative visionary world contained little room for the sufferings of Christ in comparison with other aspects of his life. Christina Ebner, when she had a vision of Christ's passion, was horrified. "On the next day after that when the priest raised up the host she saw him as he hung upon the cross and his mother and St. John were standing by him and she was very frightened by this."[31] But after the priest had received the host, "she saw his loving face . . . and he turned to both sides of choir and looked at them kindly."[32] Adelheid Langmann does not even include the passion of Christ in her *Prayer* which covers the scope of salvation history. Of all the mystics of Engelthal, Friedrich Sunder seems to have been the one who devoted a good deal of his meditation to the passion of Christ. He had five specific meditations on the crucifixion: "The first, that our Lord hung upon the cross with arms outstretched, the second that he was naked and uncovered, the third that he was crucified alone, the fourth that he was wounded, the fifth that he bowed his head."[33] When the writer goes on to describe precisely how Friedrich meditated upon each point, he shows that with each one Friedrich is transported into a mystical state. With the first meditation Friedrich is drawn into the divine Being, with the second into the divine power, the third into the divine heart, the fourth into divine love, and the fifth into the divine majesty. Also with each experience Friedrich acquires knowledge. In meditating upon Christ hanging on the cross with arms outstretched, he is drawn into the divine essence and learns that "he must order his life according to God's will more than he had before."[34] The next day while pondering Christ's nakedness, Friedrich is drawn into divine power and learns "that he must follow God more than he had done before."[35] While standing before a crucifix and thinking about Christ's isolation, he is drawn into the divine heart and receives the revelation that he has "certainty of eternal life."[36] On the fourth day he reflects on the wounds of Christ and the shedding of his blood and is drawn into divine love. From this experience Friedrich desires "to be shot with the ray of divine love so that his heart would be wounded and he would never be able to praise anyone again except God alone."[37] Finally when he thinks about Christ bowing his head, Friedrich is drawn into the divine majesty and loses all his strength, yet new strength is given him so that he will never do anything against God again.[38]

With each meditation Friedrich is rendered speechless and enters into a mystical state. The progression of the meditations over the period of five days also shows a progression in Friedrich's spiritual life and becomes an exemplar to the reader for entrance into the mystical life. In imitation of Christ's ultimate obedience to the Father's will on the cross, the believer must seek to order his or her life according to God's will. Friedrich connects the nakedness of Christ with his own lack of virtue (not clothed with virtues) and, lamenting this lack, has compassion for Christ whereby he learns to acquire virtues by following Christ's example. In pondering Christ's isolation on the cross, Friedrich desires that his heart and senses be moved to praise God alone, that is, to have no other gods in his life. As a result he enters into the divine heart for which he is given certitude of everlasting life, for his will is given and his actions and worship are performed in virtue of God alone. With the fourth meditation on the martyrdom of Christ Friedrich is initiated into the mystic state because he wishes to be united with Christ by love and because his praise, like the love of a spouse, is reserved for just one person. With the fifth meditation this mystic state is completed, for it is no longer Friedrich who lives but Christ who lives in him. This Christ is not the suffering Christ of Calvary but the glorified Christ reigning in majesty.

While realizing that the crucifixion of Jesus occupies a pivotal place in salvation history, the writers and mystics of Engelthal favor the images of Jesus as Child, Lover, and Lord when writing of their own visions. These three images nurture the spiritual life of the mystics of Engelthal and show their preference for relating to Christ under aspects other than crucifixion. All three images relate to the coming of Christ in history. As Child, the second person of the Trinity took on human flesh uniting the divine and human and making salvation for human beings possible. As Lover, Christ unites himself mystically with an individual soul, whether male or female. As glorified Lord, he returns to gather all who belong to him into one gift for the Father. Each case highlights the union of human and divine. This schema underlies the writings of Engelthal. Adelheid Langmann's understanding of Christ's identity was theologically astute. In her *Prayer* she writes about the Virgin's consent to become the Mother of God:

> I remind you, Lord, that when she spoke this word, you became true God and true Man in that hour in her womb, just as mighty, as good, and as powerful as you are in heaven and yet you became a little child, body and soul, God and Man together. I ask you, Lord, by that same love, to fill up my soul, my body and all my senses with the abundance of your mercy, of your divinity and of your humanity so that all my thoughts, my words, my deeds, my will and the way of my whole life be godly and always be pleasing in your sight.[39]

Here, too, the union of human and divine is reflected in the union of Adelheid and Christ by which she will become deified.

The visions of the Christ Child usually occur in connection with the celebration of the Eucharist. Perhaps the small size of the host suggests the small size of Christ as a youth. The prevalence of this connection for medieval nuns in particular has already been noted by many scholars.[40]

Writing on the nine extant Sister-Books, G. Lewis notes however that the childlike aspect of Christ is not exclusively a female concern, since many male authors wrote about the Child Jesus.[41] Siegfried Ringler asserts that the vision of the Christ Child in the host is probably the most frequent vision in the Sister-Books.[42] He categorizes these vision into four types, all of which occur in the visions of Engelthal: those associated with the liturgical feasts such as Christmas, those that show Christ as the Son of Mary, those that portray the Christ Child as playing with the soul, and those having to do with visions associated with the Eucharist.[43]

Adelheid Langmann records a vision during the singing of the *Gloria* at midnight Mass on Christmas in which the Virgin Mother carries her Son through the choir of Engelthal showing him to each of the nuns.[44] Another time at Christmas she sees "Our Lord in the form of a small child and he was the same size and form as when he was born from Our Lady and from his feet to his shoulder was only nine inches long. And he lay in her lap and was so beautiful and lovable that he could not have been more beautiful. And when she looked upon him and thought about what she should say to him and what she should ask for suddenly she saw him no more."[45] Advent and Christmastide seem to be favored times of meditation on and therefore of visions of the Christ Child. The Dominican nuns delighted in showing a statue of the Infant Jesus for veneration at Christmas. This artistic representation also gave impetus to their visionary experience.

During the Christmas vision of Adelheid Langmann, the Virgin Mother carries her Son specifically to Adelheid. "Our Lady placed herself in front of the sister and it seemed to this sister that her own heart opened up and Our Lady took her little Child and placed him in her heart. Then her heart closed up again and Our Lady made the sign of the cross over her heart saying, 'You will remain in this heart forever.'"[46] Mary is the agent of union between her Child and Adelheid for Christ now dwells in the nun's heart. Mary also plays a crucial role in the visionary and mystical experience of Friedrich Sunder. The Child Jesus asks her to make a bed strewn with beautiful flowers for him and Friedrich. On this bed, Mary "unites the holy soul" with Jesus and oversees the consummation of their mystical union.[47]

By extension, the divine Christ also plays with the soul, thus uniting the soul to himself and to the Trinity. In a revelation to Christina Ebner, she hears Christ say: "I play a game with you in my divinity."[48] The idea of Christ playing with her soul not only indicates union of the two but also predates Christina's earthly existence. "Before the beginning I played with you."[49] This same vocabulary appears also in Christina's *Sister-Book*.[50] The image of Christ playing with the soul also occurs in Adelheid Langmann's *Revelations*.

Ulrich of Kaisheim explains to her, "he plays a game of love with you and yet never has enough."[51]

Siegfried Ringler rightly asserts that "the appearance of the child in the host . . . is the pictorial expression for the presence of Christ in his supernatural existence."[52] In the *Gnaden-vita of Friedrich Sunder, Chaplain of Engelthal*, the author reports Gertrud of Engelthal's vision of the Christ Child in the host.[53] Toward the end of her autobiographical manuscript, Christina Ebner also reports such a vision: ". . . three times she saw our Lord in the form of a little child in the priest's hands. One time he was a small as the host, but the next time he was bigger than the host by the size of a finger and the third time he was as large as a hand."[54]

Aside from these four categories already noted, the Christ Child also appears as a revealer to the nuns. Shortly before her death, Sister Peters of Birkensee has a vision of the Christ Child. She interrogates him to establish his identity, and since he answers her questions correctly, she proclaims, "So you are Jesus Christ!" to which the Child responds, "You are a child of the eternal kingdom."[55] The same interrogation is repeated in the sketch on the life of Sister Elisa.[56] A third instance occurs in the story of Sister Kunigunde of Eichstätt.[57]

The powerful impact of the image of Christ as Lover numbers the writers of Engelthal among bridal mystics. Christ speaks of himself as a "prisoner of love" who "cannot resist the beauty of the Beloved." He is portrayed as being out of control because of his fiery love. In such a state the Beloved may ask for anything she wishes and he will grant it. Ulrich of Kaisheim writes in just this vein in one of his letters to Adelheid Langmann. Speaking of Christ, he says:

> He cools his love with you. With you he forgets all the suffering that happened to him from other people. He has become uncontrollable toward you out of love and wants to have praise and honor before his friends and is ashamed of nothing before his enemies. In brief, he has become drunk with love and behaves toward you like a child. Therefore, ask and command him immediately. Whatever you want, he wants and whatever he will not grant to you according to his will, he will give you something much better.[58]

Christina Ebner also uses the image of Christ as the "prisoner of love." He reveals to her: "I am your prisoner because of love and come willingly to you."[59] Aside from conventional bridal mystic vocabulary and terms of address, Christina employs varied and numerous images to convey the union of herself with her Lover. Christina becomes "drunk" with love for him. He tells her: "My great love has ignited yours. From my outflow you have become drunk. My divinity has glorified you . . ."[60] The image of "flowing" features prominently in much of the discourse about their union. Christ intimates to her, "I flow into you. I flow out of you, I will make many hearts burn through you."[61] Related to the image of "flowing" is Christ's portrayal as a fountain: "I am an overflowing fountain. I have given you grace, goodness and mercy which have enriched you. I have united myself with you and will never leave you."[62] The many and varied images of Christ as Lover makes Christina's *Revelations* seem to be the account of a love story, a personal appropriation of the love of Bride and Bridegroom expressed in the Song of Solomon.

The images of Lover and Lord combine in Adelheid Langmann's visions of the Lamb of God. She makes reference to her mystical marriage with the Lamb of God three times: on the Epiphany while the *Agnus Dei* was being sung, again one year later, and once more on St. Matthias Day. The image of Christ as Lamb connects his eucharistic presence, the marriage of the Lamb (Rev. 19:6-8), his union with the soul, and his coming at the end of time. As Lamb of God Christ is the new sacrificial lamb whose death is the cause of the world's redemption. This one sacrifice is perpetuated in the celebration of the eucharist at the command of Christ, and through reception of Christ's Body and Blood the believer is united with him. Those who are united with Christ have no fear of the Last Judgment.

Adelheid also reports a vision of Christ in glory on Christmas Day. "At the third Mass he came as a mighty king and was beautiful beyond all measure."[63] Christina likewise shows Christ as the Lord Sabaoth.[64] As ruler of heaven and earth Christ nonetheless has deigned to stoop down to a lowly creature such as Christina.[65] He is also a strict judge. "I am a king in heaven and on earth, the Lord of lords on earth and a strict judge of all those who die in their sins."[66] As strict as he is portrayed, he is merciful as well: "I am a strict judge of my enemies, but a loving one to my friends.[67] Even though he is clothed in awesome majesty and splendor, the face and particularly the eyes and gaze of Christ show mercy and dispense grace.[68] To Adelheid he says, "I have poured into you the outflowing of my mercy and I have looked upon you with my merciful eyes. I have given many hearts sweetness by your will."[69] He has turned his face toward Adelheid and made what is impossible possible by his grace.[70] He proclaims, "Do not fear me. I have heaven and earth to give and I am an inexhaustible sea. The angels and saints cannot explain my wonders.[71] His lordship reflects the credal statement that he will come to judge the living and the dead. His judgment incites fear in sinners but causes joy for the righteous.

In the *Sister-Book of Engelthal,* Sister Anna Vorchtlin sees the Lord in glory in one of her visions.[72] A more detailed vision description comes from Sister Eilsa: "On Easter Day after matins it is the custom of many sisters to pray in the cloister walk. Then she bent down in the niche where the Judgment of Our Lord is. Then she was enraptured and saw Our Lord sitting on a throne in his majesty and the twelve apostles were with him and all the world was beneath him. And a radiant brilliance shone from his face that was as bright as a thousand suns and the heavens were opened above him and a great host of angels and saints came also."[73]

THE MOTIF OF BEING CHOSEN

Christina Ebner frequently adverts to the theme of "being chosen" by God/ Christ, either to be in a special relationship with God or to fulfill some mission. She also strongly asserts that religious are a chosen group, as are Christians in general and the Friends of God in particular. Such notions have strong precedents in Scripture.

Most commonly the term *chosen* applies to the biblical Hebrew tribes collectively. Isaiah calls them a "chosen people" (Isa. 43:20), but usually the various Scripture authors refer to the people collectively as chosen by descent: "O offspring of Abraham his servant, sons of Jacob, his chosen ones!" (1 Chron. 16:13).[74] The psalmist likewise employs such vocabulary: "So he led forth his people with joy, his chosen ones with singing (Ps 105:43) and again in Ps. 106:5: ". . . that I may see the prosperity of thy chosen ones, that I may rejoice in the gladness of thy nation, that I may glory with thy heritage." The most important aspect of being chosen as a people is the unique election of the Hebrews to enter into a special relationship with God that no other people on earth enjoy. The foundation for this election first occurs in the second book of Moses: "For you are a people holy to the Lord your God, and the Lord your God has chosen you to be a people for his own possession, out of all the peoples that are on the face of the earth" (Deut. 7:6). The Scripture writer wishes to emphasize this election and repeats this description of the people verbatim in Deuteronomy 14:2. Similar descriptions of election occur elsewhere in the Old Testament.[75]

This collective election of a people by blood descent undergoes a development in the New Testament. No longer does God base election upon blood descent from Abraham, Israel, and Jacob, but rather on those washed in the blood of Christ. The identification as being chosen by God applies now in a particular way to Christians. Paul addresses the Colossians using such terms: "Put on then, as God's chosen ones, holy and beloved, compassion, kindness, lowliness, meekness, and patience" (Col. 3:12) and to the Thessalonians he writes, "For we know, brethren beloved by God, that he has chosen you" (1 Thess. 1:4). The most famous passage, however, occurs in the first letter of Peter, for it clearly attributes the prerogatives and definition of the chosen people to the Christian Church composed of both Jew and Gentile: "But you are a chosen race, a royal priesthood, a holy nation, God's own people, that you may declare the wonderful deeds of him who called you out of darkness into his marvelous light" (1 Pet. 2:9). Finally, this notion of election occurs in the apocalyptic literature in prediction of the end times: "They will make war on the Lamb, and the Lamb will conquer them, for he is Lord of lords and Kings of kings, and those with him are called and chosen and faithful" (Rev. 17:14). The Hebrews in the Old Testament and baptized Christians in the New Testament both function out of their special status to be an example to those peoples who are not chosen, such as the Egyptians or Assyrians. In the Christian dispensation this identification functions as an invitation to become Christian through belief in Christ and acceptance of baptism in the name of the Trinity. Paul addresses a group of neophytes in the letter to the Colossians: "Put on then, as God's chosen ones, holy and beloved, compassion, kindness, lowliness, meekness, and patience" (Col. 3:12). The chosen people have an obligation to behave in a manner pleasing to God, as described in the quote.

In the writings of Christina Ebner, the idea of the special status of Christian nations and of all Christendom is firmly established. In a revelation to Christina, Christ announces: "I am the true Love in my eternal faithfulness . . . whenever I give grace as I have done to my beloved people. My beloved people, you have this outpouring [of grace] from my passion."[76] This quote clearly connects the new definition of the chosen people as defined by the blood of Christ. This change in definition brings about many other changes as well. Christ continues: "They said in the Old Testament that no one could forgive sins, but God alone. That is now not so in the era of grace. I proved that in the Gospel . . . when I gave St. Peter the power."[77] As was often the case with the chosen people of the Old Testament, those of the new dispensation could act contrary to the will of God, be disobedient to divine law, and resent their special status by wishing to be like those not chosen by God. It is necessary even in the Christian era for Christina to pray for Christendom, especially during the period of the interdict and because of the dissension among warring factions of Christians.[78]

The idea that a smaller group from among the chosen people could also be chosen for a special task for the benefit of the whole people is best exemplified by the establishment and perdurance of the Levitical priest-hood. The priests of the Old Testament were already established in the Book of Deuteronomy. After giving directions as to what they may possess, the writer of Deuteronomy speaks of the Levitical priests. "For the Lord your God has chosen him out of all your tribes, to stand and minister in the name of the Lord, him and his sons for ever" (Deut. 18:5). Throughout the Old Testament this formula is repeated in various ways: "And the priests, the sons of Levi shall come forward, for the Lord your God has chosen them to minister to him and to bless in the name of the Lord, and by their word every dispute and every assault shall be settled" (Deut. 21:5). This caste of men was clearly described as chosen to perform ritual tasks— to minister before God, to bless the people, and to act as arbitrators in contentious situations. They also minister to God as guardians of the Ark: "And Moses wrote this law, and gave it to the priests the sons of Levi, who carried the ark of the covenant of the Lord, and to all the elders of Israel" (Deut. 31:9). Their ritual functions increased with the establishment of the Temple in Jerusalem, for now they must offer sacrifices of various sorts as part of their ministry to God. Even among this chosen group defined by a narrower blood descent than even that of the entire people, there was also a yet more select group: " . . . these are the sons of Zadok, who alone among the sons of Levi may come near to the Lord to minister to him" (Ezek. 40:46). Like the people, the sons of Levi, despite their status, often neglected their duties or sinned against the law of God. And because of this, "he will sit as a refiner and purifier of silver, and he will purify the sons of Levi and refine them like gold and silver, till they present right offerings to the Lord" (Mal. 3:3). In addition to the priests, other groups of selected individuals also functioned in distinctive ways—the elders of Israel, the judges, the royal line, the prophets of the Lord.

The concept of specially chosen, distinct groups among the people continues with the spread of the Christian Church. This formulaic order begins with apostles and continues with martyrs, virgins, and confessors. In a revelation to Christina Ebner, a list of special groups appears in standard form: "The twelve apostles said, 'Lord we praise you because Christian life comes from our seed.' Then the martyrs said, 'For the sake of the . . . blood we shed by your will, give them victory."[79] This passage continues, mentioning confessors and virgins as well. The natural progression from such distinct groups includes hermits, monastics (monks and nuns), canons and canonesses, and later mendicant friars and nuns. In several passages the importance of the contemplative monastic life as led by Dominican nuns receives firm affirmation as being a distinct and special group. In another revelation Christ tells Christina: "Because you have sought me from your youngest days I have been true to you and because you have been true to me I have given you a contemplative life beyond all human senses."[80] Christina thinks of her unworthiness to lead such a life. Responding to her thought, Christ asserts: "How had David deserved a contemplative life as is shown of him by the psalms? How had his son, the Lord Solomon, deserved me giving him such great wisdom? How had Moses deserved the great grace I gave him? How had Peter deserved to become a prince over heaven and earth? How had Paul deserved to be taken up to the third heaven?"[81] The implication here and in many other places is that no one has ever deserved any of these special positions, but Christ is free to grant them as he wishes. The analogy of Christina and the nuns being heirs of past greatness also occurs in a revelation in which the desert and the monastic choir are compared: "I have chosen you. You did not choose me. I told the prophets to go into the desert so that I may speak with them. Go into the choir so that I may speak to you!"[82]

In the writings of the Dominican nuns, the idea that the nuns themselves had been chosen from among the people to assume a special relationship with Christ was very strong. They understood entrance into the monastery as marking a special conversion. They conceived of religious profession as almost a second baptism. It numbered the nuns among an elect few.

The idea of an individual being chosen by God to assume a special relationship or to perform an assigned task occurs frequently in the Bible. Of the many individuals recorded in Scripture as being chosen by God, the most important are Moses, David, and Christ. In Psalm 106:23, the psalmist remembers Moses as a "chosen one."[83] His being chosen to lead the Israelites out of Egypt and to deliver the commands of the Decalogue depend upon the unique experience of the revelation of God to Moses on Mt. Sinai (Exod. 3:1-16). Moses is attracted by the burning bush, hears the voice of God, discovers he is on holy ground and in the presence of the God of Abraham, Isaac and Jacob, meets God face to face, and receives a commission to free the people. The pattern of this encounter will be replicated in the revelations to Christina Ebner and others, who in her visions, auditions and dreams encounters God/Christ, recognizes him as Lord, and receives some message or task to perform.

The power of the Lord's choice is emphasized in the story of David. The chosen prophet Samuel acts in the Lord's stead to choose the future king. Among the sons of Jesse he is the least likely candidate, but after the rejection of all his older brothers, it is clear whom the Lord had chosen: "Now he was ruddy, and had beautiful eyes, and was handsome. And the

Lord said, 'Arise, anoint him; for this is he.' Then Samuel took the horn of oil, and anointed him in the midst of his brothers; and the Spirit of the Lord came mightily upon David from that day forward" (1 Sam. 16:12-13). The choice is clearly attributed to the Lord. The anointing sets David aside and marks him as the chosen one of God, much as the oil used in baptism sets aside the baptized for Christ. David's election and the Lord's blessing continue with the story of his combat with Goliath. The young boy's confidence is in God: "The Lord who saved me from the lion and the bear will save me from this Philistine" (1 Sam. 17:37). David fights without armor and kills the giant. His fame and status are sung in Psalm 89:3, in which the Lord proclaims, "I have made a covenant with my chosen one, I have sworn to David my servant." David, despite his blessings as chosen, and his anointing as king, nevertheless sins against God by lusting after Bathsheba, committing adultery with her, and thus causing the deliberate and premeditated death of her husband Uriah the Hittite (2 Sam. 11). Even after this, Scripture records God's constancy to his election: "Yet to his son I will give one tribe, that David my servant may always have a lamp before me in Jerusalem, the city where I have chosen to put my name" (1 Kings 11:36).[84] The motif of being chosen continues in the life of Christina and others. She wonders why she receives revelations and so many signs of love and favor from Christ. The answer is always the same—he is free to choose. "I am a free God, whom no one can coerce."[85]

The use of a vocabulary of chosenness occurs most significantly with Christ. At the baptism in the Jordan, a scene rehearsed in the writings of the nuns of Engelthal, Christ is proclaimed to be the chosen one: "And when Jesus was baptized, he went up immediately from the water, and behold, the heavens were opened and he saw the Spirit of God descending from heaven saying, 'This is my beloved Son, with whom I am well pleased'" (Matt. 3:15-17).[86] This verse conflates two related sources. The first occurs in Psalm 2:7: "You are my son, today I have begotten you." The second is from Isaiah 42:1: "Behold my servant, whom I uphold, my chosen, in whom my soul delights." Similar formulations occur also as Christ is transfigured in the sight of Peter, James, and John. They have been overshadowed by a bright cloud from which a voice speaks: "'This is my beloved Son, with whom I am well pleased; listen to him'" (Matt. 17:5).[87] Significantly, in this scene the three disciples witness Moses and Elijah, representing the Law and the Prophets, deferring to Christ in this theophany. He fulfills and supercedes even such great figures as Moses and Elijah. Reflecting on Christ, Peter exhorts his audience to "come to him, to that living stone, rejected by men but in God's sight chosen and precious." (1 Pet. 2:4).

The centrality of Christ for the nuns is unmistakable. He is *the* Chosen One of God, the very manifestation of God. He portrays himself in such terms. Speaking to Christina he says, "I come to you as the splendor of the heavenly Father and I have set you on fire just like one passes a light from one to another."[88] Later he repeats this image with a slightly different intent: "I am the splendor of my heavenly Father. I have enlightened you as much as is possible for a human being."[89] For Christina all grace comes to her by virtue of Christ's love, which reflects the Father's love and is brought about by the Holy Spirit. The motive for all of God's revelations and Christ's actions is love.[90]

Not only people or distinct groups or individuals could be chosen, but places as well. Preeminent among these is Jerusalem or Mt. Zion and specifically the Temple. In his dedicatory prayer, King Solomon twice refers to the "chosen" city, Jerusalem (1 Ki. 11:13,32,36). In the second Book of Chronicles, the Lord says: "I have chosen Jerusalem that my name may be there and I have chosen David to be over my people Israel" (2 Chron. 6:6).[91] The vocabulary of chosenness also applies specifically to the Temple building itself. "Then the Lord appeared to Solomon in the night and said to him: 'I have heard your prayer, and have chosen this place for myself as a house of sacrifice" (2 Chron. 7:12). Further on he says, "For now I have chosen and consecrated this house that my name may be there for ever; my eyes and my heart will be there for all time (2 Chron. 7:16). Later a summary statement combines all of these elements: "'In this house, and in Jerusalem, which I have chosen out of all the tribes of Israel, I will put my name for ever (2 Chron. 33:7).[92] The various motives of choice converge in Christ here as well. Not only is Christ the *Chosen One* by virtue of his singular status as Son and Savior, but even the imagery of the Temple is appropriated to the person of Christ. Peter writes metaphorically about Christ using the vocabulary of God's choice of a place to dwell. "For it stands in scripture: 'Behold, I am laying in Zion a stone, a cornerstone chosen and precious, and he who believes in him will not be put to shame (1 Pet. 2:6).'" The Temple housed the Ark of the Covenant within the Holy of Holies. It was on Mt. Zion that the Lord had chosen to dwell.[93] There the chosen priests offered sacrifices and prayers to God for themselves and for the people, for God, who was present in the tabernacle, had expressly willed this to be his new meeting place with his people in the holy city. The indwelling of God within the Temple also accrues to Christ, who preeminently became the new Temple. In the revelations to Christina this imagery is appropriated to Christina herself. Christ announces to her: "I have chosen you and therefore I do great things for you. I have loved you, therefore you receive my sweet speech. You are my temple, therefore I treat you lovingly."[94] The temple becomes a metaphor for the indwelling of divinity. The God who dwelt within the Temple, Christ who is the Temple, and Christina who becomes the Temple of God become one.

Understanding Christ as the summit to which all history tends and from which all history proceeds, the same dynamics of being chosen continue in a fulfilled and surpassing way in the age of the New Testament. Now the concept of the people of God embraces all those who believe in Christ as Son of God and who are baptized. No longer is the definition of "chosen people" limited to those of blood descent: it includes those "washed in the blood of Christ." When writing to the Thessalonians, Paul shows an appreciation for the chosen status of the entire community: "For we know, brethren beloved by God, that he has chosen you . . . " (1 Thess. 1:4). The same applies to his sentiments expressed to the Colossians: "Put on then, as God's chosen ones, holy and beloved, compassion, kindness, lowliness, meekness, and patience (Col. 3:12).

There are also distinct groups chosen from among the baptized. Scripture reports that the apostles form a new group by the will of Christ: ". . . until the day when he was taken up, after he had given commandment through the Holy Spirit to the apostles whom he had chosen" (Acts 1:2). Their status is reiterated in Peter's first sermon: ". . . not to all the people but to us who were chosen by God as witnesses, who ate and drank with him after he rose from the dead" (Acts 10:41). The apostles form a distinct group separate from the people by God's choice through their intimate contact with Christ, particularly after his Resurrection. As the Church developed, other groups formed—elders, presbyters, virgins, martyrs, confessors. While none of these bears the unqualified descriptive details and vocabulary of being chosen by God, they do show the tendency to group individuals in a similar way and certainly the group, while not bearing the approbation of Scripture, continues the same dynamic as that established in Scripture and can be interpreted as such. Paul differentiates distinct groups by function: "And God appointed in the church first apostles, second prophets, third teachers, then workers of miracles, then healers, helpers, administrators, speakers in various kinds of tongues" (1 Cor. 12:28). Martyrs are "chosen by God" to share in the shedding of Christ's blood by giving witness to their faith and shedding their own blood. Scripture describes the Christian protomartyr Stephen as "full of grace and power," who performed "great wonders and signs among the people" (Acts 6:8). The description of his death at the hands of the authorities becomes a model for holiness and martyrdom. "Now when they heard these things they were enraged, and they ground their teeth against him. But he, full of the Holy Spirit, gazed into heaven and saw the glory of God, and Jesus standing at the right hand of God" (Acts 7:54-56).

Christina understands the nuns as a distinct group of chosen individuals. As religious women and as Dominicans, the nuns understand themselves in terms of the *vita apostolica*. The form of their life set off as a distinct group under obedience to a superior assigned with the task of praising God and interceding for the people shows them to be heirs of the apostles by imitating them as well as heirs of the priests whose function is to intercede and even by extension to exercise the function of sacrifice by the monastic martyrdom of their lives.

Another distinct group would be the priests who continue Christ's very own task: "For every high priest chosen from among men is appointed to act on behalf of men in relation to God, to offer gifts and sacrifices for sins" (Heb. 5:1). The New Testament interpretation links the Old Testament Levitical priesthood, Christ, and the priests of the New Testament by reason of the function and their being chosen to perform that function.

Also, individuals are chosen in the New Testament to perform certain tasks. Ananias wishes not to seek out Saul, the agent of the chief priests and persecutor of Christians: "But the Lord said to him, 'Go, for he is a chosen instrument of mine to carry my name before the Gentiles and kings and the sons of Israel . . .'" (Acts 9:15). Saul becomes Paul and undertakes the conversion of the Roman world.

Christina and Adelheid likewise understand that they and others have been especially chosen by God/Christ to be in a love relationship with him and to have power to influence him by that love in order to help strengthen believers in faith, convert sinners and release souls from purgatory. Christina's intercessory influence is recognized by the world—King Charles, the burgrave of Nuremberg, Henry of Nördlingen, the flagellants, and others.

For Christina, the Christian people have become the Chosen People. The apostles (bishops and priests) inherit the role of the Levitical priesthood as well as being given the task to proclaim the Good News. Nuns are a distinctly chosen group marked by profession of vows to live a sacrificial life of praise and petition. Some individuals are chosen to be in a special relationship with Christ, to be his brides, his beloved ones, and to exercise power over him.

COMMUNION AND IMAGES OF UNION

The basis of much that will be said and reported by Christina about the Eucharist is the firm belief that Christ is truly present, body and blood, soul and divinity in the bread and wine consecrated at the Mass. His presence is real, not symbolic, and it perdures even when housed in a tabernacle. Further, the Mass celebrates salvation history, for it not only incorporates the present moment but also perpetuates the singular sacrifice of Christ on the cross. The action of the Mass unites the living and the dead. It benefits all present and all for whom they pray, both in purgatory and on earth. The Mass is the central act of worship, the meeting place of heaven and earth, time and eternity, the past, present, and future. It unites saints, believers, sinners, and angels in the worship of the Triune God. For the nuns it is "the most prominent, characteristically female concern."[95]

The nuns believe in the presence of Christ in the Eucharist. They express their belief in the desire to receive communion and in the miraculous experiences they have in relation to the celebration of the Mass, the elevation of the host, and the reception of communion.

Although these authors occasionally employ vocabulary associated with essence mysticism *(Wesenmystik)* to write about the union of Christ with the soul, overwhelmingly they use the vocabulary, imagery, and patterns of thought associated with bridal mysticism *(Brautmystik)*. Using bridal mystic categories, the nuns seek to express an unmediated experience of the Divine. The imagery of bridal union between the soul and God is more humanly natural and theologically safer than the cerebral and pantheistic-prone expression of mystical union used in essence mysticism, for bridal imagery more successfully describes the union of God and the soul while respecting the individuality and maintaining the separateness of the two. However, since bridal imagery is necessarily erotic, many people have found the literary expression of it objectionable in religious writings. The Latin translation of Margaret Ebner's *Revelations*, produced for the first attempt at beatification, sanitized the text by expunging the "naughty bits." Likewise, as Siegfried Ringler has shown, the manuscript progression of the *Revelations* of Adelheid Langmann displays an attempt to abbreviate by de-eroticizing the text. Christina Ebner's *Revelations* have never been transcribed from the manuscripts, so erotic were they thought to be.[96] The same element that so powerfully expresses the union of Christ and the nun has also kept these texts in obscurity.

Each nun consciously understands herself as chosen by Christ to enter with him into a spousal relationship that far surpasses the experience of the ordinary Christian. Each nun also discovers a corollary power for intercession. The manner in which each becomes chosen reveals the nature of the relationship as a mixture of suffering and love. From the beginning Adelheid Langmann describes her relationship with Christ in just that way. He wishes her to be "one with him" by becoming a nun, but she fears the rigors she will have to endure in a monastic setting. Christ allays her fears promising that he will never abandon her and will guide her to lead a perfect and a holy life with him. To the aging Christina Ebner, Christ reveals that the very fact that she had been born on Good Friday symbolizes her destiny to share in the passion of Christ in both senses of the term—in his suffering and in his love. Christ also assures her, "I have chosen you, you did not choose me and those whom I choose win heaven and earth."[97] The admixture of suffering and love not only forms the basis of the relationship but also defines its progress.

The development of the relationship between Christ and each nun demonstrates growth in unity of will and love. Adelheid Langmann undergoes a progression in the battle of wills between herself and Christ. At every stage he has to win her by assuring her that he will never abandon her. Christ also tests her love for him. When asked for a third time whether she wishes to go to heaven or remain on earth, Adelheid responds to Christ by saying simply, "I want whatever you want." This, of course, is finally the correct answer, for immediately Christ addresses her as "Beloved!" and delivers the lengthiest profession of love to her in the text to that point.

Christina Ebner constantly hears from Christ that she is one of his most beloved in all the world. More readily than the other nuns, she accepts Christ's will and conforms herself to it. At the outset she feels so full of grace that she compares herself to a pregnant woman. At the beginning of her autobiography she is already celebrating Easter, presumably having gone through the passion, and even writes of visits to the heavenly Jerusalem. She is fully aware of her chosen status and grieves for those who do not know such love from Christ.

In their works both nuns describe their relationship to Christ as a *minnespil* or a game of love. For example, Christ tells Christina, "I play a game with you."[98] Later he expands on this statement: "I play a game of love with you."[99] To help Adelheid understand this same process, Ulrich Niblung writes to her describing a similar dynamic, "You are loved by your Bridegroom, totally loved from the heart . . . He will not let you be away from the bridal bed . . . He plays a game of love with you yet never has enough."[100] Margaret Ebner, a contemporary mystic known to both Adelheid and Christina, describes and expands on a similar experience when Christ spoke to her: "I have a lovely work in you that is a sweet game to me. Your love compels me to let myself be found so that your soul is satisfied and yet your body will be unharmed . . . your burning love binds me . . . your fiery love keeps me near . . . I want to give you the kiss of love."[101]

Evidently the progression of union in will and love is not one-sided. The nuns portray Christ almost as being at the mercy of his beloved bride. Adelheid's beauty has drawn him into the heated chamber (*kemenate*) to be with his beloved. He finds rest in the garden of her heart. He is trapped in this enclosed space and only Adelheid has the key to unlock the door. The Divine Lover places himself at the mercy of his beloved. Whatever she wishes and prays for, he will grant, even the release of all the souls from purgatory. The nuns take Queen Esther as their model, for like her they enjoy the status as bride of the king and dare to enter into the royal chamber in order to save the people. Both nuns receive the gift of release of souls from purgatory whenever they ask for it. Both Adelheid and Christina frequently receive a certain number of souls delivered from purgatory, sinners converted to Christ, and believers strengthened in faith. Their privileged status as brides of Christ, along with Christ's surrender to their love for him, gives each nun the power of intercession for the living and the dead.

In each case the relationship with Christ leads the nun inexorably into mystical, ecstatic union with him. The professions of love, the granting of prayers, and the increase of intensity in mystical phenomena climax in moments of union with Christ. Adelheid Langmann prays for mystical union with Christ: "Lord, unite yourself to me and me to you so that our union will last forever without any separation." Christ responds: "Just as little as I can ever be separated from my Father, so little will I ever be separated from you."[102] Adelheid describes her union with Christ in an episode during Advent when she thinks her heart will burst for love of Christ and, falling into ecstasy in choir, has to be carried to her cell where she meets two virgins Spes and Caritas, who accompany her on the arduous mystical journey to meet the Beloved. Eventually they reach a city bathed in bright light and

the virgins put her down on the bed. While she was lying on the bed she saw her Lord approaching and he was so beautiful that I had never really heard of his beauty since he was a thousand times more beautiful. His face shone brightly and his light outshone the light that filled the city. He came up to me and his beauty shone into my heart and went through all my limbs . . . In all his joyous beauty he knelt before the bed and his face was turned toward mine. I looked up and gazed at him. He was so beautiful that I could not bear it and it seemed to me that my soul would dissolve from true love. He said, 'My Beloved!' With that same word that so sweetly came out of his mouth he drew my poor, sinful soul into his Godhead and I can say nothing more about this vision . . .[103]

Christina Ebner shares the same intimacies with Christ, who tells her: "I have loved you with an eternal love."[104] He further clarifies her position: "You are in the highest degree of love."[105] Christ also portrays himself as a "prisoner" of her love.[106] He repeatedly exclaims, "I come to you as one who is dead from love, as your bridegroom to your bridal bed."[107] To allay her fears he also states, "I come to you not as a judge, I come to you as a bridegroom to his bridal bed."[108] The union of Christ and Christina is imaged as a dissolving or a flowing into: "I flow into you and flow out of you because you are a temple in which I have placed my heavenly treasure. I have embraced you with my loyalty and given you the kiss."[109] This quote combines the vocabulary of union in four distinct ways. Christ flows into Christina and subsequently flows forth for the benefit of others. She is a temple like the Temple in which God had come to dwell. Christ "embraces" her in love and gives her the "kiss," an image taken from the Song of Solomon and from Bernard's sermons.

In the biography of Friedrich Sunder, the image of union is strikingly erotic:

> After he had received the Body of our Lord, and the soul had been fed and conformed by the Lord our God, then spoke the infant Christ, the child of our lady: "Dear mother, make a joyous bed for me and my beloved spouse where I and my much beloved bride can take our pleasure with each other." Then the bed was made with lots of beautiful flowers (that were to be spiritual virtues), then Jesus advanced to the little bed, and Mary, his holy mother, joined the holy soul with the little Jesus. And they had such loving joy and pleasure with one another of embraces and kisses, and laughter and with all divine pleasure that the angels and the saints, who were gathered about, were altogether amazed that such a man still on this earth was living with body and soul, with whom our Lord worked such a wonder.[110]

Jeffrey Hamburger comments on this passage: "Christ refers to Sunder's soul as his bride in the conventional language of bridal mysticism. The mystical marriage is consummated in the lectulus noster floridus (Song of Sol. 1:16), whose flowers, according to the text, stand for Sunder's spiritual virtues. Mary, the angels, and the saints surround the bed like witnesses at the consummation of an actual medieval wedding.[111]

Another aspect of this sort of eroticism has to do with the exemplary role of St. John. The writers of Engelthal assume the apostle John was the "disciple whom Jesus loved."[112] That he lived the longest of all the apostles and eventually recorded his unique reminiscences of Christ in his own version of the Gospel, sent letters that were included in the scriptural canon, and left an account of a vision in his Book of Revelation assured for him a prominent place in the spirituality of the writers of Engelthal. As beloved, John enjoys a unique relationship with Christ signified by his presence at important events—the Transfiguration, the Agony in the Garden, but most importantly at the Last Supper, where he leaned on the breast of Christ and alone learned the identity of the traitorous disciple. This moment in John's life bears tremendous importance for the Engelthal community. It symbolizes John's utterly unique status as beloved of Christ and shows him to be the receiver of hidden mysteries from Christ that he reveals in his Gospel and in the Book of Revelation. This image of John occurs in the *Speculum virginum* where he is repeatedly identified with the spouse in the Song of Solomon and is shown as drinking and suckling from the side of Christ.[113] The author of the fourteenth-century *Das Buch von geistlicher Armut* describes John as the apostle who "slept on the breast of Jesus Christ and sucked out from there all the wisdom and the hidden mystery of God."[114] A more reserved formulation of this is preserved in the liturgy for the Office of John the Evangelist: 'This is John, who reclined on the breast of the Lord at the Last Supper, the blessed apostle to whom were revealed heavenly mysteries."[115]

Adelheid Langmann describes an experience like John's in her *Revelations*. While listening to the reading in refectory, Adelheid sees Christ, accompanied by Mary and Mary Magdalen, standing before her. "He said, 'My Beloved,' and sat down on her right side. Then she leaned down against his heart and lay against his breast until the sister stood up."[116] After she had been taken back to her cell, the author writes that our Lord "granted her many good things beyond all measure and stayed with her and revealed many things to her."[117] Adelheid's leaning against the breast of Christ is an imitation of St. John at the Last Supper (John 13:23-25). Like him she has been called "Beloved" by Christ and has sucked wisdom from his breast, gaining secret knowledge of heavenly things that she can then reveal to others. Her replacement of John in this episode is emphasized by the presence of Mary and Mary Magdalen, the only people other than John who were present at the death of Jesus on the cross. Adelheid assumes John's role and nourishes others with her own *Revelations*.

Writing about this phenomenon, Christina Ebner extends this image to the angels and the saints, who "kiss the feet of Christ and then suck from the wound of his divine heart."[118] Specifically she also writes of her own experience. Christ says to her: "I have given you to suck with my sweetness from the breast of my delight."[119] In a passage closely associated with Christ's crucifixion, Christina experiences the same. Standing before the Father with arms outspread, Christ says, "Father, thus have I stood on the holy cross until my soul left my body. Therefore I want to embrace everyone in the arms of my mercy and want to give them the kiss of my love."[120] After that the angels and saints fall down in worship before him. The author writes: "After that he [Christ] granted her to suck from the wounds of his divine heart like the bees suck from the flowers."[121] These exact words as reported on the vigil of St. Elizabeth are repeated later in the manuscript after St. Cecilia's Day.[122] This portrayal of John, and therefore of the mystics, is not singular. Previously John was portrayed as *sponsa Christi* and the image of sucking at the breast of Christ appeared in the *Speculum virginum*. According to Jeffrey Hamburger, this imagery appears also in the prayer book of Arnulph of Milan, in the writings of Elizabeth of Schönau, and Mechthild of Magdeburg, among others.[123]

This image of sucking can also function as an image of maternity and nourishment in which Christ weans the nun with wisdom from his own milk. It is complemented by the image of the Christ child sucking from the breast of Adelheid, Christina, Friedrich Sunder, or their contemporary mystic, Margaret Ebner. Christina is directed by Christ to tell John Tauler and Henry of Nördlingen that Christ is their friend (*friundin*), that is, female friend, perhaps a more acceptable notion than the alternative homoeroticism implied in the biography of Friedrich Sunder.

The number of images used to express the union of Christ and the soul is astounding. Aside from the erotic and maternal images, the writers of Engelthal also use images from nature. Christ reveals images of union to Christina after she has received him in communion. "I live in you like honey in wax. I dwell in you like a bird in the air. I live in you like a fish in water."[124] Christina protests that she does not understand this revelation. He clarifies it: "Your body is like the wax that has received my sweetness so often. The bird in the air means that I have often shown you heavenly things. The fish in water is that as little as one knows about the ground so little does one know about the great grace that I do for you and this is unbelievable to humans."

The ultimate expression of union beyond any momentary experience is the indwelling of God in the soul. The writers of Engelthal express this permanent habitation of the divine in the soul of the mystic using vocabulary and images taken from Scriptures. Christ reveals to Christina Ebner that she has become his temple: "I have chosen you and therefore I do great things for you. I have loved you and therefore you have my sweet conversation. You are my temple and therefore I treat you lovingly."[125] This revelation continues, "I dwell in you as the fragrance in roses. I dwell in you as the brightness in lilies. I, noble fruit, have blossomed from you. You suck my sweetness like a bee sucks from flowers."[126] All of these images seek to express the union of Christ and Christina. The images from nature all show qualities that are integral to the thing or a natural and necessary activity of the creature. The use of temple imagery comes explicitly from the Scriptures and connotes a fullness of meaning not immediately apparent without further explanation. The God of the Hebrews had chosen the Temple on Mt. Zion in Jerusalem in which to dwell. There he was truly present to the people in the Holy of Holies. His presence made a mere structure built by human hands a holy place to which the people came to pray, sing the psalms, and worship, and in which the priests offered daily sacrifices to the Lord. The Hebrews expressed their love and reverence for the Temple in many psalms and other writings. The prophet Ezekiel's vision of the temple portrays it as an edifice that gives life to everything around it:

> The angel brought me back to the entrance of the temple of the Lord, and I saw water flowing out from beneath the threshold of the temple toward the east, for the facade of the temple was toward the west; the water flowed down from the southern side of the temple, south of the altar. . . . Wherever the river flows, every sort of living creature that can multiply shall live, and there shall be abundant fish, for wherever this water comes the sea shall be made fresh. Along both banks of the river fruit trees of every kind shall grow; their leaves shall not fade, nor their fruit fail. Every month they shall bear fresh fruit, for they shall be watered by the flow from the sanctuary. Their fruit shall serve for food, and their leaves for medicine. (Ezek. 47)

The Temple is the visible embodiment of the invisible God. The presence of the Holy One of Israel brings blessings and abundance to the people and the land. Above all it gives life to and sustains all creatures and makes them flourish. The understanding of the presence of God in the temple clearly undergoes a process of interiorization and personalization. In the Gospel according to John, Christ, after having expelled the merchants and moneychangers, declares: "Destroy this temple . . . and in three days I will raise it up" (John 2:19). The Gospel writer interprets this response: "Actually he was talking about the temple of his body. Only after Jesus had been raised from the dead did his disciples recall that he had said this, and come to believe the Scripture and the word he had spoken (John 2:21-22)." Jesus appropriates the qualities of the Temple to himself, for in him Divinity dwells. And the grace that he bestows gives eternal life to everyone who accepts him and sustains all in that life. This gift is conveyed primarily through the reception of holy communion. The nun receives Christ himself into her body and soul, is made one with him, and becomes by that action a temple of the Lord, and in turn shares the graces received with others. For Christina the indwelling is not a result of infrequent reception of the sacrament: it becomes a permanent condition begun with the reception of communion, but independent from it. For this reason the images to express her union with Christ are so numerous and expressed in such a rich variety of vocabulary. Christina is "Bride," "spouse," "a bee," "a rose," and "a lily." The image of inflowing also plays a role here: "I flow into you and from you. You are a temple in which I have placed my heavenly treasure."[127] Christina appropriates the characteristics of the Temple. Within her dwells Christ, who declares, " I will never depart from you."[128]

Adelheid Langmann prefers to use other images to express the reality of her union with Christ and his indwelling. After Christ professes that he will never abandon her, Adelheid makes a request: "Dearly beloved Lord, for the sake of the love you showed me yesterday, let me see you." In response Christ reveals to her: "Look into your own heart!"[129] There will he be found; such is the unity between them. Adelheid's soul wishes never to be separated from Christ. In response to this desire he says, "As little as I can separate myself from my heavenly Father, so little do I want to separate myself from you."[130] The indwelling is also expressed in this passage in terms of the writing of Christ's name on Adelheid's heart. At the beginning of Advent Christ reveals to her: "I want to write your name in the book of life so that it will never be erased from it . . ."[131] Adelheid does not understand what that means and asks what the "book of life" is. He answers: "It is my divine heart that is the book of life. Whoever has been written down there can never be erased."[132] Later Christ further clarifies his desire to do this and embellishes the experience with descriptive detail: "Then he raised his right hand and wrote the name 'Jesus' on her heart. Four of the letters were in gold.[133] Using the same means Adelheid also wishes to complete the union between the two. "Lord, write my name on your heart also!"[134] To her request Christ acquiesces demonstrating their union symbolically by the carving of their names on each other's hearts.

The high point of the progression of mystical espousals occurs in the episode in which the virgins Caritas and Spes lead her to the bed of love where mystical union will take place:

The Lord now approached the bed. In all his joyous beauty he knelt down before the bed and his face was turned toward mine. I looked up and gazed at him. He was so beautiful that I could not bear it and it seemed to me that my soul would dissolve from true love. He said, "My Beloved!" With the same word that so sweetly came out from his mouth he drew my poor, sinful soul into his Godhead and I can say nothing more about this vision . . .[135]

The importance of this passage rests not only on the content but on Adelheid's sudden shift in person. Rarely does she relate her narrative in the first person, usually preferring to refer to herself impersonally as a "sister" or by using the third-person singular pronoun. It seems that the ecstatic exultation in remembering this event compels her to personalize the account, perhaps because the experience was and remains so powerful to her as she writes about it in retrospect.

OTHER CHARACTERISTICS OF ENGELTHAL SPIRITUALITY

One of the most striking common *topoi* in the literature of Engelthal is the *Gnadenfrucht Topos*, the *topos* of the fruits of grace. Every biographical document except for the fragmentary *Vita* of Gertrud produced at this center of mysticism contains multiple references to this *topos*. The formula of the *topos* remains consistent throughout the works. This consistency in formulation and frequency in use shows the importance that this *topos* has for the spirituality of the mystics of Engelthal. The form of the *topos* indicates the breadth of the spiritual vision of the writers, shows a keen sense of the communion of the saints, and bespeaks a firm conviction of the power of intercessory prayer. The standard form for the *topos* can be quoted from any of the works. The *topos* occurs fifteen times in the autobiography of Adelheid Langmann, but one example from each work will demonstrate its formulation. After receiving communion on the feast of St. Mary Magdalen, Adelheid meditates upon the passion of Jesus Christ. She prays for him to come to her, and when he appears he says: "For the sake of those for whom you have prayed I give you thirty thousand souls from purgatory and as many sinners for conversion and the same number of devout people for strengthening in faith."[136] The formula varies somewhat as does the number of souls, sinners, and devout people mentioned. During a Mass in honor of the Trinity, Christina Ebner receives assurance from the Heavenly Father: "This Mass should make one aware of heaven and earth and purgatory. I let a thousand times a thousand souls and as many sinners to be converted and as many good people to be strengthened . . ."[137] On the Feast of St. Dionysius, God announces to Friedrich Sunder: "And fifty souls should be saved by your mass, and as many sinners converted, and as many good people should grow in virtue."[138] In the biographical sketch of Sister Reichgard contained in the *Sister-Book of Engelthal*, the *Gnadenfrucht Topos* appears in the following form: "The first *Ave Maria* she recited was for the convent and all good people, the second *Ave Maria* for all sinners, and the third *Ave Maria* for the souls in purgatory."[139] In each case the context of the *topos* is intercessory prayer, often after communion, when God or Christ promises to Adelheid, Christina, Friedrich, Reichgard, and others that he will grant their prayers for others in a very specific way. The three categories of recipients show an ingrained appreciation for the communion of saints whose membership includes all souls, living or deceased, who have not been damned to the fires of hell. The *topos* contains a consistent progression from souls in purgatory to sinners to good people, all of whom will be aided in a specific and appropriate way by the prayers of the mystic.

Medieval people were almost obsessed with the need to pray for the souls in purgatory; they offered funds for celebrating Masses for souls in perpetuity and established chantries or funded benefices to assure their remembrance in prayer by the beneficiaries of such gifts and offices. , The Dominicans in particular prayed for the dead, especially for the deceased friars and nuns. In a monastery or priory, the deceased members of the house were commonly buried under the cloister walk and any time a nun walked over the graves, she would recite the *Miserere* for the repose of the souls of the dead buried below. Other remembrances also perpetuated the practice of praying for the dead—masses on the anniversary of the death of an individual, masses to be celebrated for the dead members of entire families or groups of families, the special practices associated with All Souls' Day, and the establishment of special days in the Dominican calendar to remember all deceased members of the Order, deceased parents, and deceased benefactors of the monastery. Adelheid Langmann learns of the power of the prayers of living individuals to deliver souls from purgatory in her descent into purgatory on All Saints' Day: "There she was also led to those souls who had already done penance for everything but still did not yet see God. There she saw various sisters from her monastery, who were thought to be already above in heaven, but were not yet there. She saw the soul of her mother among them. She too was thought to have already reached heaven a long time ago. She saw innumerable souls there. If just one *Ave Maria* or a *Pater noster* or *Miserere* were to be said for them they would go immediately to heaven."[140] Adelheid Langmann suffers the pains of this purgatory and becomes convinced of the necessity of praying for the souls: "In purgatory when an *Ave Maria* was recited for someone it benefited all other souls and all became happy as when someone who is very thirsty is given a drink of water.[141] It should not be surprising in any way that the mystics of Engelthal prayed frequently for the souls in purgatory. However the consistent connection of it with prayer for the living makes the *Gnaden-frucht Topos* a paradigm for a world view that transcends time into eternity and indicates an interpretation of human life as the progression from bad to good, from pain to joy, a constant process of conversion or change of heart that begins on earth and ends in eternal life.

Conversion of sinners and personal conversion of life concerned monastics; indeed such conversion is the *raison d'être* of the monastic life, admission to which represented a conversion from worldly to spiritual concerns. Monastic life also had as its goal the interior conversion of the monk or nun. Entrance into a monastery did not assure the monastic of salvation, it only offered the monk or nun the opportunity to strive for salvation and even perfection. That a monastic should begin to struggle with all aspects of life in confronting his or her own sinfulness in a monastic context was the expected course of events. Without such spiritual turmoil, no progress could be made. To aid anyone in this process of conversion, the prayer of others helped immensely. The laity believed the prayers of the nuns, monks, or friars to be particularly helpful. Friedrich Sunder learns that God has appointed special nuns and friars to pray for the welfare and conversion of the Dominican Order.[142] The group known as the Friends of God, whose membership consisted of nuns, monks, friars, merchants, peasants, nobles, and a queen, had as its task the mutual assistance of the members through prayer, advice, and the sharing of books in order to support each member in living a life committed to Christian values and the constant conversion of life. This second petition in the *Gnadenfrucht Topos* demonstrates the deep appreciation of the nuns for the need to pray for each other in order to be led not into temptation but rather to a deeper conversion of heart.

The third part of the *Gnadenfrucht Topos* shows the conviction of the nuns that the monastic life represents a dynamic progression in holiness. Entry into a monastery and the taking of the veil represent no end to a process, no static degree of blessedness, but a beginning of a process of deeper conversion to Christ and a commitment to the things of heaven. All of monasticism depends upon this insight: that progress or growth in Christian life is possible and indeed necessary for salvation and to fulfill the Gospel command to "be perfect as your heavenly Father is perfect" (Matt. 5:48).

Siegfried Ringler points out other forms of the *Gnadenfrucht Topos*. It may also occur in the form of two petitions, omitting at times either "good people" or "sinners." This abbreviation occurs three times in the *Gnaden-Vita of Friedich Sunder*. On St. Stephen's Day "from his [Friedrich Sunder's] mass on the same day one hundred souls were delivered from purgatory and as many sinners were converted."[143] The devils complain about Friedrich Sunder and rejoice at his death, not because they have won his soul but because he can do them no more harm by his prayer. They almost shout: "Now lead him away because it is a long time since we are so happy at the death of someone on earth. He has exercised great power over the sinners on earth. Whenever we thought we had them for sure, he took away a small portion of them. And in purgatory he often did that to us. When we thought we should have them for a longer time, he came and took a great number of souls away from us. Therefore we are glad that he is dead."[144] The sinners do not appear once in the formula in the *Gnaden-Vita*. The Lord promises Friedrich that, "many good people will be made better by you and many souls will be delivered."[145] The abbreviated form of the *topos* also appears four times in Christina Ebner's autobiography and twice in her biography. On the feast of the Annunciation when she receives communion, Christ makes known to her his blessings: "In the Old Testament I was a lord, but in the New Testament I am a lover of the world. Before the beginning I played with you, with the people I wanted to do great things with and to whom I wanted to give great gifts for all those for whom you have prayed today . . . I will give you a thousand times a thousand souls from purgatory and a hundred sinners to be converted."[146] Later he gives her "one hundred thousand souls and one hundred thousand sinners."[147]

The use of this *topos* is not unique to the literature of Engelthal, as Siegfried Ringler has shown.[148] Adoplh Franz has already offered evidence that the origin of the *Gnadenfrucht Topos* lies in the ten fruits of the Mass interpreted prevalently in the fourteenth and fifteenth centuries.[149] Ringler points out other instances of the *topos* from Franz's work. "That in each Mass a soul is delivered from the pain of purgatory and a sinner is converted from sin and the just person will be protected against the mass of mortal sins."[150] Ringler concludes, however, that the *topos* with only two petitions is the oldest form and the basis of the triple version.[151] Ringler goes on to write that the association of specific and higher numbers marks the usage at Engelthal. In the autobiography and the biography some reader in the past added all the numbers of souls delivered by Christina Ebner's intercession—

23,710,200![152] The most common number associated with the *topos* was thirty or thirty thousand. Adelheid Langmann asks about the number after having received 30,000 each of souls, sinners, and good people: "'Lord, I wonder why you always like to give by thirties?' Our Lord said, 'I was betrayed for thirty pennies.'"[153] This explanation may have satisfied Adelheid, but it does not convince Ringler, who theorizes that the number has to do with Gregorian Masses, the celebration of Mass on thirty consecutive days for the release of a soul from purgatory.[154] Not surprisingly, the use of the *topos* and the numbers in the biography of the priest, Friedrich Sunder, stays close to the original source—the Mass, while Christina Ebner expands the sense of the *topos*.[155] For her the deliverance of souls, the saving of sinners, and the strengthening of believers is a sign of God's faithfulness.[156] For her it is no longer a fruit of the Mass but the graced life of an individual that invites God to give this gift.[157] Christina Ebner however, continues to associate the event with communion and thus with the Mass. Ringler himself quotes the following text as the most instructive of the formulations in the literary output of Engelthal. "'These are thirty-thousand of the souls that have waited to be delivered on this day' [. . .] Then she thought: Oh no Lord, you have never given me this without giving me as many sinners and spiritual people to be warmed in your love.' Then he answered her and said, 'I will give them to you.'"[158]

In a more complete study, other elements of the spirituality of Engelthal might be pursued. Among these would be the role of angels in the writings. It seems significant that the name of the monastery was chosen to be Engelthal (the valley of the angels). Angels do appear frequently in the writings of Engelthal and some are even named—Gloriosus, for example, who is identified as a guardian angel. Certainly more could be done in connecting the writers of Engelthal with Dominican contemporaries such as Tauler, who is mentioned several times by Christina Ebner, or Eckhart, who exercised a tremendous influence over many of the early nuns in Germany. Some scholar could pursue a study of possible influences of other Sister-Books. The influence of the liturgy needs to be further investigated. Was the imaginative visionary experience of a particular day connected with the prayers, Scripture readings, or even readings from texts such as the Martyrology?

BEYOND THE WALLS: ENGELTHAL'S INFLUENCE

RECENTLY GERMANISTS, THEOLOGIANS, AND HISTORIANS have begun to rediscover the monastery of Engelthal and the literary production of the nuns. These scholars have begun to produce studies from the perspectives of history (Gustav Voit), literature (Siegfried Ringler), linguistics (Philipp Strauch), spirituality (Margarete Weinhandl), and women's studies (Ursula Peters). This is a welcome development since scholars have taken very little interest in the nuns, mystics, and writers of Engelthal since the surrender by the last two nuns to the Protestant authorities of Nuremberg in 1565 and the subsequent closing of the other monasteries associated with it. However, documentary evidence shows that the nuns of Engelthal exercised a strong literary and spiritual influence in the fourteenth and fifteenth centuries. Because of the secularization of all the relevant monasteries, most documentary evidence of the influence of Engelthal on other groups of monastics has been lost. What is extant merely hints at the importance of the writings of Christina Ebner, Adelheid Langmann, Friedrich Sunder, and others for their contemporaries and spiritual progeny. Two of the most significant places and groups of persons influenced by the writings of the nuns, friars, and chaplains of Engelthal were other convents of nuns, particularly Pillenreuth and Inzigkoven.

The Augustinian hermitesses founded the monastery of Pillenreuth near Nuremberg in the fourteenth century. Presumably Henry of Nördlingen played an important role in connecting the women of Pillenreuth with the nuns of Engelthal. The hermitesses were well connected in mystical circles and, as Siegfried Ringler has proven, there are clear literary links between Pillenreuth, Engelthal, Inzigkoven, and St. Katharina in

Nuremberg.[1] In 1422 the Augustinians underwent a reform that consequently inaugurated a period of great literary activity especially under the superior (*Pröpstin*) Anna Ebin. The Augustinians became known for their copies and translations of mystical texts.[2] They enjoyed close ties with the Dominican nuns both of Engelthal and of St. Katharina, as well as with the Augustinian canonesses at Inzigkoven near Sigmaringen. This literary flowering as a result of the reform movement produced Manuscript W. As Ringler points out, it is certain that Pillenreuth possessed a description of Christina Ebner's life.[3] This may well have been something close to CES.

Other connections between Pillenreuth, Engelthal, and Inzigkoven exist. The inaugural sermon at Pillenreuth was delivered by a Dominican preacher.[4] The Library Catalogue of Engelthal lists a book by the chaplain at Pillenreuth.[5] The nuns of Engelthal also possessed manuscripts of many of the same works included in Manuscript W, which had Pillenreuth as its source and Inzigkoven as its producer. The Engelthal Catalogue includes a manuscript on the sisters of Weiler, the *Sister-Book of Kirchberg*, and a Sister-Book of a Dominican monastery near Ulm, all of which appear in Manuscript W.[6]

Originally two women from Sigmaringen founded Inzigkoven in 1354 following the rule of the Third Order Franciscans.[7] This foundation gradually won more followers, and a church dedicated to St. John the Baptist and a new cloister were erected in 1388. After the founding sisters died, those who remained wished to associate themselves with a stricter order. Consequently the community became Augustinian canonesses in 1394. After 1412, under the prioress Anna Schmid, strict enclosure was made possible by certain privileges the canonesses had gained, such as the choice of their own confessor and permission to receive the sacraments in their own chapel. Thereafter followed a period of intense literary activity spurred on by the visions of the prioress, Anna Schmid (d. 1420). The monastic scriptorium gained a reputation by producing fine missals and choir books. In 1431 the canonesses adopted the statutes of Pillenreuth. Thereafter their confessors came from the monasteries of Langenzenn and Indersdorf. Inzigkoven's library contained many mystical texts from the fourteenth century, having been copied by Anna Jäck and later by Elisabeth Muntprat. In 1498 Justina Blarer translated the lives of the Dutch leaders of the Devotio Moderna. Eventually the monastery, like so many other religious houses was suppressed in 1802 in the era of enlightened despots.[8] The last sister died in 1856. After the secularization, the library holdings were either destroyed or dispersed. The extant works show the great value the monastery must have placed on the preservation of mystical texts from various sources.

Siegfried Ringler and others claim that the cause of this great flowering of mysticism and literary activity at Inzigkoven was the adoption of the statutes of the hermitesses of Pillenreuth. These new statutes gave clear and strict guidelines to the members of the community that led ultimately to the adoption of private cells for each sister, unlike the majority of monastics, who slept in dormitories. This change fostered and facilitated deeper and more frequent private prayer and therefore supported the development of contemplation. Strict enclosure helped to focus the attention of the sister, especially on work in the scriptorium. Another cause of the literary flowering related to the adoption of a stricter rule was the entrance of women from the nobility who were already educated and eager for the religious life.[9]

More than 30 manuscripts from Inzigkoven have been identified thus far. Among them are texts from some of the greatest mystical writers of the Late Middle Ages: Bonaventure, Rulman Merswin, Pseudo-Bonaventure, Meister Eckhart, Gertrude the Great, Marquard of Lindau, Jan van Roesbroeck, Henry Suso, and John Tauler. Ringler draws the conclusion that the manuscript containing the works from Engelthal was copied in the same time frame and for the same audience of those writers listed above.[10] With this treasure of mystical texts, the canonesses of Inzigkoven possessed the thoughts and teachings of the greatest men and women mystics of the age, a source that helped, no doubt, to keep the women of Inzigkoven fervent and devout, without any need for reform, up to the day of the monastery's secularization.

Inzigkoven is particularly important for showing the influence of the literature of Engelthal because a collection of these works was included in a major manuscript *(Sammelhardschrift)* produced for the canonesses of Inzigkoven in the fifteenth century by Hans Probst.[11] This manuscript includes Christina Ebner's *Sister-Book of Engelthal* (f.84[r]-119[v]), the *Revelations* of Adelheid Langmann (f.120[r]-168[r]), the *Gnaden-vita of Friedrich Sunder, Chaplain of Engelthal* (f.174[v]-227[r]), and the *Vita of Sister Gertrud of Engelthal* (f. 227[r]-229[r]) by Conrad Friedrich and Heinrich of Engelthal. These Engelthal texts, recorded in close proximity to each other and all included in the second half of the manuscript, comprise two-thirds of this grand collection of mystical texts. They represent the largest selection of texts from a singular source—Engelthal.

Siegfried Ringler underscores the importance of this manuscript for three reasons: 1) Hans Probst compiled this work for the monastery of Inzigkoven. It was not a manuscript brought by one of the novices, nor was it a gift from someone outside the monastery. A portion of the manuscript was written later by Anna Jäck, a member of the community of Inzigkoven. Since these facts draw one to the conclusion that the *Sammelhandschrift* was produced for Inzigkoven, it must also reveal specifically important mystical interests of the community. 2) Because this manuscript is a collection of previously written works, it shows what literary works influenced the community at Inzigkoven. 3) Since this manuscript can be definitely identified as a production of Inzigkofen, it can help in identifying other manuscripts as belonging to this monastery by reference to the scribes or to the content.[12]

THE MONASTERY OF ST. KATHARINA IN NUREMBERG

It should not be surprising that the Dominican monastery of St. Katharina in Nuremberg exerted a certain influence over other reform-minded monasteries in southern Germany. St. Katharina promoted the reform of Dominican monasteries and successfully exported its own reform to other Dominican houses—especially to its "mother" house, Engelthal. When Engelthal grew too large a daughter house was founded in 1267 at Frauenaurach. The first prioress was Mechthild Krumpsit, a nun of Engelthal, whose biographical sketch is included in the *Sister-Book of Engelthal* written by Christina Ebner. In 1295, sixteen nuns from Frauenaurach moved to Nuremberg to begin a new foundation known as St. Katharina. In 1428, the monastery was first reformed by nuns from the monastery of Schönensteinbach and afterwards led the reform of many other Dominican monasteries.[13]

Siegfried Ringler demonstrates in particular correspondence between the texts of Manuscript W, produced at Inzigkoven and containing important lengthy texts from Engelthal, with passages from numerous manuscripts belonging to the Dominicans of St. Katharina.[14] Further, he shows specific connections between the Inzigkoven manuscript and others from St. Katharina, thus demonstrating interdependence and influence of these monasteries.

While Pillenreuth promoted mystical literature and Inzigkoven disseminated manuscripts, some of the most important texts for both monasteries were the biographical and autobiographical texts written at Engelthal. While it is true that Engelthal was just one monastery in a complexus of religious houses of men or women, all of whom believed, practiced, taught, and promoted the reality of mystical experience, still, it is rural Engelthal that produced powerful documents of faith and mystical experience that found a ready audience in this circle of like-minded individuals. It is precisely in the biographical and autobiographical nature of the texts that they are so fascinating to others. These texts preach in a concrete way from personal experience what Meister Eckhart, John Tauler, and Henry Suso expressed in their homilies and tracts. The Engelthal texts incarnate the word of God in living contemporaries who record their sometimes beautiful, sometimes frightening, and sometimes bizarre experiences in literary texts so that others may believe and follow in their way.

The extent of Engelthal's influence cannot really be judged for several important reasons. It is not certain how many manuscripts were ever produced by the writers of Engelthal or how many were copied for use in monasteries elsewhere. The destruction of these religious houses and the dissemination or destruction of their library holdings caused during the Reformation, the Thirty Years War, and the great period of secularization in the early nineteenth century make it impossible to judge the influence that the texts of Engelthal might have had on contemporaries or on subsequent readers. The manuscripts that survived were written in a German that became progressively more difficult to read and understand. In addition, the theology expressed in the texts and the reports of what in any age would be considered fantastical mystic experiences made the texts unpalatable to all but a few. With a renewed sense of the contribution of women's experience to theology, these texts will no doubt take their place among the great biographical spiritual works of Christianity.

NOTES

INTRODUCTION

1. Siegfried Ringler, *Viten-und Offenbarungsliteratur in Frauenklöstern des Mittelalters* (München: Artemis Verlag, 1980), 383.
2. Ringler, *Viten*, 384.
3. None of these works has been translated into English, except as excerpts in scholarly articles. I have already translated the *Offenbarungen* of Adelheid Langmann and plan to translate all the texts produced at Engelthal for publication.
4. Gustav Voit, *Engelthal: Geschichte eines Dominkanerinnenklosters im Nürnberger Raum* (Nürnberg: Verlag Korn und Bern, 1977), 25; Karl Schröder, ed., *Der Nonne von Engelthal Büchlein von der Gnaden Überlast* (Tübingen: H. Laupp, 1871), 7.
5. Voit. *Engelthal, Nürnberger Urkundenbuch*, 172.
6. ESB, 6; Schröder, *Der Nonne*, 3:4-10.
7. Voit, *Engelthal*, 23.
8. Schröder, *Der Nonne*, 3.
9. Ibid., 5f.
10. Voit, *Engelthal*, 24.
11. Gustav Voit, "Geschichte des Klosters," *750 Jahre Engelthal* (Simmelsdorf: Altnürnberger Landschaft e.V., 1994), 11.
12. Voit, *Engelthal*, 25, fn 69.
13. Ibid., 25.
14. Schröder, *Der Nonne*, 7; Voit, *Engelthal*, 25.
15. Voit, *Engelthal*, 25.
16. Ibid., 26.
17. Schröder, *Der Nonne*, 7; Voit, *Engelthal*, 27.
18. Voit, *Engelthal*, 27.
19. Ibid.
20. Ibid., 207-209.
21. Philipp Strauch, *Die Offenbarungen der Adelheid Langmann: Klosterfrau zu Engelthal* (Straßburg: Karl J. Trübner, 1878), 73. Henceforth, this will be cited as *Adelheid Langmann*, but when I refer to the manuscript transcription, it will appear as AL. Unless specifically referenced as Strauch, *Margaretha Ebner*, all references to Strauch refer to his book on Adelheid Langmann.
22. Voit, *Engelthal*, 35.
23. Voit, "Geschichte des Klosters," 16.
24. Ibid., 16-17.

25. Ibid., 44. Charles IV (1315-78) became king of Bohemia in 1346 and assumed the imperial dignity in 1355.

26. Voit, *Engelthal,* 44; G. W. K. Lochner, *Leben und Gesichte der Christine Ebnerin: Klosterfrau zu Engelthal* (Nürnberg: August Recknagel's Buchhandlung, 1872), 25.

27. Voit, *Engelthal,* 44; Lochner, *Leben,* 26.

28. Voit, *Engelthal,* 44; Lochner, *Leben,* 27f., 35f.

29. Voit, *Engelthal,* 40.

30. Ibid., 41.

31. Voit, "Geschichte des Klosters," 20.

32. Hieronymus Wilms, *Das Älteste Verzeichnis der deutschen Dominikanerinnenklöster* in *Quellen und Forschungen zur Geschichte des Dominikanerordens in Deutschland* (Leipzig: Otto Harrassowitz, 1928), 71.

CHAPTER ONE

1. Marie-Humbert Vicaire, *St. Dominic and His Times,* translated by Kathleen Pond (New York: McGraw Hill, 1964), 122.

2. "The Primitive Constitutions of the Monastery of San Sisto," *Early Documents of the Dominican Sisters.* Vol. I. (Summit, N.J.: Dominican Nuns of Summit, 1969), 7.

3. *Early Documents,* II, 1.

4. Ibid., II, 1-2.

5. Ibid., II, 2.

6. Ibid., II, 5.

7. Karl Schröder, *Der Nonne von Engelthal Büchlein von der Gnaden Überlast.* Tübingen: H. Laupp, 1871), 30.

8. Ibid., 17.

9. AL, 178a; Philipp Strauch, *Die Offenbarungen der Adelheid Langmann, Klosterfrau zu Engelthal* (Straßburg: Karl J. Trübner, 1878), 68:11. Henceforth, this will be cited as *Adelheid Langmann,* but when I refer to the manuscript transcription, it will appear as AL. Unless specifically referenced as Strauch, *Margaretha Ebner,* all references to Strauch refer to his book on Adelheid Langmann.

10. Margarete Weinhandl, *Deutsches Nonnenleben: Das Leben der Schwestern zu Töß und der Nonne von Engelthal Büchlein von der Gnaden Überlast in Katholikon Werke und Urkunden,* II (München: O.C. Recht Verlag, 1921), 29.

11. Ibid., 18-19.

12. AL, 103a; Strauch, 13:24f.; AL, 117b; Strauch 23:24.

13. Leonard P.Hindsley, *Margaret Ebner: Major Works* (New York: Paulist Press, 1993), 93.

14. *Early Documents,* II, 33.

15. Weindhandl, *Deutsches Nonnenleben,* 21.

16. AL, 154b; Strauch, 48:29.

17. AL, 151a; Strauch 46:10f.; AL, 186b; Strauch, 76:18.

18. AL, 151a; Strauch, 48:29.
19. *Early Documents*, II, 38.
20. Ibid., II, 38.
21. *Early Documents*, II, 12.
22. Weinhandl, *Deutsches Nonnenleben*, 36.
23. *Early Documents*, II, 15.
24. Ibid., II, 16-17.
25. Ibid., II, 17.
26. Simon Tugwell, O.P., *Early Dominicans: Selected Writings* (New York: Paulist Press, 1982), 70.
27. *Early Documents*, II, 33.
28. Ibid., II, 34.
29. Ibid., II, 7.
30. Ibid., II, 22-23.
31. Cod. Cent. VII, 79, Nuremberg, Staatsbibliothek.
32. Ibid., VII, 25. 1-48.
33. Paul Ruf, ed., *Mittelalterliche Bibliothekskataloge— Deutschlands und der Schweiz* 3,1, 1932, (München: Beck'sche Verlag, 1932), 645.
34. Martin Grabmann, "Deutsche Mystik in Kloster Engelthal" *Sammelblatt des Historischen Vereins Eichstätt* 25/26, (1912), 33- 44.
35. Weinhandl, *Deutsches Nonnenleben*, 17.
36. Hieronymus Wilms, *Geschichte der deutschen Dominikanerinnen, 1206-1916* (Dulmen i.W.: Laumann'sche Buchhandlung, 1920), 75-76.
37. Weinhandl, *Deutsches Nonnenleben*, 35.
38. Grabmann, "Deutsche Mystik," 34.
39. Margot Schmidt in Hindsley, *Margaret Ebner*, 46-47.
40. Grabmann, "Deutsche Mystik," 39.
41. CEN, XVIv (my translation).
42. Wilhelm Preger, *Geschichte der deutschen Mystik im Mittelalter* (Leipzig: Dorfling & Francke, 1881, 3 vols.; reprint Aalen: Otto Zeller Verlagsbuchhandlung, 1962), 275-276; AL, 122b; Strauch, 27:14f.
43. Siegfried Ringler, ed., *Die Deutsche Literatur des Mittelalters Verfasserlexikon* (Berlin: Walter de Gruyter, 1985), 602; Strauch, *Adelheid Langmann*, 61:12-66:7.
44. Henri Denifle, "Über die Anfänge der Predigtweise der deutschen Mystiker," *Archiv für Literatur und Kirchengeschichte des Mittelalters* (Berlin/Frieburg: B. Herder, 1886), 645.
45. Tugwell, *Early Dominicans*, 327-329.
46. Wilms, *Dominikanerinnen*, 72.
47. Ibid., 73.
48. Otto Langer, "Zur Dominikanischen Frauenmystik im spätmittelalterlichen Deutschland," in Peter Dinzelbacher and Dieter K. Bauer, eds., *Frauenmystik im Mittelalter* (Ostfildern bei Stuttgart: Schwabenverlag, 1985), 342-343.
49. AL, 112a; Strauch, 19:29.
50. Weinhandl, *Deutsches Nonnenleben*, 33.
51. Langer, "Frauenmystik," 342-343.

52. AL, 107a; Strauch, 16:25-26.
53. AL, 173a; Strauch, 63:5-6.
54. AL, 173b; Strauch, 63:14-17.
55. AL, 98b; Strauch, 9:26f.; AL, 106b, Strauch, 16:13f.
56. AL, 132a; Strauch, 33:25-26.
57. AL, 106a; Strauch, 16:2-4.
58. Langer, "Frauenmystik," 346.
59. Philipp Strauch, *Margaretha Ebner und Heinrich von Nördlingen* (Freiburg i.B. and Tübingen: Akademische Verlagsbuchhandlung von J. C. B. Mohr, 1882; reprint Amsterdam: Verlag P. Schippers, N.V., 1966), 270-271.
60. Alois Haas in Preface to Josef Schmidt, ed, and Maria Shrady, trans., *Johannes Tauler: Sermons* (New York: Paulist Press, 1985), xii.
61. Ibid., xiii.
62. Ibid., xxiv.
63. Shrady, *Johannes Tauler*, 164.
64. Ibid., 165.
65. Nicholas Heller, *The Exemplar: Life and Writings of Blessed Henry Suso*, O.P. (Dubuque, I.A.: The Priory Press, 1962), II, 117-127.
66. AL, 112b; Strauch, 20:15.
67. AL, 106b; Strauch, 16:13f.
68. Heller, *The Exemplar*, II, 335.
69. Weinhandl, *Deutsches Nonnenleben*, 36-37.
70. AL, 139b; Strauch, 38:23-27.
71. AL, 198a; Strauch, 85:12-13.
72. AL, 157b, Strauch,, 51:13-15.
73. AL, 150b; Strauch, 45:23-26.
74. AL, 178a; Strauch, 68:25-27.
75. AL, 139b; Strauch, 38:23-27.
76. AL, 110a; Strauch, 18:25-28.
77. Weinhandl, *Deutsches Nonnenleben*, 37-38, quoting Engelbert Krebs, "Die Mystik in Adelhausen: Eine vergleichende Studie über die Chronik der Anna von Munzingen und die Thaumatographische Literatur des 13. und 14. Jahrhunderts als Beitrag zur Geschichte der Mystik im Predigerorden," *Festgabe Heinrich Finke* (Münster: Aschendorff, 1904), 87.

CHAPTER TWO

1. Manuscript W is f. 84^r-119^v of the *Codex Scotensis Vindobonensis*, 234.
2. Gertrud Jaron Lewis, *By Women, for Women, about Women: the Sister-Books of Fourteenth-Century Germany* (Toronto: Pontifical Institute of Medieval Studies, 1996), 287.

3. See Siegfried Ringler, *Viten- und Offenbarungsliteratur in Frauenklöstern des Mittelalters* (München: Artemis Verlag, 1980), 19-28, for a detailed description of the contents, the history of the manuscript and its features.

4. Ringler, *Viten*, 21.

5. Lewis, Willaert, and Govers. *Bibliographie zur deutschen Frauenmystik des Mittelalters*, #10 in the series *Bibliographien zur deutschen Literatur des Mittelalters*, ed. Wolfgang Bachofer, (Berlin: Erich Schmidt Verlag, 1989), 418.

6. Manuscript W 118r.

7. Karl Schröder, *Der Nonne von Engelthal Büchlein von der Gnaden Überlast* (Tübingen: H. Laupp, 1871), 1:1.

8. Ibid., 1:11-13.

9. Ibid., 4:1-2.

10. Ibid., 10:9-10.

11. Ibid., 13:1-2.

12. Ibid., 7:12-14.

13. Ibid., 1:1-5.

14. Ibid., 1:5-10; Paragraph 1 refers to paragraph numbers of the text and is used here simply to indicate relative position in the manuscript.

15. By contrast, the *Sister-Book of Engelthal* reports this event, perhaps a betrothal, as taking place in 1214, whereas the historical documentation records the years of the marriage as 1220 or 1221.

16. Schröder, *Der Nonne*, 1:21; *3.

17. Ibid., 1:24-25, *4.

18. Ibid., 2:1-2, *4.

19. Ibid., 1:26-28.

20. Ibid., 2:2-4; Acts 2:44-45: "And all who believed were together and had all things in common and they sold their possessions and goods and distributed them to all, as any had need." See also Acts 4:34-35: "There was not a needy person among them, for as many as were possessors of lands or houses sold them, and brought the proceeds of what was sold and laid it at the apostles' feet; and distribution was made to each as any had need."

21. Schröder, *Der Nonne*, 2:5, *5.

22. Ibid., 2:5-6.

23. Ibid., 2:9-10.

24. Ibid., 2:11-14, *5.

25. Ibid., 2:16, *5.

26. Ibid., 2:17-23.

27. Ibid., 2:25.

28. Ibid., 2:27, *5.

29. Ibid., 2:5f., *5.

30. Ibid., 3:24f., *9.

31. Ibid., 4:3f., *10.

32. Ibid., 3: 19-20. Various scholars have assumed that "gray Order" refers to Cistercians, but Ulrich's response to the proposal implies that it may refer to Franciscans, Poor Clares, who wore sacks and a cloak, not the normal attire

33. Ibid., 6:12f., *18.
34. Ibid., 42:28-34. Christina quotes from the response after the fifth nocturne at matins on the fourth Sunday of Advent: "Virgo Israel revertere ad civitate tuas; usquequo dolens averteris? Generabis Dominum Salvatorem oblationem novam in terra ambulabunt homines * In salvationem . . . In caritate perpetua dilexi te: ideo attraxi te miserans."
35. Ibid., 7:7-10, *20.
36. Ibid., 7:20-21, *20.
37. Ibid., 37:33-38:11, *126.
38. John 1:12: "Quotquot autem receperunt eum, dedit eis potestatem filios Dei fieri, his qui credunt in nomine ejus." All English translations of the Bible text are from the Revised Standard Version.
39. See Lewis, By Women, 59, n. 4, 169, 170.
40. Schröder, Der Nonne, 42:28-34, *147.

CHAPTER THREE

1. VGE, 227v: ". . . wann wir es daz tusent tail nicht geschriben haben daz sie vns gesait het."
2. VGE, 227r; Siegfried Ringler, Viten- und Offenbarungsliteratur in Frauenklöstern des Mittelalters (München: Artemis Verlag, 1980), 445.
3. Gustav Voit, Engelthal: Geschichte eines Dominikanerinnenklosters in Nürnberger Raum (Nürnberg: Verlag Korn und Bern, 1977), 105-109.
4. Ibid., 108; M RN 352.
5. Voit, Engelthal, 108; M RN 507.
6. Voit, Engelthal, 108; M RN 891.
7. VGE, 227v: "Nun heb ich hie an von diser swester leben."
8. Voit, Engelthal, 216.
9. Ibid., 219-220.
10. FS, 176r; Ringler, Viten, 393.
11. FS, 176v; Ringler, Viten, 393.
12. Ibid.
13. Ibid.
14. FS, 177r; Ringler, Viten, 393.
15. FS, 177v; Ringler, Viten, 394.
16. Ibid. Reference to this incident appears in Matt. 26:39, 26:42; Mark 14:36; John 18:11; John 19:26ff; Luke 22:42, 23:34, 23:46.
17. Ibid.
18. Ibid.
19. FS, 178v; Ringler, Viten, 394: 150f.
20. VGE, 227r: "Ain wenig von der hailigen Gerdruden."

21. VGE, 229r: "Gedenckend durch got her Hansen Bropscz von Byberach mit ainem Aue Maria, schriber diss buchs."

22. VGE, 227r: "Die wunder gottes vnd die gnad, die er tut und wurcket mit gutten luten, die sind gut zewissen, da von daz vnser herre da von gelobt werd vnd die lut da von gebessert werden."

23. VGE, 227v: "Daz tat sie etwen vnserm herren zy lob vnd durch vnser sel hail, daz wir vns da by solten bessren . . ."

24. VGE, 227v: "Vnd och gar oft vberkam sie vnser herr, kum daz sie vns etlich ding sait."

25. VGE, 227v: ". . . da trumpt ir daz ain liechter stern fur von himel herab vf ir hopt, als got wolt da mit zerkennen geben, daz daz kint, daz die frou trug, solt ain liecht werden jn der cristenheit, als och geschach."

26. VGE, 227v-228r: "Da by gab sie zerkennen, daz sie sich dez kindes wolt vnderwinden vnd wolt dez pflegen, als sie och tet allwegen."

27. VGE, 228r: "Vnd des tromes verstunden sie sich nit was er betutet, vncz hin nach da sie sahen, was got gross gnaden an das kint leit."

28. Of particular relevance for monastics would have been the account of the birth of Christ given in the *Legenda aurea* by Jacobus de Voragine: "The mode of the birth [of Christ] was also miraculous. It was above nature . . . in that the birth was painless" (39); Thomas Aquinas likewise teaches that Mary suffered no pain in giving birth to Christ (ST III, q. 35, art. 6), basing his argument from authority on the *Sermo de Nativitate* by St. Augustine.

29. VGE, 228r: "Daz kind was also gut, als wir vernumen, daz sin mutter kain nacht von seinem wainen nie uf gestund: wann wo es sin mutter hingeseczt jn siner wiegen tag oder nacht, da lag es still vnd gutlichen."

30. VGE, 228r: "Vnser herr got der hub fru an, dem kind sin gnad mit zetailen."

31. VGE, 228v: "Die selben gewonheit volbracht vnser herr an ir vncz jn ir alter, daz er sie spiset mit gotlicher sussikait, daz si es liplichen enpfand, nit all tag och oft, vnd tat ir kunt, daz er daz het getan an ir von kinthait."

32. For Margaret Ebner, see Leonard Hindsley, *Margaret Ebner: Major Works* (New York: Paulist Press, 1993), 134, where Mary gives Margaret the Christ Child to let him suck from her heart; for Christina Ebner, see CEN, 56rv, 145v, and VGE, 88r, 141r.

33. VGE, 228v: "Gelobet siest du, zarte, werde, hcohgelobste kungin, vnser fro!"

34. VGE, 228v-229r: "Als du sprichest 'Gelobet siest du', so lobest du mich mit dem engeln, der mir von himel her ab ward gesant vnd mir bracht den gruss von got. Als du denn sprichest 'zartes', so lobest du mich mit dem hailigen gaist, der ain anvaher was mit mir siner zarten werk. Als du denn sprichest 'werde', so lobest du mich mit minem lieben sun, dem ich ward was vor allen frowen. Als du denn sprichest 'hochgelobte', so lobest du mich mit dem himelschen vatter, der mich hochgelobt hat ob allen hailigen jn dem himel. Als du denn sprichest 'kunigin, vnser frou', so lobest du mich mit allen hailigen, der kungin ich hin."

35. VGE, 229r; Ringler, *Viten*, 447.

36. VGE, 229r: "Vnd wenn du daz sprichest, so sicht dich ie als oft vnser fro an."

37.   VGE, 229r; Ringler, *Viten*, 446.

CHAPTER FOUR

1.   AL, 87a; Philipp Strauch, *Die Offenbarungen der Adelheid Langmann, Klosterfrau zu Engelthal* (Straßburg: Karl J. Trübner, 1878), 1:4-6. Henceforth, this will be cited as *Adelheid Langmann*, but when I refer to the manuscript transcription, it will appear as AL. Unless specifically referenced as Strauch, *Margaretha Ebner*, all references to Strauch refer to his book on Adelheid Langmann.

2.   AL, 87a; Strauch, 1:6-14.

3.   AL, 185b-186b; Strauch, 75:22-76:9.

4.   AL, 188b; Strauch, 77f.

5.   AL, 106b; Strauch, 16:13-18.

6.   AL, 170a; Strauch, 61:12 f.

7.   Gustav Voit, *Engelthal: Geschichte eines Dominikanerinnenkloster im Nürnberger Raum* (Nürnberg: Verlag Korn und Bern, 1977), 192.

8.   Ibid., 192.

9.   Strauch, *Adelheid Langmann*, xvi.

10.   AL, 126b; Strauch, 29:28.

11.   Voit, *Engelthal*, 194.

12.   Strauch, *Adelheid Langmann*, xvi.

13.   *Geschlecht-Buch der stadt Nürnberg*, British Museum Library, German manuscript 10,009, 1559, s.v. Langmann.

14.   Strauch, *Adelheid Langmann*, xvi.

15.   Ibid.

16.   Voit, *Engelthal*, 192.

17.   Johann Christoph Martini, *Historisch-geographisch Beschreibung des ehemaligen berühmten Frauenklosters Engelthal* (Nürnberg/Altdorf, 1762; 2. Aufl. 1798), 80, 86.

18.   Ibid., 114. Geut Sechsin is the same name as Jutta Sachsen.

19.   Voit, *Engelthal*, 193.

20.   AL, 150b-151a; Strauch, 45:31-46:9.

21.   AL, 148a; Strauch, 43:27-44:3.

22.   AL, 162ab; Strauch, 55:3-16.

23.   AL, 164b; Strauch, 56:20-26.

24.   AL, 165b; Strauch, 57:14-17.

25.   AL, 166a-167b; Strauch, 57:20-58:12.

26.   AL, 168b-169a; Strauch, 60:10-13.

27.   Wilhelm Oehl, *Deutsche Mystikerbriefe des Mittelalters 1100-1550* (München: Georg Müller Verlag, 1931), 393.

28.   See Strauch, *Adelheid Langmann*, xii-xv, for further details about the manuscripts.

29.   Ibid., xx.

30. For Adelheid's *Prayer* see AL, 191b-207b and Strauch, 80-91; for the letters see AL 207b-215 and Strauch, 91-96; for the school episode see AL, 103b-104a and Strauch, 14:8-15.

31. For Eberhard see AL, 160b and Strauch, 53; for Elsbet see AL, 178a and Strauch, 68; See Siegfried Ringler, *Viten- und Offenbarungsliteratur in Frauenklöstern des Mittelalters* (München: Artemis Verlag, 1980), 64-73, where he compares these manuscripts in detail.

32. For temptation see AL, 185b-187a and Strauch, 75-76; for profession see AL, 97a and Strauch, 8.

33. Ringler, *Viten*, 19-28.

34. Ibid., 73.

35. For lack of faith see AL, 95b-96b and Strauch, 7:25-8:16; for wounds see AL, 178a and Strauch, 67:33-68:3.

36. Ringler, *Viten*, 74.

37. Library Catalogue, Staatsarchiv Nürnberg, Nürnberger Saalbücher, Nr. 45a, fol. 7.

38. For prayer see AL, 191b and Strauch, 80:20f.

39. The new section begins at AL, 209a; Strauch, 92:26f.

40. AL, 87a; Strauch, 1:1-15.

41. AL, 87b-88a; Strauch, 1:20-2:8.

42. AL, 88b-90a; Strauch, 2:19-3:22.

43. AL, 91a; Strauch, 4:7-26; AL, 92a-93a; Strauch, 4:27- 5:26.

44. Josef Schmidt, Introduction to Joseph Schmidt, ed., and Maria Shrady, trans., *Johannes Tauler: Sermons* (New York: Paulist Press, 1985), 12.

45. AL, 87a; Strauch, 1:1-4.

46. AL, 170a-177a; Strauch, 61-66.

47. AL, 191b; Strauch, 80.

48. AL, 191b-192b; Strauch, 80-81.

49. AL, 193b; Strauch, 82:7f.

50. AL, 191b; Strauch, 80.

51. AL, 193b; Strauch, 82:7f.

52. AL, 195b; Strauch, 83:15-18.

53. AL, 205b-206a; Strauch, 90:18-24.

54. AL, 194b-195a; Strauch, 82:34-38; AL, 194bf.; Strauch, 82:23-32.

55. AL, 193a; Strauch, 81:30-33; and again AL, 202b; Strauch, 88:4f.

56. For bridegroom see AL, 193a and Strauch, 81; for child see AL, 196ab and Strauch, 83:34-84:3.

57. AL, 207b, Strauch, 91:23-28.

58. Oehl, *Mystikerbriefe*, 394-396; for Letter 1 see AL, 211b-212b and Strauch, 94:1-19; for Letter 2 see AL, 212b-214a and Strauch, 94:20-95:17; for Letter 3 see AL, 214a-215b and Strauch, 95:18-96:3; for the rest of the text of letters see AL, 209a-211b and Strauch, 92:26-93:36.

59. Philipp Strauch, *Margaretha Ebner und Heinrich von Nördlingen* (Freiburg i.B. and Tübingen: Akademische Verlagsbuchhandlung von J. C. B. Mohr, 1882; reprint Amsterdam: Verlag P. Schippers, N.V., 1966), Letter LIX, 272:10-11.

60. AL, 212b; Strauch, 94:20f.
61. AL, 214ab; Strauch, 95:18f.
62. AL, 214a; Strauch, 95:18.
63. AL, 215ab; Strauch, 96:1-3.

CHAPTER FIVE

1. "Daz gehort almol dem elczten Ebner an daz ez almol pey vnderm namen belieben schol."
2. "Das leben der heiligen Christina Ebnerin."
3. "Tobias Ebner ist es zustaendig."
4. Ursula Peters judges this to be from the eighteenth century, but the librarians in Stuttgart prefer sixteenth or seventeenth century. See Ursula Peters, *Religiöse Erfahrung als literarisches Faktum: Zur Vorgeschichte und Genese frauenmystischer Texte des 13. und 14. Jahrhunderts* (Tübingen: Max Niemeyer Verlag, 1988), 157.
5. CES, 75v.
6. CES, 154v-155r.
7. Peters, *Erfahrung*, 157, fn 102: Ursula Peters believes this manuscript comes from the fifteenth century.
8. Johannes Traber, *Die Herkunft der selig genannten Dominikanerin Margareta Ebner, geboren zirka 1291, gestorben 20. Juni 1351* (Donauwörth: Historischer Verein Donauwörth, 1910), 12.
9. Sebastian Schlettstetter, *Dass Wunderbarliche Leben, Hoche und unerhorte Wunderwerck der Seligen Gottgeweichten Jungfraw Margarethae von Maria Medingen*—a manuscript dated 1662 and housed in the archives of the Monastery of Maria Medingen, Mödingen.
10. Peters, *Erfahrung*, 158.
11. Ibid., 159; Md1, 321.
12. Md1, 107f.; Peters, *Erfahrung*, 158.
13. Md1, 282f.; Peters, *Erfahrung*, 158.
14. Md1, 262f.; Peters, *Erfahrung*, 158.
15. Md1, 356; Peters, *Erfahrung*, 158.
16. Md1, 326f.; Peters, *Erfahrung*, 159.
17. Md1, 422, Peters, *Erfahrung*, 159.
18. Md1, 392ff.; Peters, *Erfahrung*, 159.
19. Md1, 371; Peters, *Erfahrung*, 159.
20. Peters, *Erfahrung*, 159.
21. Md1, 319; Peters, *Erfahrung*, 159: "herr nün las mich, das ich ims sag."
22. Md1, 320; Peters, *Erfahrung*, 160: "vnd das hat sy offt mer getan: dz sie got pat das er sie liess zü im, wenn si in vberflussigen gnaden wz got ze einem lob, dz disw grossw ding nicht verdilget wurden, sunder das sie geoffent wurden got ze eim lob."

23. Peters, *Erfahrung*, 161: "Diese für die Entstehung des Lebensberichts so wichtige Beichtvater bleibt freilich anonym."

24. Md1, 4; Peters, *Erfahrung*, 161: "wunder, die ir got het getan."

25. Md1, 27; Peters, *Erfahrung*, 163.

26. Peters, *Erfahrung*, 164.

27. Philipp Strauch, *Margaretha Ebner und Heinrich von Nördlingen* (Freiburg i.B. and Tübingen: Akademische Verlagsbuchhandlung von J. C. B. Mohr, 1882; reprint Amsterdam: Verlag P. Schippers, N.V., 1966), for Letter XXVI (1338), see 210:21; for LII (1348-49), see 266:62.

28. Gustav Voit, *Engelthal: Geschichte eines Dominikanerinnenklosters im Nürnberger Raum* (Nürnberg: Verlag Korn und Bern, 1977), 108.

29. CEN, XXVIIIr: "Wan si waz perolin und was in grozen noten daz si vergult. Do het her ir gelobt er wolte perol sein und si in einen noten lassen alz er tet." *Prioress* is the title of the superior of a monastery of Dominican nuns. *Prior* designates the superior of a convent of Dominican friars.

30. Engelthal Library Catalogue, Staatsarchiv Nürnberg, Nürnberger Saalbcher, Nr. 45a.

31. CEN, XXXIIIIv.

32. CEN, Ir: ". . . dise genade einer heiligen person die wol bekant ist in himel und in ertrich."

33. CEN, Ir: "Sich mert die gnade in irem hertzen in unsprechenlicher reicheit also daz sich die gnade uber goz uz der sel in den leip und in alle ire glider daz si von gnaden besezzen und beswert waz alz ein swangere graw eins kindes . . ."

34. CEN, Ir-Iv.

35. CEN, IIr.

36. Ibid.

37. Ibid.

38. CEN, IIv.

39. CEN, Iiv: "O du hertzenlicher innerster freunt, wie weistu so wol wenn du dir ewiclichen erwelt hast den kanst auch wol ruffen. So si komen in di zeit di horen auch snelliclich dein stimme und volgent dir nach. Also taten auch die erwelten kinder ditz convents die in vollem glauben die potschft gotez enpfingen von ir getrewen muter."

40. CEN, IIIr.

41. CEN, IIIrv.

42. CEN, IIIv.

43. CEN, Vv.

44. CEN, VIrv.

45. CEN, VIIv.

46. CEN, VIIIr.

47. CEN, LXXXXVIIIIv.

48. Ibid.

49. See, among others, CEN, XXXIr, XXXIIIIv, CVv, CVIIr, CXIIr, CXIIIr, CXXVIIr, CXXXVIIIIr.

50. CEN, LXXXXv.
51. CEN, CXLVrv.
52. CEN, CXLVv.
53. CEN, LXIIIr-LXIIIIr.
54. CEN, LXXXXVIv-LXXXXVIIIr.

CHAPTER SIX

1. Siegfried Ringler, *Viten- und Offenbarungsliteratur in Frauenklöstern des Mittelalters* (München: Artemis Verlag, 1980), 144.
2. Ibid., 364.
3. Ibid., 156.
4. FS, 203v; Ringler, *Viten*, 1057.
5. FS, 179v; Ringler, *Viten*, 396:184.
6. FS, 175v; Ringler, *Viten*, 392:41.
7. Ringler, *Viten*, 364.
8. CES, 111rv; Ringler, *Viten*, 448.
9. CES, 111rv.
10. CES, 96r.
11. See Peter Lechner, *Bericht aus dem mystischen Leben der gottseligen Ordensjungfrauen Christina und Margareth Ebner aus Nürnberg* in *Das mystische Leben der heiligen Margareth von Cortona* (Regensburg, 1862), 210.
12. CES, 116r.
13. Ibid.
14. Ibid., 78v-79r.
15. Ibid., 78v-79r.
16. Ibid., 78v-79r; Ringler, *Viten*, 448.
17. Karl Schröder, ed., *Der Nonne von Engelthal Büchlein von der Gnaden Überlast* (Tübingen: H. Laupp, 1871), 15, 21-25; ESB, 38.
18. Schröder, *Der Nonne*, 40, 20-41, 23; ESB, 103-104. This alludes to Eph. 4:26-27: "Be angry but do not sin; do not let the sun go down on your anger, and give no opportunity to the devil."
19. Schröder, *Der Nonne*, 41:22-23; ESB, 105.
20. Ringler, *Viten*, 449-450.
21. Wilhelm Preger, *Geschichte der deutschen Mystik im Mittelalter*. 3 vol. (Leipzig: Dorfling & Francke, 1881, reprint Aalen: Otto Zeller Verlagsbuchhandlung, 1962), 135; Ringler, *Viten*, 450; CES, 99v.
22. Ringler, *Viten*, 450; ESB, 27:27f.
23. Ringler, *Viten*, 450; HstAMü, NR 230; StAN, Nürnb. Salb. (Rep. 59) Nr. 207, f. 106r.
24. Ringler, *Viten*, 146-150.
25. FS, 174v; Ringler, *Viten*, 391:1-4.

26. John 20:31: ". . . but these are written that you may believe that Jesus is the Christ, the Son of God, and that believing you may have life in his name."

27. FS, 174v; Ringler, *Viten*, 391:5-8.

28. FS, 174v; Ringler, *Viten*, 391:9-10.

29. FS, 174v; Ringler, *Viten*, 391:12.

30. FS, 174v; Ringler, *Viten*, 391:16-17.

31. FS, 174v-175r; Ringler, *Viten*, 391:16-26.

32. See Dominic's Ninth Way of Prayer in particular; Simon Tugwell, "The Nine Ways of Prayer of St. Dominic: A Textual Study and Critical Edition," *Medieval Studies* 47 (1985), 91-92.

33. FS, 175r; Ringler, *Viten*, 391:27-29.

34. FS, 175r; Ringler, *Viten*, 391:28-392:35.

35. FS, 175r; Ringler, *Viten*, 392:36.

36. FS, 175v; Ringler, *Viten*, 392:37-43.

37. FS, 175v; Ringler, *Viten*, 392:43-52.

38. FS, 175v-176r; Ringler, *Viten*, 392:53-59.

39. William A. Hinnebusch, *The History of the Dominican Order*. Vol. I: *Origins and Growth to 1500* (Staten Island, N.Y.: Alba House, 1966), 51.

40. Simon Tugwell, *Early Dominicans: Selected Writings* (New York: Paulist Press, 1982), 95.

41. Ibid., 96.

42. John Cassian, *The Institutes and the Conferences* in C. S. Gibson, trans. *Nicene and Post-Nicene Fathers*, vol XI, (Oxford: Parker and Co., 1894, reprint 1982), 285.

43. Tugwell, *Early Dominicans*, 102.

44. Boniface Ramsey, O.P., trans., *John Cassian: The Conferences* in Ancient Christian Writers No. 57; (Mahwah and New York: Paulist Press, 1997), 375; Conf. X. VI. 4.

45. Ramsey, *Cassian*, 339; Conf. IX.XV.2; Gibson, *Cassian*, 392.

46. Ramsey, *Cassian*, 345, Conf. IX.XXV.1.

47. Ramsey, *Cassian*, 385, Conf. X.XI.5.

48. Ringler, *Viten*, 201.

49. FS, 1393-1398; Ringler, *Viten*, 430, *110.

50. FS, 184r; Ringler, *Viten*, 401:369-373.

51. FS, 184v; Ringler, *Viten*, 401:372-381.

52. FS, 185r-185v; Ringler, *Viten*, 402:409-413.

53. FS, 185v-186r; Ringler, *Viten*, 402-403:417-433.

54. FS, 218r; Ringler, *Viten*, 435:1577-1581.

55. FS, 174v-175v; Ringler, *Viten*, 391-392, *1-5.

56. FS, 176r; Ringler, *Viten*, 392-393, *7.

57. The Gertud section is FS, 176r-179r; Ringler, *Viten*, 393-395, *8-15.

58. Entenberg is located five kilometers from Engelthal. The monastery possessed lands around Entenberg and gradually assumed the spiritual care of the village. Testimony about a dispute over the spiritual care of Entenberg in 1319 states that the chaplains of Engelthal had been celebrating Mass there for over thirty years (Ringler, *Viten*, 186).

59. FS, 176r; Ringler, *Viten*, 393, *8.
60. Ibid.
61. Ibid., *9.
62. Ibid.
63. Ibid.
64. Ibid.
65. FS, 177r; Ringler, *Viten*, 393, *10.
66. FS, 179r, Ringler, *Viten*, 393, *16.
67. FS 177v; Ringler, *Viten*, 394:116f., *12; Matt. 18:21-22: "Then Peter came up and said to him, 'Lord, how often shall my brother sin against me, and I forgive him? As many as seven times?' Jesus said to him, 'I do not say to you seven times, but seventy times seven.'"
68. FS, 177v; Ringler, *Viten*, 394:119f., *12; Matt. 26:42: "Again for the second time, he went away and prayed, 'My Father, if this cannot pass unless I drink it, thy will be done;'" and Mark 14:36: "And he said, 'Abba, Father, all things are possible to thee; remove this cup from me; yet not what I will, but what thou wilt;'" and Luke 22:42: "Father, if thou art willing, remove this cup from me; nevertheless, not my will, but thine be done.'"
69. FS, 177v; Ringler, *Viten*, 394:120f., *12; John 19:26-27: "And when Jesus saw his mother, and the disciple whom he loved standing near, he said to his mother, 'Woman, behold your son!' Then he said to the disciple, 'Behold, your mother!' And from that time the disciple took her to his own home."
70. FS, 177v; Ringler, *Viten*, 394:122f., *12; Luke 23:34: "And Jesus said, 'Father, forgive them, for they know not what they do.' And they cast lots to divide his garment."
71. FS, 177v; Ringler, *Viten*, 394:124; *12; Luke 23:46: "Then Jesus crying out with a loud voice, said, 'Father, into thy hands I commit my spirit.'" And having said this he breathed his last."
72. FS, 178v; Ringler, *Viten*, 395:148-149, *13: This passage reveals the date of St. Caritas's feast day, the day before the feast of SS. Crispin and Crispinianus, October 24.
73. FS, 179v; Ringler, *Viten*, 396, *18.
74. FS, 180r; Ringler, *Viten*, 397, *21.
75. FS, 181v; Ringler, *Viten*, 398, *26.
76. FS, 181v; Ringler, *Viten*, 398, *27.
77. FS, 182r; Ringler, *Viten*, 399, *28.
78. FS,183v; Ringler, *Viten*, 400:346, *33.
79. FS, 183v-184r; Ringler, *Viten*, 400-401, *33.
80. FS, 184v; Ringler, *Viten*, 401:380-381, *34.
81. FS, 187r; Ringler, *Viten*, 404:475-485, *43.
82. Echtermeyer/Benno von Wiese, eds., *Deutsche Gedichte*, (Düsseldorf: August Bagel Verlag, 1973), 40.

You are mine, I am yours;
Of that you may be sure.

You have been locked up within my heart
And the key has been thrown away.
Within you must always stay.
(Translation my own.)

83. Allusions to this same poem occur in Adelheid Langmann's *Revelations* (103f; 47:911; 46:24-30) as well as in Mechthild of Magdeburg's *The Flowing Light of the Godhead.*
84. FS, 187r; Ringler, *Viten,* 404:483, *43.
85. FS, 181r; Ringler, *Viten,* 398:260, *25.
86. FS, 218v-219r; Ringler, *Viten,* 436:1607f, *132,
87. FS, 225r; Ringler, *Viten,* 442:1828-1836, *147.
88. FS, 219r; Ringler, *Viten,* 436:1618f, *133.
89. The feast day is 25 August; St. Louis died in 1270 and was already canonized by 1297.
90. FS, 188r-189r; Ringler, *Viten,* 406:518-406:560; *47.
91. Ringler, *Viten,* 231.
92. FS, 194v; Ringler, *Viten,* 398, 412:755f., *63.
93. FS, 194v; Ringler, *Viten,* 398., 412:763-766, *64.
94. FS, 194v; Ringler, *Viten,* 398., 412:766-771, *64.
95. FS, 195r; Ringler, *Viten,* 412:772-413:779, *65.
96. FS, 195r; Ringler, *Viten,* 413:780-785, *66.
97. FS, 196v; Ringler, *Viten,* 414:824-836, *69.
98. FS, 197r-197v; Ringler, *Viten,* 415:848f., *72.
99. FS, 198r; Ringler, *Viten,* 415:878f., *75.
100. FS, 198r; Ringler, *Viten,* 416:889f, *75.
101. FS, 198r-198v; Ringler, *Viten,* 416:889-898, *76.
102. Jeffrey F. Hamburger, *The Rothschild Canticles* (New Haven: Yale University Press, 1990), 108-109.
103. FS, 197v; Ringler, *Viten,* 415:866-870 *73.
104. Ringler, *Viten,* 257.
105. Hamburger, *Canticles,* 109.
106. FS, 198v; Ringler, *Viten,* 416:904f., *77.
107. FS, 198v; Ringler, *Viten.,* 416:906-910, *77.

CHAPTER SEVEN

1. Christina also quotes the Latin text of Psalm 10:7 (Vulgate; Ps. 11:6 RSV); Ps. 45:10, Ps. 86, Ps. 126:6; and Jer. 1:5, among others. The writer of the *Gnadenvita of Friedrich Sunder, Chaplain of Engelthal* also quotes directly in Latin: Gen. 32:24-29; Matt. 8:7; Ps. 44:3, 5; Ps. 45:6; Gal. 4:19. Deut. 32:5.
2. Luke 5:1: "Factum est autem, cum turbae irruerent in eum, ut audirent verbum Dei, et ipse stabat secus stagnum Genesareth." ("While the people pressed

upon him to hear the word of God, he was standing by the lake of Genesaret" [RSV].)

3. CEN, LXXXXIIIv.
4. FS, 221v; Siegfried Ringler, *Viten- und Offenbarungsliteratur in Frauenklöstern des Mittelalters* (München: Artemis Verlag, 1980), 438; Gal. 4:19: "My little children, with whom I am again in travail until Christ be formed in you!" [RSV]
5. FS, 222v; Ringler, *Viten,* 439.
6. CEN, CXLVIIr.
7. CEN, XXXr; CXXXIIIIv.
8. CEN, CXXXIIIIv.
9. ESB, 91; Karl Schröder, ed., *Der Nonne von Engelthal Büchlein von der Gnaden Überlast* (Tübingen: H. Laupp, 1871), 35: "Swer gotes joch tregt, dem macht er ez gern süez und leiht." Matt. 11:29-30: "Take my yoke upon you, and learn from me; for I am gentle and lowly in heart, and you will find rest for your souls. For my yoke is easy, and my burden is light" (RSV).
10. German paraphrases occur in the *Sister-Book of Engelthal*: 1 Cor. 13:12; in the autobiography of Christina Ebner: Isa. 66:12-13; Ps. 42: 1; 1 Cor. 2:2, 9-10; 2 Cor. 12:9; John 13:7; Matt. 5:18 and 11:11; (Luke 7:28); Luke 2:25-26; Luke 24:10.
11. CEN, LIIIr: "La dich meiner gnaden benugen. Ich briche meiner worte niht."
12. CEN, XIIIIv, LVv.
13. FS, 177v; Ringler, *Viten,* 394:110f.
14. FS, 224r; Ringler, *Viten,* 441:1800f.
15. ESB, 15-16; Schröder, *Der Nonne,* 6:33-7:3: "Da sie nu komen zu dem virden suntag im advent, da sie sungen die metin, da sie nun komen hintz dem funften respons 'Virgo Israel', und der vers 'In caritate perpetua', daz sank sie teutsch und sank so unmenschlichen wol, daz man brufet, sie sunge mit engelischer stimme. Der vers teut sich also: 'Ich han dich gemint in der ewigen minne, da von han ich dich zi mir gezogen mit meiner barmhertzikeit.'"
16. Schröder, *Der Nonne,* 60; note 6,35.
17. ESB, 76-77; Schröder, *Der Nonne,* 29-30: "Frew dich, tohter von Syon./schone botschaft kumet dir:/su solt singen suzzen don/nach allez dinez hertzen gir./ Du bist worden gotez schrin:/ do von solt du frolich sin/ und solt niht leiden hertzen pin. Wol her an den raien/ den schone kint wol sehen./ Jubiliren, meditiren,/ jubiliren, contempliren,/ jubiliren, speculieren,/ jubiliren, concordiren."
18. Schröder, *Der Nonne,* 65-66, note 29,30.
19. *Codex 2686,* Wien, Nationalbibliothek.
20. Paul Ruf, ed., *Mittelalterliche Bibliothekskataloge—Deutschlands und der Schweiz* (München: C. H. Beck'sche Verlag, 1932), 3,1,638-650.
21. AL, 116a; Philipp Strauch, *Die Offenbarungen der Adelheid Langmann, Klosterfrau zu Engelthal* (Straßburg: Karl J. Trübner, 1878), 22:16f., *35. Henceforth, this will be cited as *Adelheid Langmann,* but when I refer to the manuscript transcription, it will appear as AL. Unless specifically referenced as Strauch, *Margaretha Ebner,* all references to Strauch refer to his book on Adelheid Langmann.

22. AL, 121b; Strauch, 26:24f., *42.
23. AL, 122a; Strauch, 26:24f., *42.
24. AL, 193b; Strauch, 82:13f., *98.
25. AL, 141a-b; Strauch, 39:26f., *55.
26. AL, 129b; Strauch, 31:23f., *48.
27. AL, 129b; Strauch, 31:26f., *48.
28. AL, 124b; Strauch, 28:19, *43.
29. AL, 124b; Strauch, 28:19f., *43.
30. AL, 101a; Strauch, 12:2f; *19.
31. AL, 102a; Strauch, 13:3f.; *20.
32. For Beloved see *27,*35, *36, *38, *43, *51; for Love see *41, *56, *62, *65, *76.
33. AL, 198b; Strauch 85:23f., *119.
34. AL, 170b; Strauch, 61:21f., *72.
35. for "never be separated" see *5, *14, *19, *26, *50; for "Just as little" see *24.
36. AL, 211a; Strauch, 93:32f., *158.
37. AL, 122a; Strauch, 26:26f, *42.
38. AL, 122b; Strauch, 27:1f., *42.
39. AL, 122b-123a; Strauch, 27:10f., *42.
40. AL, 123a; Strauch, 27:15-19, *42.
41. AL, 99b; Strauch, 10:26f., *17.
42. AL, 99b; Strauch, 10:27-11:2, *17.
43. AL, 100a; Strauch, 11:9f., *17.
44. AL, 101a; Strauch, 12:5f., *19.
45. AL, 112a; Strauch, 20:4f., *32.
46. AL, 139b-140a; Strauch, 38:27f., *55.
47. AL, 140b; Strauch, 39:9f., *55.
48. AL, 175a-b; Strauch, 64:28-65:10, *72.
49. AL, 106a; Strauch, 16:4, *25.
50. AL, 122b-123a; Strauch, 27:10f., *42.
51. AL, 151b-152a; Strauch, 46:24, *62.
52. AL, 176b; Strauch, 65: 27f., *72
53. AL, 98b; Strauch, 9:26f., *15.
54. AL, 98b; Strauch, 10:1f., *15.
55. AL, 106a; Strauch, 16:13-14, *25
56. AL, 115a; Strauch, 21:24-26, *33; AL 126b; Strauch, 29:24- 27, *45.
57. AL, 103a; Strauch, 13:26f., *22.
58. AL, 103b; Strauch, 14:2f., *22.
59. AL, 108b; Strauch, 17:22f., *29.
60. AL, 203a; Strauch, 88:21-22, *138; Matt. 3:17: "This is my beloved Son with whom I am well pleased."

CHAPTER EIGHT

1. Philipp Strauch, *Die Offenbarungen der Adelheid Langmann, Klosterfrau zu Engelthal* (Straßburg: Karl J. Trübner, 1878), 115. Henceforth, this will be cited as *Adelheid Langmann*, but when I refer to the manuscript transcription, it will appear as AL. Unless specifically referenced as Strauch, *Margaretha Ebner*, all references to Strauch refer to his book on Adelheid Langmann.
2. Josef Haupt, ed., *Das Hohe Lied übersetzt von Williram, erklärt von Rilindis und Herrat, Äbtissinnen zu Hohenburg in Elsaß (1147-1196)* (Wien: Wilhelm Braumüller, 1864), 8-9 (my translation).
3. Ibid., 10.
4. Ibid., 10-11.
5. AL, 204a, Strauch, 89:3; Haupt, *Das Hohe Lied*, 25:1f.
6. Song of Sol. 5:1b: "Comedite, amici, et bibite; et inebriamini, carissimi."
7. Haupt, *Das Hohe Lied*, 66:10; "Grow and eat me, not that I will be changed into you through your eating of my body, but rather you will be changed into me."
8. AL, 134a; Strauch, 35:5-7; "'I will not be changed into you, rather you should be changed into me.'"
9. Haupt, *Das Hohe Lied*, 66.
10. Ibid., 1.
11. AL, 104ab; Strauch, 14:16f.
12. AL, 112b; Strauch, 20:12f.
13. AL, 129b; Strauch, 31:26-28.
14. AL, 135a; Strauch, 35:28-30.
15. AL, 141b; Strauch, 39:26-27.
16. AL, 193a; Strauch, 81:30-33.
17. Haupt, *Das Hohe Lied*, 16; Strauch, *Adelheid Langmann*, 1,36,42,72,79.
18. Haupt, *Das Hohe Lied*, 23; for crown see Strauch, *Adelheid Langmann*, 11 and 55, among other passages; for shows see 79; for dresses see 11.
19. Haupt, *Das Hohe Lied*, 27; Strauch, *Adelheid Langmann*, 65.
20. Haupt, *Das Hohe Lied*, 136.
21. Ibid., 136: The text in the Haupt edition differs slightly from the Vulgate: "Pone me ut signaculum super cor tuum ut signaculum super brachia tua. Quia fortis est delictio ut mors dura sicut inferus emulatio."
22. AL, 87b-90a; Strauch, 1:20-3:22.
23. AL, 122a; Strauch, 26:27.
24. AL, 92ab; Strauch, 5:8-12.
25. Bernard of Clairvaux, *Song of Songs*, trans. Kilian Walsh (Kalamazoo: Cisterican Publications, 1971-1976), I, 6:9; Bernard of Clairvaux, *S. Bernardi Opera, Vol. I, Sermones super Cantica Canticorum*, 2 vols., ed. Jean Leclerq (Romae: Editiones Cistercienses, 1957), 30: "Datum est et mihi misero nonnumquam sedere secus pedes Domini Jesu . . ."
26. Friedrich Ohly, "Geist und Formen der Hoheliedauslegung im 12. Jahrhundert," *Zeitschrift für Deutsches Altertum* 85 (1954), 187.

27. Bernard of Clairvaux, *Song of Songs*, I, 7:2; Bernard of Clairvaux, *Sermones*, I, 31: "Quis dicit? Sponsa. Quaenam ipsa? Anima sitiens Deum."

28. AL, 93ab; Strauch, 6:1-3.

29. AL 104a-107a, Strauch, 14-16; AL, 118ab, Strauch, 23-24.

30. AL, 98ab; Strauch, 9-10.

31. AL, 105a-107a; Strauch, 15-16; AL. 98ab; Strauch, 9-10.

32. AL, 122a-123b; Strauch, 26-27.

33. AL, 140a; Strauch, 38:27-28.

34. AL, 151b-152a; Strauch, 46:25-26.

35. AL, 152b; Strauch, 47:9-10.

36. AL, 90b; Strauch, 3:25f.

37. AL, 91a; Strauch, 4:16f.

38. AL, 91ab; Strauch, 4:7f.; AL, 169a-170a; Strauch, 60-61; AL, 185b-187a; Strauch, 75-76; AL, 91ab; Strauch, 4-5.

39. AL, 100a; Strauch, 11:9-11.

40. AL, 101a; Strauch, 12:2-4.

41. AL, 104b; Strauch, 15:1.

42. AL, 107a; Strauch, 16:25-26.

43. AL, 107b; Strauch, 16:31-17:6; AL, 108a; Strauch, 17:9; AL, 114b; Strauch, 21:15f.

44. AL, 118a; Strauch, 23:29f.

45. AL, 123b-124a; Strauch, 27:27f.

46. AL, 133b; Strauch, 34:19.

47. AL, 134a; Strauch, 35:5-7.

48. AL, 134b-135a; Strauch, 35:21f.

49. AL, 136b; Strauch, 36:25f.

50. Bernard of Clairvaux, *Song of Songs*, II, 27:1; Bernard of Clairvaux, *Sermones*, I, 182: "Quomodo ergo sicut pelles Salomonis formosa, quasi vero Salomon in omni gloria sua quidquam habuerit condignum decore sponsae et gloria ornatus eius?"

51. Bernard of Clairvaux, *Song of Songs*, II, 27:1; Bernard of Clairvaux, *Sermones*, I, 182: "Quid, inquam, tale in se ostendit ea quae praeterit figura huius mundi, quod aequare speciem animae possit illius, quae exuta terreni hominis vetustatem, eius qui de caelo est decorum induit, ornata optimis moribus pro monilibus, ipso purior, sicut et excelsior aethere, sole splendidor?"

52. AL, 95a; Strauch, 7:9f.

53. AL, 105a; Strauch, 15:13.

54. See, among others, AL, 104a; Strauch, 14:21-23; AL, 106b; Strauch, 16:8-10; AL, 118b; Strauch, 24:78.

55. AL, 109a; Strauch, 18:2f.

56. AL, 113b-114a; Strauch, 20-21.

57. AL, 129b; Strauch, 31:25f; AL, 135a; Strauch, 35:29-30.

58. AL, 143a-144a; Strauch, 40:31-41:14.

59. AL, 151b; Strauch, 46:16f.

60. AL, 112b; Strauch, 20:13-14.

61. AL, 115b; Strauch, 22:29-23:2.
62. AL, 129b; Strauch, 31:26f.
63. AL, 141ab; Strauch, 39:26-27.
64. For profession see AL 98b-99a; Strauch, 10:9f; for marriage ceremony see AL 101b-102a; Strauch, 12:22f; Al, 121ab; Strauch, 26:7f.; for marriage bed see AL 170a-177a; Strauch, 61:12-66:7.
65. Bernard of Clairvaux, *Song of Songs*, II, 23:3; Bernard of Clairvaux, *Sermones*, I, 140: "Sit itaque hortus plana ac simplex historia, sit cellarium moralis sensus, sit cubiculum arcanamu theoricae contemplationis."
66. Bernard of Clairvaux, *Song of Songs*, II, 23:17; Bernard of Clairvaux, *Sermones*, I, 150: "At vero tertio isto in loco non plane terribilis, nec tam admirabilis quam amabilis apparere dignatus, serenus et placidus, suavis et mitis, et multae misericordiae omnibus intuentibus se.
67. AL, 104a; Strauch, 14:18-21.
68. AL, 121a-123b; Strauch, 26:1-27:26.
69. AL, 152b; Strauch, 47:8-9.
70. AL, 165b; Strauch, 57:15-16.
71. AL, 176b-177a; Strauch, 65:22-66:3.
72. AL, 123a; Strauch, 27:15-19.
73. Bernard of Clairvaux, *Song of Songs*, I, 9:2; Bernard of Clairvaux, *Sermones*, I, 43: "Gratias de osculo pedum, gratias et de manus; sed si cura est ei ulla de me, osculetur me osculo oris sui."
74. Bernard of Clairvaux, *Song of Songs*, I, 3:2; Bernard of Clairvaux, *Sermones*, I, 15: "Huius igitur beatae paenitentis exemplo porsternere et tu, o misera, ut desinas esse misera: prosternere et tu in terram amplectere pedes, placa osculis, riga lacrimis, quibus tamen non illum laves, sed te, et fias una de grege tonsarum."
75. Bernard of Clairvaux, *Song of Songs*, I, 4:2; Bernard of Clairvaux, *Sermones*, I, 19: "Osculum, pacis indicium esse omnes novimus."
76. AL, 179a; Strauch, 70:12-23.
77. Bernard of Clairvaux, *Song of Songs*, I, 4:1.
78. AL, 178ab; Strauch, 69:31f.
79. AL, 179b; Strauch, 70:28f.
80. Bernard of Clairvaux, *Song of Songs*, I, 2:9; Bernard of Clairvaux, *Sermones*, I, 14: ". . . porro ipsum osculum esse non aliud quam mediatorem Dei et hominum, hominem Christum Iesum, qui cum Patre et Spiritu Sancto vivit et regnat Deus per omnia saecula saeculorum. Amen."
81. Bernard of Clairvaux, *Song of Songs*, I, 8:7b-8; Bernard of Clairvaux, *Sermones*, I, 40: "Audi siquidem osculum de ore: Ego et Pater unum sumus; item: Ego in Patre, et Pater in me est. Osculum est ore ad os sumptum; sed nemo appropiat. Osculum plane dilectionis et pacis, sed dilectio illa supereminet omni scientiae, et pax illa omnem sensum exsuperat. Verumtamen quod oculus non vidit, nec auris audivit, nec in cor hominis ascendit, Paul revelavit Deus per Spiritum suum, hoc est per osculum oris sui."
82. AL, 106b-107a; Strauch, 16:19f; AL, 128ab; Strauch, 31:2f.; AL, 178a; Strauch, 67:15f.; AL, 192b; Strauch, 81:15f.

83. Bernard of Clairvaux, *Song of Songs*, I, 8:1:2; Bernard of Clairvaux, *Sermones*, I, 37: "Nempe si recte Pater osculans, Filius osculatus accipitur, non erit ab re osculum Spiritum Sanctum intelligi, utpote qui Patris Filiique imperturbabilis pax sit, gluten firmum, individuus amor, indivisibilis unitas."

84. AL, 103b; Strauch, 14:5-7.

85. Bernard of Clairvaux, *Song of Songs*, II, 38:5; Bernard of Clairvaux, *Sermones*, II, 17: "'Mirabilis facta est,' inquit, 'visio ista ex te, o sponsa, quam tibi postulas demonstrari, nec modo praevales intueri meridianam et miran, quam inhabito, claritatem.'"

86. Bernard of Clairvaux, *Song of Songs*, I, 38:5; Bernard of Clairvaux, *Sermones*, II, 17: "Erit, cum apparuero, quod tota pulchra eris, sicut ego sum pulcher totus; et simillima mihi, videbis me sicuti sum. Tunc audies: Tota pulchra es, amica mea, et macula non est in te."

87. AL, 141b; Strauch, 39:26-27.

88. AL, 193b; Strauch, 82:9-12.

89. AL, 124b; Strauch, 28:19.

90. Bernard of Clairvaux, *Song of Songs*, IV, 67:1; Bernard of Clairvaux, *Sermones*, II, 188: "Dilectus meus mihi, et ego illi" (Song of Sol. 2:16).

91. AL, 152b; Strauch, 47:9-10.

92. Bernard of Clairvaux, *Song of Songs*, II, 27:8; Bernard of Clairvaux, *Sermones*, I, 188: "Confirmat me in hoc sensu maxime illa fidelis promissio: Ego et Pater, ait Filius, ad eum, id est ad sanctum hominem, veneimus, et mansionem apud eum faciemus. Prophetam quoque non de alio dixisse caelo arbitror: Tu autem in sancto habitas, laus Israel. Manifeste autem Apostolus dicit habitare Christum per fidem in cordibus nostris" (Eph. 3:17).

93. AL, 106a; Strauch, 16:4.

94. Bernard of Clairvaux, *Song of Songs*, II, 27:8. See above for quote from his *Sermones*.

95. Bernard of Clairvaux, *Song of Songs*, IV, 71:10; Bernard of Clairvaux, *Sermones*, II, 221: "Ergo cum undique inhaerent sibi homo et Deus,—inhaerent autem undique intima mutuaque dilectione inviscerati alterutrum sibi—, per hoc Deum in homine et hominem in Deo esse haud dubie dixerim."

96. AL, 140b; Strauch, 39:10-12.

97. AL, 178a; Strauch, 67:27f.

98. AL, 115a; Strauch, 21:24.

99. Bernard of Clairvaux, *Song of Songs*, IV, 71:8; Bernard of Clairvaux, *Sermones*, II, 220: "Quam quidem unitatem non tam essentiarum cohaerentia facit, quam conniventia voluntatum."

100. CEN, XVIv: "Ich hon dir daz buch dar umb zu gefuget daz dein geistliche frewde dester grozzer sein."

101. CEN, XIVv: "Und maint das buch daz da heisset ein uzfliezzendes liht der gotheit."

102. CEN, LXXr: "Mein ewige liep, ich hon dir daz buch gesant daz so heizzet ein ausflissendez liht der gotheit vor dem tot dor umb daz du dester kuner seist

in dem gnaden nit allein durch dich. Du solt dar von reden di weil du lebest di ich dir tu dester gelewiger sei."

103. Strauch, *Margaretha Ebner und Heinrich von Nördlingen* (Freiburg i.B. and Tübingen: Akademische Verlagsbuchhandlung von J. C. B. Mohr, 1882; reprint Amsterdam: Verlag P. Schippers, N.V., 1966), 246:117f; Letter XLIII

104. Leonard P. Hindsley, *Margaret Ebner: Major Works* (New York: Paulist Press, 1993), 46-47.

105. Margarete Weinhandl, *Deutsches Nonnenleben: Das Leben der Schwestern zu Töß und der Nonne von Engelthal Büchlein von der Gnaden Überlast* in *Kathlokon Werke und Urkenden.* II. (München: O.C. Recht Verlag, 1921), 14.

106. Strauch, *Margaretha Ebner*, 247:1-3; Letter XLIII.

107. The basic text stems from the Einsiedeln Manuscript 277, which had been sent from a friend of Henry's, Margaretha "zum Goldenen Ring" in Basel as a gift to Swiss hermitesses. See Margot Schmidt, *Mechthild von Magdeburg: Das fließende Licht der Gottheit* (Mystik in Geschichte und Gegenwart, Band 11), (Stuttgart-Bad Canstatt: Fromann-Holzboog, 1995), ix-x.

108. Margot Schmidt in Hindsley, *Margaret Ebner*, 33.

109. Strauch, *Margaretha Ebner*, 247.

110. Ibid., 248-249; *156-159.

111. Ibid., 210.

112. Ibid., 266.

113. CEN, CLXVIIr, CLXVIIIrv, CLXXIv.

114. Ringler in Langosch, *Verfasserlexikon*, col. 298.

115. CEN, XVIv, LXXr.

116. Strauch, *Adelheid Langmann*, 100.

117. Ibid., 18:21-19:3; *91.

118. Gall Morel, *Offenbarungen der Schwester Mechthild von Magdeburg oder das fliessende Licht der Gottheit* (Darmstadt: Wissenschaftliche Buchgesellschaft, 1963), 33; M. Schmidt, *Das Fließende Licht*, 47. All translations from Mechthild's *The Flowing Light of the Godhead* are mine.

119. FS, 176r; Ringler, *Viten*, 393.

120. CES, 116r: "do er gesegnet . . . do erschein ir in eins indes wis daz wz unzalich schön . . ."

121. CEN, XIIv-XIIIr: "In dem selben iar an sant Remigien tag unter der messe do saz di selbe swester hinten in dem kor und do man daz prefacio an hub do erschien ir unser herre in eins cleinen kindeleins weise und lof vorn uz dem kor hin hinter zu ir und stunt fur di pan und sahs an."

122. CEN, LXVr: "An dem montag in der kreuzwoche do laz ein prediger messe in dem kor do sah si in des priesters handen daz er in auf hub in dem oblat sein minncliches antlutz do nach verwandelt er such in eins cleinen kindeleins weise und waz in ein weisses tuch gewindelt . . . Diz gesiht daz sah si oft im sacramente."

123. Strauch, *Adelheid Langmann*. 77:27-30, *30.

124. Morel, *Offenbarungen*, 40; Schmidt, *Das Fließende Licht*, 56.

125. Weinhandl, *Deutsches Nonnenleben*, 41; AL *91.

126. Morel, *Offenbarungen*, 184; Schmidt, *Das Fließende Licht*, 226:10f.; Hans Neumann, *Mechthild von Magdeburg 'Das fließende Licht der Gottheit'* (München: Artemis Verlag, 1990), Book VI.8; Weinhandl, *Deutsches Nonnenleben*, 42.

127. AL 152b; Strauch, 47:9-10, *63.

128. Morel, *Offenbarungen*, 66; Schmidt, *Das Fließende Licht*, 89.

129. FS, 187r; Ringler, *Viten*, 404:483-485, *43.

130. Morel, *Offenbarungen*, 85; Schmidt, *Das Fließende Licht*, 11.

131. Strauch, *Adelheid Langmann*, 57:8f.,*70.

132. Morel, *Offenbarungen*, 56; Schmidt, *Das Fließende Licht*, 77.

133. Morel, *Offenbarungen*, 56; Schmidt, *Das Fließende Licht*, 78.

134. Ibid.

135. Strauch, *Adelheid Langmann*, 61-66. This signifies the *unio mystica* of Christ and Adelheid.

136. AL, 175a; Strauch, 64:25f., *72.

137. AL, 176b; Strauch, 65:25f., *72.

138. ESB, Karl Schröder, ed., *Der Nonne von Engelthal Büchlein von der Gnaden Überlast* (Tübingen: H. Laupp, 1871), 7:30-32, 20: 24f., 27:32f., 36:14f.

139. AL, 178a; Strauch, 67:16-20.

140. CES 92r; CES 110r, which is similar to Neumann's *Mechthild of Magdeburg*, 68:22f.

141. Neumann, *Mechthild*, 75:69-71: "Oben in dem throne siht man den spiegel der gotheit, das bilde der menscheit, das lieht des heiligen geistes und bekennet, wie die drie ein got sint und wie si sich fugent in ein." See also Neumann, *Mechthild*, 227:52f.

142. AL, 105ab; Strauch, 15:16f., *25.

143. AL, 154b-156a; Strauch, 48:29-50:5, *65.

144. FS, 202r; Ringler, *Viten*, 419-420.

145. FS, 202r; Ringler, *Viten*, 420.

146. M. Schmidt, *Das Fließende Licht*, xxi-xxvi.

147. AL 204a; Strauch, 89:1-4, *141.

148. Neumann, *Mechthild*, 16:7-8 (Book I, Ch. 22: "Die brut ist trunken worden von der angesihte des edeln antlutes"); see also Morel, *Offenbarungen*, 11, 64; Schmidt, *Das Fließende Licht*, 20, 86.

149. CEN, LXXXXVr: "An dem obersten tag do nam si unseren herren do sprach er mein grozz minn hat von dem deine enzunt von mein ausfluzz bistu trunken worden."

150. Morel, *Offenbarungen*, 8, 28, 33, 41; Schmidt, *Das Fließende Licht*, 15, 43, 47, 57; AL *11, *80, *11, *55, *61, *80, *29, *32, *55, *87.

151. For a printed version of the Latin text, see Karl Weinhold, *Lamprecht von Regensburg: Sanct Francisken Leben und Tochter Syon.* (Paderborn: Ferdinand Schöningh, 1880), 285-291.

152. See Wiltrud Wichgraf, "Der Traktat von der Tochter von Syon und seine Bearbeitungen," in Wilhelm Braune, ed., *Beiträge zur Geschichte der Deutschen Sprache und Literatur* (Halle: Max Niemeyer, 1922), Band 46, 173-231.

153. For a printed version of Lamprecht's text, see Weinhold, *Lamprecht*, 261-544.

154. See L. Wolff, s.v. "Tochter Sion," in Karl Langosch, ed., *Die Deutsche Literatur des Mittelalters Verfasserlexkion*, (Berlin: Walter de Gruyter & Co., 1953), Band IV., 479-80.

155. For a printed transcription of manuscript Cgm 29 (Bayerische Staatsbibliothek zu München), see Wichgraf, *Traktat*, 177-181.

156. Engelthal Library Catalogue, fol. 7-8.

157. Weinhold, *Lamprecht*, 305.

158. Strauch, *Adelheid Langmann*, 108, note to 62, 12ff. He draws his conslusion from a comparison with a text not available to me: *Heidelberger Jahrbuch der Literatur*, 1816, 2, 715f.

159. Wolff, *Verfasserlexikon*, 481.

160. Ringler, *Viten*, 373: "Bisher sah man in diesem Werk meist (mit höchst unsicherer Begründung) die sogenannte "alemannische Tochter Syon", auf diese Dichtung findet sich jedoch bei F[riedrich] S[under] kein einziger stichhaltiger Hinweis."

161. Ibid.

162. Engelthal Library Catalogue (1444), f. 8: "Item das sein dye tewczen pucher des klosters zu Engeltal der sein an der sum kleiner und großer LIIII pucher."

163. Ringler, *Viten*, 232.

164. FS, 189r; Ringler, *Viten*, 406:550f.

165. Weinhold, *Lamprecht*, 345: "din wille ouch, swie guot er ist,/ dern mac doch in einem muote,/ die wile dir so manege huote/ das glesich und diu werlt leit und des tiuvels kündecheit."

166. Ringler, *Viten*, 373.

167. FS, 195v; Ringler, *Viten*, 413.

168. Weinhold, *Lamprecht*, 441; it is "Karitas" in this text.

169. Ibid., 441-442.

170. AL, 178a; Strauch, 61-66, *72.

171. CEN, CLXVIIv: "An eim freitag sprach er, 'ich pin von minnen dein gefangner und kum willicliche zu dir. ich wil dich kronen mit meiner parmhertzikeit. ich pin ein uberwinter deiner sinne.'"

172. AL, 122ab; Strauch, 26:26-27:4, *42.

173. AL, 210ab; Strauch, 93:15-21, *159.

174. FS, 202v; Ringler, *Viten*, 420: "Sich, liebe sel, wenn got din herre kum zu dir, so vmb vahe jn mit dinen armen zertlichen vnd lieblichen vnd sprich zue im: 'Veniat dilectus meus in ortum suum ut comedat fructus pomorum suorom.' The Latin quote is the beginning of chapter five of the Song of Solomon: "Come to my garden, my sister, my bride. I gather my myrrh with my spice. I eat my honeycomb with my honey. I drink my wine with my milk."

175. Weinhold, *Lamprecht*, 492.

176. Ibid., 291.

177. Ibid., 181: "von irs hertzen andacht ward offt gesprochen: 'kum zü mir in den garten meyner sel, mein tröst, mein herzenlyeb, aller wlt schöpfer, durch den mein hertz verwuntt ist, und hab ein wolgefallen daryn und mach grünen mein vernunfft, und lass wachsen nach [d]einem gevallen allerlaj plümen, besunder

feyol und lilgen mit wolsmeckenden rösen: das ist dyemütikajt, lawtrikajt, götliychew lieb. Und belejb daryn als lang, pis das ich dy tzeyr meynes lebens verpring und den schaten diser welt gönzleych vernicht, und das mir darnach scheyn das ewig lyecht, das ist Kristus Jhesus, ayner yedliechen gelaubigen sel gemachel."

178. AL, 151ab; Strauch, 46:10-18, *62.
179. AL, 122ab; Strauch, 26:24-26, *42.
180. CEN, XIr.
181. FS, 177r; Ringler, Viten, 194.
182. FS, 178v; Ringler, Viten, 195.
183. Ringler, Viten, 191.
184. Ibid., 191.
185. Ibid., 193.
186. AL, 170ab; Strauch, 61:12-17, *72.
187. AL, 170b-171a; Strauch, 61:21-62:1, *72.
188. Cgm 29; Weinhold, Lamprecht, 178.
189. AL, 173b-174a; Strauch, 62:3-4, *72.
190. AL, 173b; Strauch, 63:16-17, *72.
191. Cgm 29; Weinhold, Lamprecht, 178-179.
192. AL, 175a; Strauch, 63:24, *72.
193. AL, 174ab; Strauch, 64:1-13, *72.
194. Cgm 29; Weinhold, Lamprecht, 180.
195. AL, 175a; Strauch, 64:20-28, *72.
196. Weinhold, Lamprecht, 477-478: ". . . zu im also vaste/ mit des schines glaste,/ den sin schoen antlütze treit. Vür war si dir geseit:/ sin antlütze ist gnaden vol, / . . . ez ist daz ewige licht.'"
197. Ibid., 181.
198. Ibid., 418.
199. AL, 176b-177a; Strauch, 65:26-66:5, *72.
200. Weinhold, Lamprecht, 482: "der geist ziuhet durh den munt/ den adem, daz ist ouch wol kunt./ swer sich ze gote danne nahet,/ sin geist den adem vahet, der von sinem munde gat."

CHAPTER NINE

1. Ceslaus Velecky, O.P., trans., St. Thomas Aquinas: Summa Theologiæ (New York: McGraw-Hill / London: Eyre & Spottiswoode, 1965), Vol. 6, 123.
2. Siegfried Ringler, Viten- und Offenbarungsliteratur in Frauenklöstern des Mittelalters (München: Artmeis Verlag, 1980), 271.
3. T. C. O'Brien, O.P., ed., St. Thomas Aquinas: Summa Theologiæ (New York: McGraw-Hill / London, Eyre & Spottiswoode, 1976), Vol. 7, 218-219: Summa Theologiæ Ia.43.3. resp. 1: "Et ideo missio invisibilis fit secundum donum gratiæ gratum facientis et tamen ipsa persona divina datur."

4. O'Brien, *St. Thomas, Summa Theologiae (ST)*, Ia.43.3.resp. 2.: "Ad secundum dicendum quod gratia gratum faciens disponsit animam ad habendam divinam personam."

5. O'Brien, *St. Thomas*, 260.

6. Quoted in O'Brien, *St. Thomas*, 260.

7. AL, 137b; Philipp Strauch, *Die Offenbarungen der Adelheid Langmann, Klosterfrau zu Engelthal* (Straßburg: Karl J. Trübner, 1878), 37:15, *52. Henceforth, this will be cited as *Adelheid Langmann*, but when I refer to the original manuscript it will appear as AL. Unless specifically referenced as Strauch, *Margaretha Ebner*, all references to Strauch refer to his book on Adelheid Langmann.

8. CEN, XLVIIIr.

9. CEN, VIIIv-IXr.

10. Karl Schröder, *Der Nonne von Engelthal Büchlein von der Gnaden Überlast* (Tübingen: H. Laupp, 1971), 36:14.

11. Ibid., 27:30-32.

12. Ibid., 27:33-34

13. Ibid., 7:30.

14. Ibid., 7:31.

15. Ibid., 7:33.

16. CEN, Lrv.

17. CEN, XLVv.

18. CEN, IXv.

19. Ibid.

20. FS, 180v; Ringler, *Viten*, 397:237f., *23. See also other references in FS: 186v; Ringler, *Viten*, 403, *40;

21. FS, 189r; Ringler, *Viten*, 406, *47.

22. FS, 194v-195r; Ringler, *Viten*, 412-413, *63-67.

23. FS, 217v; Ringler, *Viten*, 434, *124.

24. FS, 224rv; Ringler, *Viten*, 441, *143.

25. CEN, CCCIr.

26. CEN, LXXVr.

27. CEN, LXXXXVIIIIr.

28. CEN, VIIIr.

29. CEN, XLIIIrv.

30. ESB, 86; Schröder, *Der Nonne*, 33:31f.

31. CEN, LXXXIIv.

32. Ibid.

33. FS, 207r; Ringler, *Viten*, 424:1183f.

34. FS, 207v; Ringler, *Viten*, 424:1207-1208.

35. FS, 207v; Ringler, *Viten*, 425:1216f.

36. FS, 208r; Ringler, *Viten*, 425:1224.

37. FS, 208rv; Ringler, *Viten*, 425:1230f.

38. FS, 208v; Ringler, *Viten*, 425:1237f.

39. AL, 195a; Strauch, 83:1f; *102.

40. See G. J. Lewis, *By Women, for Women, about Women: The Sister-Books of Fourteenth-Century Germany* (Toronto: Pontifical Institute of Medieval Studies, 1996), 100-105; also Carolyn Walker Bynum, "Women mystics and eucharistic devotion in the thirteenth century," *Women's Studies* 11 (1984): 179-214.

41. Lewis, *By Women*, 100.

42. Ringler, *Viten*, 187.

43. Ibid.

44. AL, 131b; Strauch, 33:5f., *50.

45. AL, 177b; Strauch, 66:17f., *74.

46. AL, 132a; Strauch, 3:21f., *50.

47. FS, 198r; Ringler, *Viten*, 415:878f.,*75.

48. CEN, 84v.

49. CEN, 95v; see also CEN, 69v, 100v, 126r, 128v, 129r, 131v; CES, 42v, 43r.

50. ESB, 29; Schröder, *Der Nonne*, 12:6f.

51. AL, 210b; Strauch, 93:21, *159.

52. Ringler, *Viten*, 288: "Die Erschienung des Kindes in der Hostie, . . . ist bildhafter Ausdruck für die Anwesenheit Christi in seiner übernatürlichen Wesenheit."

53. FS, 176r, 177r.

54. CEN, CLIv-CLIIr: "In der gnoden reichen zeit sah si dreistunt unser herren in der form eins kindleins in dez pristers handen. Eins mols waz er alz cleine alz daz oblat zu dem andern mol ging er einz vingers hin uber zu dem dritten mol waz er eins manner spann lang."

55. ESB, 82; Schröder, *Der Nonne*, 32:5f.

56. ESB, 101; Schröder, *Der Nonne*, 39:23f.

57. ESB, 109; Schröder, *Der Nonne*, 42:35-43:8.

58. AL 210b-211a; Strauch, 93: 23f, *159.

59. CEN, CLXVIIv.

60. CEN, LXXXXVr.

61. CEN, CIIr.

62. CEN, LXXXIIIv.

63. AL, 133a; Strauch, 34:9f., *50.

64. CEN, CXXXVr.

65. Ibid.

66. CEN, CXXXr; see also CEN, CXXXIv, CXXXIIr, CXLIIIIr.

67. CEN, CXLIIIIr.

68. CEN, XLIIv.

69. CEN, CXXVrv.

70. CEN, LXv.

71. CEN, CXXIIIIv.

72. ESB, 94; Schröder, *Der Nonne*, 36:30f., *121.

73. ESB, 101-102; Schröder, *Der Nonne*, 39:32-30:3, *134.

74. The term "chosen ones" occurs in Ps. 105:6, Ps. 105:43, Ps. 106:5, and Col. 3:12.

75. See also 1 Kings 3:8, Ps. 33:12, Isa. 43:20.

76. CEN, CXXXIIr.

77. CEN, CLVIv.
78. CEN, LXXVIIIIr.
79. CEN, XLVIv.
80. CEN, LXXXVv.
81. CEN, LXXXVIr.
82. CEN, CLIIr.
83. Moses as "chosen one" occurs also in Ps. 105:26, Ps. 106:23.
84. See also 1 Kings 11:13, 32.
85. CEN, CXIXv; also CXXIIIIr.
86. See also the accounts of the baptism in Mark 1:9-11, Luke 23:21,22; John 1:29-34.
87. See also 2 Pet. 1:17, Mark 1:11.
88. CEN, XLIr.
89. CEN, CXXr.
90. CEN, CXVIr.
91. See also 2 Chron. 6:34, 38.
92. See also Neh. 1:9.
93. Ps. 132:13: "For the Lord has chosen Zion; he has desired it for his habitation."
94. CEN, CXVIr.
95. Bynum, "Women mystics," 179-214.
96. Happily, Ursula Peters's critical edition of Christina Ebner's *Revelations* will appear in 1998.
97. CEN, IIr.
98. CEN, CXXVIr.
99. CEN, CXXVIIIIr.
100. AL, 210a; Strauch, 93:11f.
101. Leonard P. Hindsley, *Margaret Ebner: Major Works* (New York: Paulist Press, 1993), 122.
102. AL, 104a; Strauch, 14:21-23.
103. AL, 175b; Strauch, 65:4f.
104. CEN, CDXXXv.
105. CEN, CXXVv.
106. CEN, CLXVIIv.
107. CEN, CLXVIIIr.
108. CEN, CXXIIv.
109. CEN, CXXXVIr.
110. Jeffrey Hamburger, *The Rothschild Canticles: Art and Mysticism in Flanders and the Rhineland around 1300* (New Haven: Yale University Press, 1990), 109; Ringler, *Viten*, 415-416.
111. Hamburger, *Canticles*, 109.
112. John 19:26.
113. Hamburger, *Canticles*, 78.
114. Hamburger, *Canticles*, 78; Cited from A. Oppel, *Das Hohelied Salomonis und die religiöse Liebeslyrik*, Abhandlungen zur mittleren und neueren Geschichte 32

(Berlin, 1911) 1: "slief uf der brust Jhesu Christi ung soug alle wishait dar uz und die verborgen heimlichkeit Gottes."

115. Hamburger, *Canticles*, 78; Cited from R. Haussherr, "Über die Christus-Johannes-Gruppen: Zum Problem 'Andachtsbilder' und deutsche Mystik," *Beiträge zur Kunst des Mittelalters: Festschrift für Hans Wenzel zum 60. Geburtstag* (Berlin, 1975), 90: "Iste est Johannes, qui supra pectus Domini in coena recubuit: beatus Apostolus, cui revelata sunt secreta coelestia."

116. AL, 36, Strauch, 23.20f.

117. AL, 36; Strauch, 23:20f.

118. CEN, CXLVv

119. CES 141r: "ich hon dich gesogt mit meiner sussikeit von den brüsten miner wollustiekeit."

120. CEN, CXLVv.

121. Ibid.

122. CEN, CLIIIr.

123. Hamburger, *Canticles*, 78.

124. CEN, LXVIIr.

125. CEN, CXLVIr.

126. Ibid.

127. CEN, CXXXVIr.

128. CEN, CXIIIv.

129. AL, 106a; Strauch, 16:4.

130. AL, 106b; Strauch, 16:8-10.

131. AL, 98b; Strauch, 9:26-28.

132. AL, 98b; Strauch, 10:1-3.

133. AL, 106b; Strauch, 16:15-17.

134. AL, 107a; Strauch, 16:17-18.

135. AL, 176b; Strauch, 65:22-30.

136. AL, 117a; Strauch, 23:10-15.

137. CEN, 50v; my translation.

138. FS, 210v; Ringler, *Viten*, 427.

139. ESB, 67-68; Schröder, *Der Nonne*, 26:18f.

140. AL, 188b; Strauch, 77:27f.

141. AL, 189b; Strauch, 78:22f.

142. FS, 182v; Ringler, *Viten*, 399:312f.

143. FS, 199r; Ringler, *Viten*, 417.

144. FS, 226v; Ringler, *Viten*, 443-444.

145. FS, 224v; Ringler, *Viten*, 441-442.

146. CEN, LXXXXVIr

147. CEN, CIr.

148. Ringler, *Viten*, 196-197.

149. Ringler, 197; Adolph Franz, *Die Messe im Deutschen Mittelalter* (Freiburg i.B., 1902; reprint Darmstadt, 1963). 43, # 9.

150. Franz, *Messe*, quoted in Ringler, *Viten*, 197; my translation.

151. Ringler, *Viten*, 197.

152. Ibid., 197; CES, 39r = CEN, IIr.
153. AL, 120b; Strauch, 25:17-19, *38.
154. Ringler, *Viten,* 198.
155. Ibid.
156. Ibid.; CEN, 151v: "daz all tag vom ertrich zu himel varent on alle weis und daz all tag sünder bekert werdent und daz all tag sel vz dem fegfewr zu himel farent."
157. Ringler, *Viten,* 198.
158. CES, 123v, Ringler, *Viten,* 198.

EPILOGUE

1. Siegfried Ringler, *Viten- und Offenbarungsliteratur in Frauenklöstern des Mittelalters* (München: Artemis Verlag, 1980), 48-49.
2. G. J. Lewis, F. Willaert, and M. Govers, eds., *Bibliographie zur deutschen Frauenmystik des Mittelalters* (Berlin: Erich Schmidt Verlag, 1989), 418.
3. Ringler, *Viten,* 50.
4. Ibid.
5. Engelthal Library Catalogue, f. 8.
6. Hieronymus Wilms, *Das älteste Verzeichnis der deutschen Dominikanerinnenklöster,* Quellen und Forschungen zur Geschichte des Dominikanerordens in Deutschland (Leipzig: Otto Harrassowitz, 1928), 34.
7. For the historical background of the monastery, I have taken most of the information on this page from Ringler, *Viten,* 38-44.
8. Lewis, *Bibliographie,* 418.
9. Ringler, *Viten,* 42.
10. Ibid., 44.
11. Ibid., 36. Hans Probst came from Biberach, where a family by that name lived. Two canonesses of Inzigkoven in the fourteenth century bear the surname.
12. Ibid., 38.
13. Wilms, *Das älteste Verzeichnis,* 85-86.
14. Ringler, *Viten,* 45.

SELECT BIBLIOGRAPHY

MANUSCRIPTS

Vienna, Bibliothek des Schottenstifts
    Codex Scotensis Vindobonensis 308 (234) contains the Gnaden-vita of
Friedrich Sunder (FS), the Life of Sister Gertrud of Engelthal (GE) and the Revelations of Adelheid Langmann (AL)

The Sister-Book of Engelthal:

Nuremberg, Germanisches Nationalmuseum
    codex 1338. = ESB

Codex Scotensis Vindobonensis
    codex 308, fol. 84r-119v.

Christina Ebner:

Nuremberg, Staatsbibliothek
    codex Cent. V., App 99. = CEN

Stuttgart, Württembergische Landesbibliothek
    codex theol. Et phil. 2^0 282. = CES

Mödingen/Dillingen—Kloster Maria Medingen
    Hs Christina Ebner = Md1

Schloß Eschenbach (E), Codex 90 der Ebnerischen Bibliothek

Adelheid Langmann:

Berlin, Staatsbibliothek Preussischer Kulturbesitz
    mgq 866: 86r-215v = B; AL

Munich, Staatsbibliothek
    cgm 99: 36r-173r. = M

Vienna, Bibliothek des Schottenstifts
    Codex Scotensis Vindobonensis 308 (234): 120r-168r.

SECONDARY SOURCES

Geschlecht-buch der stat Nürnberg. British Library German Manuscript 10, 009, 1559.

Library Catalogue, Staatsarchiv Nürnberg, Nürnberger Saalbücher, Nr. 45a, fol. 7.

"The Primitive Constitutions of the Monastery of San Sisto." *Early Documents of the Dominican Sisters*. Vol. I. Summit, N.J.: Dominican Nuns of Summit, 1969: 7-22.

"Letter of Humbert of the Romans Imposing the Constitutions (1259)." *Early Documents of the Dominican Sisters*. Vol. II. Summit, N.J.: Dominican Nuns of Summit, 1969: 1-2.

Bernard of Clairvaux. *On the Song of Songs*, trans. Kilian Walsh. (Kalamazoo: Cisterican Publications, 1971-1976.)

————. *Sermones super Cantica Canticorum*, 2 vols. edited by Jean Leclerq. Romae: Editiones Cistercienses, 1957.

Biblia Sacra Juxta Vulgatum Clementinam. Romae/Tornaci/Paris: Desclee et socii, 1947.

Bihlmeyer, Karl. *Kirchliches Handlexikon*. Ed., Michael Buchberger, 2 Bde. München/ Freiburg/Berlin: Allgemeine Verlagsgesellschaft, 1907.

Blank, Walter. *Die Nonnenviten des 14. Jahrhunderts: Eine Studie zur hagiograbischen Literatur des Mittelalters unter besonderer Brücksichtigung der Visionen und ihrer Lichtphänome*. Diss. Freiburg i.B. 1962, pp. 78-88.

Buber, Martin. *Ecstatic Confessions: The Heart of Mysticism*. Ed. Paul Mendes-Flohr, trans. Esther Cameron. San Francisco: Harper and Row, 1985; originally published in German as *Ekstatische Konfessionen*. Jena: Eugen Dietrichs Verlag, 1909, excerpts of paragraphs 1-5 only.

Bynum, Caroline Walker. "Women mystics and eucharistic devotion in the thirteenth century" *Women's Studies* 11 (1984), 179-214.

Cassian, John. *The Institutes and the Conferences*. In *Nicene and Post-Nicene Fathers*. Vol. XI. Trans. C. S. Gibson. Oxford: Parker & Co. 1894, reprint 1982.

Denifle, Henri. "Über die Anfänge der Predigtweise der deutschen Mystiker." *Archiv für Literatur und Kirchengeschichte des Mittelalters*. Berlin/Freiburg: B. Herder, 1886, II.

Dinzelbacher, Peter. *Lexikon des Mittelalters* Band 3 (1986): sp. 1922.

Dinzelbacher, Peter, and Bauer, Peter R., eds. *Frauenmystik im Mittelalter*. Ostfilden bei Stuttgart: Schwabenverlag, 1985.

Doyé, Franz von Sales. *Heilige und Selige der römisch- katholischen Kirche*. Leipzig: Vier Quellen Verlag, 1929, Bd. 1., 195

Dünninger, Eberhard, and Kiesselbach, Dorothea, eds. "Weihnachtliche Motive in der Mystik der Dominikanerinnen in Kloster Maria Medingen und Engelthal." In *Bayreische Literaturgeschichte in ausgewählten Beispielen*, Bd. 1. Mittelalter (1965) 338- 348.

Echtermeyer/von Wiese, Benno, eds. *Deutsche Gedichte*. Düsseldorf: August Bagel Verlag, 1973.

Franz, Adolph. *Die Mess im Deutschen Mittelalter*. Frieburg i.B., 1902; reprint Darmstadt, 1963.

Gibson, Edgar C. S., trans. *John Cassian*. In Philip Schaff and Henry Wace, eds. *Nicene and Post-Nicene Fathers of the Christian Church*, Vol IX. Grand Rapids, M.I.: Wm. B. Erdmans Publishing Co.; reprint 1982, 183-547.

Graber, R. "Christina Ebner von Engeltal." *Historische Blätter zur Eichstätter Kurier* 6 (1957) 1-3.

Grabmann, Martin. "Deutsche Mystik in Kloster Engelthal." *Sammelblatt des Historischen Vereins Eichstätt* 25/26, 1912: 33-44.

Greith, Karl Johann. *Die Deutsche Mystik in Predigerordern von 1250-1350 nach ihren Grundlehren, Liedern und Lebensbildern aus Handschriflichen Quellen*. Freiburg: Herder, 1861; reprint Amsterdam: Ed. Rodopi, 1965.

Grundmann, Herbert. "Geschichtliche Grundlagen der deutschen Mystik." In Kurt Ruh, ed. *Altdeutsche und Altniederdeutsche Mystik*: 82ff.

Gürsching, Heinrich. *Neue urkundliche Nachrichten über den Mystiker Heinrich von Nördlingen*. In *Festgabe Karl Schornbaum*. Neustadt (Aisch): P.C.W. Schmidt, 1950, 42-57 passim.

Hamburger, Jeffrey F. *The Rothschild Chronicles: Art and Mysticism in Flanders and the Rhineland around 1300*. New Haven and London: Yale University Press, 1990.

Haupt. Josef. ed. *Das Hohelied übersetzt von Williram, erklärt von Rilindis und Herrat, Äbtissinen zu Hohenburg in Elsass (1147-1196)*. Wien: Wilhelm Braumüller, 1864.

Heller, Nicholas. *The Exemplar: Life and Writings of Blessed Henry Suso, O.P*. Dubuque, I.A: The Priory Press, 1962.

Hinnebusch, William, O.P. *The History of the Dominican Order*. 2 vols. Staten Island, N.Y.: Alba House, 1966-1973.

Hindsley, Leonard P. *Margaret Ebner: Major Works*. Mahwah and New York: Paulist Press, 1993.

Hoffmann, H. *Willirams Übersetzung und Auslegung des Hohenliedes in doppelten Texten aus den Breslauer und Leidener Handschriften herausgegeben und mit einem vollständigen Wörterbuche versehen*. Breslau, 1827

Kieckhefer, Richard. *Unquiet Souls: Fourteenth-Century Saints and their Religious Milieu*. Chicago and London: University of Chicago Press, 1984.

Kist, Johannes. *Lexikon für Theologie und Kirche* 2. Aufl. Band 3 (1959) sp. 1958.

Kramer, Dewey Weiss. "'Arise and Give the Convent Bread': Christine Ebner, the Convent Chronicle of Engelthal, and the Call to Ministry among Fourteenth Century Religious Women." In *Women as Protagonists and Poets in the German Middle Ages: An Anthology of Feminist Approaches to Middle High German Literature*. ed. Albrecht Classen, Göppingen: Kümmerle Verlag, 1991, 187-206.

Krebs, Engelbert. "Die Mystik in Adelhausen: Eine vergleichende Studie über die Chronik der Anna von Munzingen und die Thaumatographische Literatur des 13. und 14. Jahrhunderts als Beitrag zur Geschichte der Mystik im

Predigerorden." In *Festgabe Heinrich Finke* (Münster i. W.: Aschendorff, 1904), 41-105.

Krebs, Engelbert. *Verfasserlexikon.* 1. Aufl. Bd. 1 (1933) 471-482.

Langer, Otto. *"Zur Dominikanischen Frauenmystik im spätmittelalterichen Deutschland,"* in Peter Dinzelbacher, and Dieter K. Bauer, eds. *Frauenmystik im Mittelalter.* Ostfildern bei Stuttgart: Schwabenverlag, 1985:341-346.

Langosch, Karl, ed. *Die Deutsche Literatur des Mittelalters Verfasserlexikon.* Berlin: Walter de Gruyter & Co., 1985. Completed in 1985 by Karl Ruh, ed.

Lechner, Peter. *Bericht aus dem mystischen Leben der gottseligen Ordensjungfrauen Christina und Margareth Ebner aus Nürnberg.* In *Das mystische Leben der heiligen Margareth von Cortona,* Regensburg, 1862, 141-323; esp. 141-218.

Lewis, Gertrud Jaron. *By Women, for Women, about Women: The Sister-Books of Fourteenth Century Germany.* Toronto: Pontifical Institute of Medieval Studies, 1996.

Lewis, G. J., Frank Willaert, and Marie-Jose Govers, eds. *Bibliographie zur deutschen Frauenmystik des Mittelalters,* # 10 in the series *Bibliographien zur deushchen Literatur des Mittelalters,* ed. Wolfgang Bachofer, Berlin: Erich Schmidt Verlag, 1989.

Lochner, Georg Wolfgang Karl. *Leben und Gesichte der Christine Ebnerin, Klosterfrau zu Engelthal.* Nürnberg: August Recknagel's Verlag, 1875.

Martini, Johann Christoph. *Historisch-geographisch Beschreibung des ehemaligen berühmten Frauenklosters Engelthal.* Nürnberg/Altdorf 1762; 2. Aulf. 1798.

Matter, E. Ann. *The Voice of My Beloved: The Song of Songs in Western Medieval Christianity.* Philadelphia: University of Pennsylvania Press, 1990.

Menzies, Lucy, trans. *The Revelations of Mechthild of Magdeburg (1210-1297) or The Flowing Light of the Godhead.* London, New York, and Toronto: Longmans, Green and Co., 1953.

Morel, G. *Offenbarungen der Schwester Mechthild von Magdeburg oder das fliessende Licht der Gottheit.* Darmstadt: Wissenschaftliche Buchgesellschaft, 1963.

Morgan, B. Q. and F. W. Strothman, eds. *Middle High German Translation of the Summa Theologica by Thomas Aquinas.* Stanford: Stanford University Press, 1950; reprint 1967.

Neumann, Hans. *Mechthild von Magdeburg 'Das fließende Licht der Gottheit.'* München: Artemis Verlag, 1990.

O'Brien, T. C., ed., *St. Thomas Aquinas: Summa Theologiae* New York: McGraw-Hill / London: Eyre & Spottiswoode, 1976.

Oehl, Wilhelm, *Das Büchlein von der Gnaden Überlast von Christina Ebnerin* (Dokumente der Religion 11) Paderborn: Ferdinand Schöningh, 1924.

_____. *Deutsche Mystikerbriefe des Mittelalters 1100- 1550.* München: Georg Müller Verlag, 1931.

Ohly, Friedrich. "Geist und Formen der Hoheliedauslegung im 12. Jahrhundert." *Zeitschrift für Deutsches Altertum* 85 (1954):181-197.

Peters, Ursula. *Religiöse Erfahrung als literarisches Faktum: Zur Vorgeschichte und Genese frauenmystischer Texte des 13. und 14. Jahrhunderts.* Tübingen: Max Niemeyer Verlag, 1988.

————. "Das 'Leben' der Chrisine Ebner: Textanalyse und kulturhistorische Kommentar." In Kurt Ruh, ed., *Abendländische Mystik im Mittelalter* 402-422 with discussion overview 472.

Pfeiffer, F. *Die Mystiker des 14. Jhrs.* Göttingen: Vandenhoeck & Ruprecht, 1907, 2 Bände.

Pope, Marvin. *The Song of Songs: A New Translation with Introduction and Commentary—The Anchor Bible.* Garden City, N.Y.: Doubleday and Company, 1977.

Preger, Wilhelm. *Geschichte der deutschen Mystik im Mittelalter.* Leipzig: Dorfling & Francke, 1881. 3 vol.; reprint Aalen: Otto Zeller Verlagsbuchhandlung, 1962.

Prestel, Josef. *Die Offenbarungen der Margaretha Ebner und der Adelheid Langmann.* Weimar: Verlag Hermann Bohlaus Nachfolger, 1939: 113-183.

Ramsey, Boniface, O.P. *John Cassian: The Conferences* in Ancient Christian Writers Series, No. 57, Mahwah and New York: Paulist Press, 1997.

Reinitzer, Heimo. *Deutsche Bibelübersetzungen des Mittelalters.* Bern: Peter Lang Verlag, 1987-88.

Ringler, Siegfried. Die Deutsche Literatur des Mittelaters Verfasserlexikon. Berlin: Walter de Gruyter, 1985, V. s.v. "Langmann, Adelheid."

————. "Die Rezeption mittelalterlicher Frauenmystik als wissenschaftliches Problem, dargestellt am Wekr der Chrisine Ebner." In Peter Dinzelbacher and Dieter R. Bauer, eds., *Frauenmystik im Mittelalter*, 178-200.

————. *Viten- und Offenbarungsliteratur in Frauenklöstern des Mittelalters.* München: Artemis Verlag, 1980.

Rublack, Ulinka. "Female Spirituality and the Infant Jesus in Late Medieval Dominican Convents." *Gender and History*, Vol. 6, No. 1, April 1995, 37-57.

Ruf, Paul, ed. *Mittelalterliche Bibliothekskataloge—Deutschlands und der Schweiz 3, 1, 1932*, München: C.H. Beck'sche Verlag, 1932.

Ruh, Kurt. *Old German Mysticism.* Bern: Francke Verlag, 1950.

————. *Medium Aevum.* Band I Aidos Verlag 1963.

Ruh, Kurt, ed. *Altdeutsche und Altniederdeutsche Mystik* (Wege der Forschung XXIII); Darmstadt, 1964.

Scheeben, Heribert Christian. "Über die Predigtweise der deutschen Mystiker." In Kurt Ruh, ed. *Altdeutsche und Altniederdeutsche Mystik*: 101f.

Schlettstetter, Sebastian. *Dass Wunderbarliche Leben, Hoche und unerhorte Wunderwerc der Seligen Gottgewichten Jungfraw Margarethae von Maria Medingen.* Manuscript of the Monastery of Maria Medingen, Mödingen, 1662.

Schmidt, Josef, ed., and Shrady, Maria, trans. *Johannes Tauler: Sermons*. Mahwah and New York: Paulist Press, 1985.

Schmidt, Margot. *Mechthild von Magdeburg: Das fließende Licht der Gottheit* (Mystik in Geschichte und Gegenwart Abteilung I Christiliche Mystik Band 11), Stuttgart-Bad Canstatt: Frommann-Holzboog, 1995.

Schröder, Karl, ed. *Der Nonne von Engelthal Büchlein von der Gnaden Überlast*. Tübingen: H. Laupp, 1871; text 1-44; 59-71.

Seemüller, Joseph. *Willirams deutsche Paraphrase des Hohenliedes mit Einleitung und Glossar*. Straßburg: Karl J. Trübner, 1878.

Strauch, Philipp. *Die Offenbarungen der Adelheid Langmann, Klosterfrau zu Engelthal*. Straßburg: Karl J. Trübner, 1878.

――――. *Margaretha Ebner und Heinrich von Nördlingen*. Freiburg i.B. and Tübingen: Akademische Verlagsbuchhandlung von J. C. B. Mohr, 1882; reprint Amsterdam: Verlag P. Schippers, N.V., 1966.

Traber, Johannes. *Die Herkunft der selig genannten Dominikanerin Margareta Ebner, geboren zirka 1291, gestorben 20. Juni 1351*. Donauwörth: Historischer Verein Donauwörth, 1910.

Tugwell, Simon. *Early Dominicans: Selected Writings*. New York: Paulist Press, 1982.

Velecky, Ceslaus, O.P., trans., *St. Thomas Aquinas: Summa Theologiae*. New York: McGraw-Hill / London: Eyre & Spottiswoode, 1965.

Vetter, Ferdinand. *Aus der Nonne von Engelthal Büchlein von der Gnaden Überlast (Lehrhafte Literatur des 14. Und 15. Jahrhunderts)*. Berlin/Stuttgart, 1889. 74-78.

Vicaire, Marie-Humbert, O.P. *St. Dominic and His Times*. Trans. Kathleen Pond. New York: McGraw-Hill, 1964.

Voit, Gustav. *Engelthal: Geschichte eines Dominikanerinnenklosters im Nürnberger Raum*. Nürnberg: Verlag Korn und Bern, 1977.

――――. "Geschichte des Klosters Engelthal." In *750 Jahre Engelthal*. Simmelsdorf: Altnürnberger Landschaft e.V., 1994.

Walter, Wilhelm. *Die deutsche Bibelübersetzungen des Mittelalters* (188). Sp. 347.

Walz, Angelus. *Die Zeit der Mystik* (14. Jahrhundert). In *Dominikaner und Dominikanerinnen in Deutschland* (1225- 1955), 550f.

Weinhandl, Margarete. *Deutsches Nonnenleben: Das Leben der Schwestern zu Töß und der Nonne von Engelthal Büchlein von der Gnaden Überlast*. In *Katholikon Werke und Urkunden*. II. München: O.C. Recht Verlag, 1921.

Weinhold, Karl. *Lamprecht von Regensburg: Sanct Francisken Leben und Tochter Syon*. Paderborn: Ferdinand Schöningh, 1880.

Wentzlaff-Eggebert, Friedrich Wilhelm. *Deutsche Mystik zwischen Mittelalter und Neuzeit*. Berlin: de Gruyter, 1969.

Wichgraf, Wilturd. "Der Tractat von der Tochter von Syon und seine Bearbeitungen." In Wilhelm Braunne, ed., *Beiträge zur Geschichte der Deutschen Sprach und Literatur.* Halle: Max Niemaeyer, 1922, 173-231.

Wilms, Hieronymus. *Das älteste Verzeichnis der deutschen Dominikanerinnenklöster.* In *Quellen und Forschungen zur Geschichte des Dominikanerordens in Deutschland.* Leipzig: Otto Harrassowitz, 1928.

————. *Das Beten der Mystikerinnen. Dargestellt nach den Chroniken der Dominikanerinnenklöster zu Adelhausen, Diessenhofen, Engeltal, Kirchberg, Ötenbach, Töß, Unterlinden (Quellen und Forschungen zur Geschichte des Dominikanerordens in Deutschland)* 2. Aufl. Including the *Weiler Schwesternbuch* (=Bücher für Seelenkulture) Freiburg i.B.: Herder & Co., 1923.

————. *Geschichte der deutschen Dominkanerinnen, 1206- 1916.* Dülmen i.W.: A. Laumann'sche Buchhandlung, 1920.

————. "Von der Stiftung des Klosters Engeltal." In *Geschichte der deutschen Dominikanerinnen, 1206-1915.* Dülmen i. W.: Laumann'sche Buchhandlung, 1920, pp. 42-44, 104-107.

INDEX